Happy Birthday
Enjoy these I
Lots of love,
Pam xxx

18/12/23
s!

CW00536942

THE
COUNCIL
of LIGHT

"This book teaches us how to use the most powerful manifesting tools of our time."

MARIE MANUCHEHRI, RN, AUTHOR OF *INTUITIVE SELF-HEALING*

"Danielle has done it again! *The Council of Light* invites us to live in the space that is our Divine Birthright, JOY. This is more than a book—it is an experience! It is one of the much-needed reads of our time to move beyond fear, shame, guilt, and blame. This book is transformative for anyone who chooses a life of happiness and abundance."

PAT BACCILI, PhD, HOST OF *THE DR. PAT SHOW*

"Extraordinary guidance is here to support us as we shift into unified consciousness. *The Council of Light* reminds us that raising our vibration is all we need to do to change our experience, and our reality. A wonderful and wise handbook for personal and life transformation!"

SARA WISEMAN, AUTHOR OF *WRITING THE DIVINE*

"Danielle's capacity to transmit higher vibrational frequencies with grounded practical actions is exquisite. Access this book to receive potent activations that will help you uplevel your life!"

LISA MICHAELS, AUTHOR OF
THE PROSPEROUS PRIESTESS HANDBOOK
AND PRESIDENT OF NATURAL RHYTHMS INSTITUTE

"Danielle Rama Hoffman has produced another magical read. . . . If you are ready for a healing, enlightening experience that will forever change the way you perceive and interrelate with life and all that you can receive, this book may well be the catalyst."

ANAIYA SOPHIA, AUTHOR OF *SACRED SEXUAL UNION*

"With specific practical explanations, positive intent, and intense enthusiasm, Danielle offers the reader an opportunity to form a direct connection with the Council of Light. Anyone on a journey of soul self-discovery will find the information about the Rays not only important but also highly applicable in facilitating changes in one's levels of joy, abundance, grace, and ease."

EUGENIA OGANOVA, AUTHOR OF
AWAKENING THE HARMONY WITHIN AND *MISSION ALPHA*

"*The Council of Light* sends humanity a powerful message that will shapeshift our reality through this beautifully written book. The intergalactic council invites us to access our inner wisdom and natural state of joy to guide our journey into becoming the divine human beings we were always meant to be."

LINDA STAR WOLF, PhD,
AUTHOR OF *SHAMANIC BREATHWORK*

"Just by reading this book you will enter the vibration of light and unity consciousness. Danielle's exercises and examples are powerful and practical and her work will support you in creating a life full of joy, health, and abundance. I am so grateful for these teachings, which encourage us to shift our awareness and thus change the quality of our daily lives."

SHARLYN HIDALGO,
AUTHOR OF *THE HEALING POWER OF TREES*

"Once in a while a book comes along that shifts, uplifts, and underscores the fact that anything is possible when you choose it. Ease and joy are not simply the result of a prosperous life—they are the path to getting there. *The Council of Light*'s energetic tools and unique approach may change your finances and life for the better."

RICH LITVIN, COAUTHOR OF
THE PROSPEROUS COACH

"The author extends a beautiful invitation to join her and the Council of Light at the divine banquet of love, wealth, joy, and health! I highly encourage you to accept this seat at the love feast! Danielle embodies the teachings in this book and gives the reader practical wisdom to bring more of all good things into our lives."

KATHRYN W. RAVENWOOD,
AUTHOR OF *HOW TO CREATE SACRED WATER*

THE
COUNCIL
of LIGHT

Divine Transmissions for Manifesting
the Deepest Desires of the Soul

DANIELLE RAMA HOFFMAN

Bear & Company
Rochester, Vermont • Toronto, Canada

Bear & Company
One Park Street
Rochester, Vermont 05767
www.BearandCompanyBooks.com

Bear & Company is a division of Inner Traditions International

Library of Congress Cataloging-in-Publication Data
Hoffman, Danielle Rama.
  The council of light : divine transmissions for manifesting the deepest desires of
the soul / Danielle Rama Hoffman.
      p. cm.
  Includes index.
  Summary: "Galactic teachings and practices to raise your vibrational energy and
create a life of joy, abundance, and ease"—Provided by publisher.
  ISBN 978-1-59143-163-3 (pbk.) — ISBN 978-1-59143-834-2 (e-book)
  1. Energy medicine. 2. Vibration—Therapeutic use. 3. Galaxies—Miscellanea. 4.
Medical astrology. I. Title.
  RZ421.H64 2013
  615.8'52—dc23
                                                                    2013011522

Printed and bound in the United States

10   9   8   7   6

Text design and layout by Virginia Scott Bowman
This book was typeset in Garamond Premier Pro and Gill Sans with Centaur,
Cochin, and Avant Garde Gothic used as display typefaces

To send correspondence to the author of this book, mail a first-class letter to the
author c/o Inner Traditions • Bear & Company, One Park Street, Rochester, VT
05767, and we will forward the communication, or contact the author directly at
www.divinetransmissions.com.

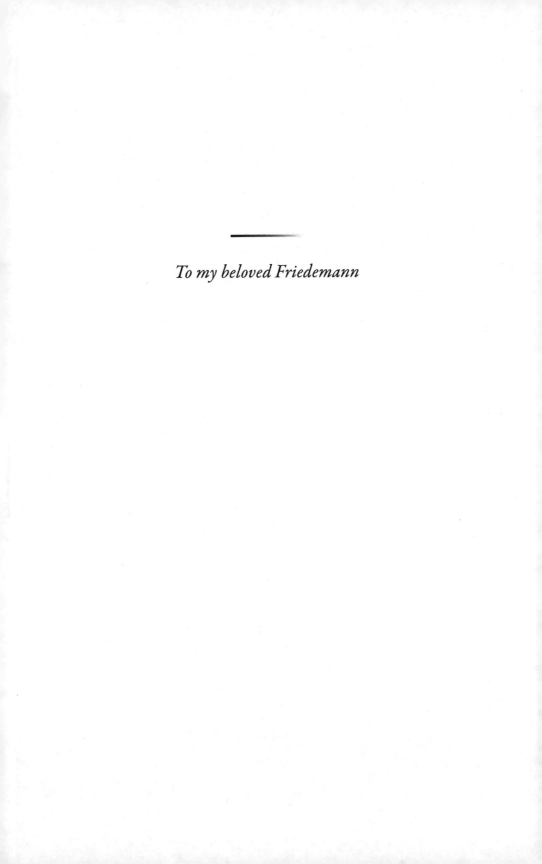

To my beloved Friedemann

CONTENTS

PART ONE

THE RAYS OF LIGHT
A Spectrum of Higher Consciousness

PART TWO

DISCUSSIONS WITH THE COUNCIL OF LIGHT

Health, Wealth, Happiness, and Other Important Topics

ACKNOWLEDGMENTS

From the altar of my heart I overflow with joyful appreciation to you the reader and all the souls who have called this stream of consciousness forth into form. I extend a special thanks to the Divine Transmissions group participants who originally participated in these teachings and for everyone who has entrusted me with the honor of being a part of their spiritual and personal evolution.

Much love and appreciation to my transcriptionist Denise Maroney for nurturing the manifestation of this beautiful being *The Council of Light* from inspiration into actualization. I extend blissful thanksgiving to everyone at Bear & Company—you are truly a stellar group of warm, bright, and adept masters of book making and publishing. Thank you Jon Graham for wholeheartedly embracing this material and the honor of receiving your highest recommendations and accolades for its publication. What a blessing. To my editors Jamaica Burns Griffin and Jennie Marx I am sending you the Joy Ray as a symbol of my appreciation for your invaluable suggestions and for co-creating an awesome manifestation of one of my soul's deepest desires—ease and grace!

Thanks to all of the mentors, friends, and family who have encouraged me to share my gifts and talents. Much love to my mom for always loving and believing in me. To my beloved Friedemann, my heart of hearts, thank you for seeing my essence and calling me to be my most empowered, joyful, and authentic self. I feel truly blessed by the wealth of happiness our love, friendship, and soul connection has brought into my life. I am in awe of your wisdom, capacity to love, and ever-present curiosity. It is a joy to co-create this magical life with you.

To the Divine in all of your magical forms, including the ones mentioned above, myself, Thoth, and the Council of Light I extend an overflowing river of joy, love, and appreciation. All is well and You are ALL!

HOW THIS MATERIAL CAME INTO BEING

As I sit down to write this in the Provence region of France in April of 2012 I am thinking back on the times when I was frequently exhausted, stressed, struggling to make money, and bogged down in deep feelings of shame, terror, and fear related to sharing my purpose and stepping into the role of the spiritual leader that I am today. The Council of Light and the material in this book have greatly contributed to the life experience I have now. I am in the vibration of joy and living in an enhanced state of health (running, hiking, and feeling incredibly vital), wealth (enjoying a multiple six-figure business sharing my soul's purpose with awesome clients around the world), and happiness (feeling blissful, fulfilled, deeply nourished, and overflowing with appreciation). And I know that this work can be transformational for you as well.

I would like to share a bit more about my spiritual and educational background and my initiatory life experiences, because this relates to how this material came into being, the benefits it can create in your life, and also demonstrates what makes me the perfect person to transmit this divine consciousness. As a young girl, as early as three years old I have memories of knowing what people were feeling and what they often weren't saying. At the age of nine and again at seventeen I had the experience of being struck by lightning, which I believe supported my system to be able to merge with the divine intelligence and infinite knowledge that I have the distinct honor of sharing with the world today.

I went to college and majored in women's studies and psychology and worked as a counselor for a few years. During this time I was feeling overwhelmed by my empathic nature and had a stint of trying to numb out with alcohol, drugs, relationships, work, travel—which landed me in alcohol and drug treatment in 1993 (I have been sober ever since).

Up until this point I would have defined myself as an atheist. My previous religious experiences included attending the Unitarian church with my family—which I left at the age of nine—and celebrating Jewish holidays with my friends with the occasional visit to synagogue. When I arrived to the twelve steps of Alcoholics Anonymous and was told I needed to find a higher power (God), my response was, "That is not going to happen." In actuality it did, and big time. At first I reconnected to nature, which I had a strong affinity with as a child. Then I went on to massage school, which helped me to feel grounded, more in my body, and less overwhelmed by other people's emotions. I went on to be an owner of a massage school in Knoxville, Tennessee, where I had a private practice and taught other practitioners massage therapy. At this point I was only twenty-four years old.

This is where it started to get interesting. During the closing prayer at AA meetings I held hands with the people next to me and energy would shoot out my hands and up their arms, often shocking both of us. When I was giving a massage, I started seeing colors inside the person's body or had a strong intuition to put my hands in a certain place and discovered that was exactly where their pain was. At the age of twenty-six I became a Reiki Master (my teachers were the same women who ran the horseback riding camp I attended for most of my childhood). This training helped me to be able to turn on and off the energy and to also direct it so I was no longer shocking folks as it ran through me.

Then I attended a workshop on the Egyptian Goddess Sekhmet led by Nicki Scully (at the same camp). Up until this point I had been introduced to guides through Reiki, yet I wasn't conscious of who my guides were. That all changed during this workshop. I felt reclaimed by Sekhmet and reconnected to my Egyptian soul lineage. Before then I didn't have any interest in Egypt per se. I continued with my business for a few more years, teaching Reiki and offering massage and energy healing sessions. I also took kundalini yoga and went to a yoga retreat in Santa Fe, New Mexico, where I met my husband, Friedemann Schaub. Very shortly after we met I moved to Seattle, Washington, and began studying with Nicki, ultimately getting certified as an Alchemical Healing teacher and receiving direct transmission into the Lineage of Thoth. During this time I rediscovered my direct connection to Thoth, the god of infinite knowledge, and my direct connection to the Divine. I went on to lead tours to Egypt and bring in my own bodies of work: the Temples of Light, the Council of Light, the Prosperous Soul, Divine Birthright Activation, and Thoth's Magic Academy.

The process of going from having a nebulous sense of energy in my hands to now downloading ancient wisdom directly from Source was an evolution. I believe through the various initiations I received in the form of Reiki attunements and the openings of energy centers through Alchemical Healing and life initiations, I had awakened my capacity to hear, see, know, feel, intuit, directly transmit, and merge with infinite knowledge (Thoth). I have come to understand my soul's purpose as a keeper and bringer forth of ancient wisdom and a scribe. What I do at this point looks similar to channeling, as I connect to a guide or guides—or directly to Source—and then I write or speak the consciousness that I am merged with. However, I prefer to call it divine transmitting or scribing.

As I mentioned in the beginning, I had a lot of fear and terror come up as I would share my purpose. I am incredibly lucky that since my early twenties I have found my calling in supporting others in their awakening process, yet until the last few years I had a push-pull relationship with it. My gifts of being highly sensitive and empathic were also my greatest challenges. I wanted to live my purpose more than anything and at the same time I was terrified to do so, especially when it came to the divine transmitting. Yet I have come to realize that it is my divine design and that I am blessed to be able to embody the Divine 100 percent, and as such, entrain others to embody their inner divinity. The fear of being persecuted or ostracized for speaking spiritual wisdom was a common sensation I had, and one I had to overcome to share this material and to be of greater service. I know I am not alone in this and that this is something that you may have had to face as well. Now I am congruent with my purpose and the energy of joy and I am thriving.

Now back to how the Council of Light material changed my life and how the material came into being. One day, while bringing in the Temples of Light material, I meditated on Luxor Temple. In my meditation I was greeted by thousands and thousands of light beings. There were so many of them I eventually asked for a representative to introduce themselves to me so that I could communicate with them. Although I didn't realize it at the time this was my first conscious meeting with the Council of Light. Yet because I was very much steeped in my connection to Egypt and Thoth it wasn't the time for us to work together intimately.

Later on Thoth formally introduced me to the Council of Light, where they shared their purpose with me. I have included in this chapter a transcription of this meeting for you to enjoy the energetics and the nuances of this first verbal contact with them. After we met I quickly realized the significance of what they had to share and arranged to meet with them on a regular basis and record our conversations on my digital recorder. In addition to my personal meditations, the Council also invited me to offer monthly group sessions with them on a variety of topics. These monthly group sessions occurred in Seattle, Washington, yet were also offered with a bilocation option: people from all over the world could participate remotely and receive the recording afterward.

The Council would introduce themselves, share their purpose, download the most pertinent messages and vibrations multidimensionally, and sometimes provide individual transmissions for the participants. These groups continued for years and participants experienced incredible results and enhanced well-being as a result of working with the Council of Light.

The personal meditation recordings and the group session recordings are the basis for the material in this book. Each chapter is a full experience in and of itself with a beginning, middle, and an end. The transmissions were transcribed from audio to written form and then edited and adjusted slightly to make sense to a larger audience. Each chapter is a vibrational transmission: it addresses all aspects of you as the multidimensional being that you are. The process of reading and experiencing the transmissions is a spiral of consciousness. When you read one chapter it spirals you into a deeper aspect of the previous chapter and it keeps moving forward like this. The Council has guided me to keep the material on each subject as it was when it was originally transmitted, because it holds the most potent divinity codes for each subject. As you continue into the transmissions remember that the words are only a small fraction of what is included in this scribed material. So allow yourself to experience and entrain to the transmissions with all of your sensations.

Why do I think this material created such amazing results in my life and will create phenomenal results for you? First of all, it is steeped in unity consciousness, which is the shift in consciousness from fear, separation, and lack, to a consciousness of joy, purpose, and oneness. It, therefore, entrained me to be able to move into and maintain a higher vibration. It also provided tools that I could employ to transcend my limiting beliefs, emotions, and unsupportive habits. The Council of Light invited me to develop a direct relationship with them and to call upon them for support, which I did and continue to do so. The material presented in this book guided me to make internal shifts in consciousness and vibration and then my outer experience had to follow. I moved into the energy of joy and this vibration enhanced my health, wealth, and happiness.

I know that you too can create awesome results and have incredible health, wealth, and happiness through joy. Joy is a high vibration, and that which you want to experience in your life is moving at a high vibration as well. In fact, I believe there is a lot more for us all to learn by embracing joy rather than repeating the pattern of lack or scarcity. Now I have the pleasure of living my life for the joy of it, offering my services and my purpose from a place of overflowing positivity rather than from a place of obligation or fear. As such I am able to have the impact I am here to have, to be of great service and support others to do the same.

The fact that this information is available to us now is very significant. It is the time where we can move our spiritual beliefs from concepts to reality. The Earth is moving at a higher speed and vibration and inviting us to entrain to a higher vibration. The galactic teachings of the Council of Light offer us a portal of joy to take a vibrational journey into greater health, wealth, and happiness.

I believe that this material came forth in response to your calling, your asking, and your desire to expand. Thank you for your contribution to this body of work. And thanks to the Council of Light for answering our call and supporting our transition during this important time. It is with great appreciation and joy that I graciously step out of the way and allow you to connect directly with the Council of Light.

MY INTRODUCTION
TO THE COUNCIL OF LIGHT

My first verbal contact with the Council of Light changed my life, and I believe it will change yours, too. Portions of this transmission were received via "light language." Light language is comprised of grids of light that when spoken take the form of sounds that are not words or full sentences; rather, they are syllables or placeholders for sacred geometry. This transmission alternated between receiving the blocks of consciousness in light language and then translating them into English right after. In my experience light language is often used to allow the conscious mind to relax so you can receive the energy transmission more fully and with greater ease.

Thoth: Hello, dear one, it is I, Thoth, that is moving more into the forefront of your consciousness. I am gathered here with the Council of beings that have important information for you and for all of those that you come into contact with. The timing of this meeting is very specific. I will be interfacing between you and the Council. Do you have any questions?

Danielle: Yes, what's the purpose of this meeting?

Council of Light: We are a Council of Light. There are more of us than you can count. We would like to support you and your planet in the process that it is undergoing. Thoth is one of our members. You have been preparing for this endeavor. It will require much attention and focus on your part. There is more of a rigorous discipline than what you have been willing to do in the past.

Danielle: What kind of discipline?

Council of Light: Well, it is a willingness discipline, a surrendering, a willingness to let go of what you have known before. We are asking you to let go and be willing to have some of the activities you are engaged in move into the background or for you to complete them. We are not saying that every area will end; however, the way that you have been interacting with your power in relationship to these areas is going to change. It is what you have been wanting.

Danielle: Yes, I agree.

Council of Light: We will take a few moments to download some consciousness. [Silence] Now we can speak more freely with you. Thoth remains the intercessor. You are safe. Anubis is around this Council. There is a code within the DNA that has been awakening. Some call this the Divinity Code and some call this the Stellar Consciousness. It is what you have been working with at the Temple of Luxor where you first met us consciously in this lifetime. We have been instrumental at different transitions on the planet and in other solar systems. You have worked with us before and you will work with us again.

As you have agreed to participate in the awakening you have agreed to become a more enlightened being. You have agreed to be masterful with your own thoughts and feelings, committed to taking the high vibrational road as often as you can. The funny thing about it to us, and perhaps to you, is that it will feel more fluid, light, and natural than the years before where you have had a conscious and disciplined spiritual practice. You will be living your life in some ways in a more normal or mainstream way; however, the undercurrent of that is much deeper and connected to Source energy.

What is it, dear one, that you want most from your life?

Danielle: Oneness. Freedom. Abundance. Love.

Council of Light: All of these things are true. Yet, on the deepest level, we feel that you most desire to be you, and to love who you are. You are unlike anyone on the planet. Your energy has been configured in a very unique way so that you are able to interface purely with pure love consciousness. It is time that you owned your power and your place on the planet. We will be sending you many disciples. Have confidence. It is imperative that you focus on the now. [Humming]

There is an emerald green energy light stream that is coming into your universe. This light stream holds the resonance of unity in its natural state. What has happened, as you know, is that there has been a separation and a split of energy. Molecules have been dense in physicality and light has been fast moving on the energetic levels, soul levels, and spirit realms. There has been a variance that is quite vast between the density of these objects.

As this light is coming in harmonic resonance is achieved. The Energy Support Program's* primary objective is to prepare people for this unity. It is our desire to assist as many people as possible for a smooth transition into oneness. You can intend that those who are attracting this consciousness and are in alignment with your resonance find you with ease and grace. Be prepared for the vast amount of people that will be drawn to you.

You need to let go of everything that you've known so far and we are asking that you let go of your tendency to overthink and control. We will download more of this light through you today. This is the discipline aspect that we are speaking of, for it is a process of steeping. A sponge in water can only absorb so much water. When it is saturated it cannot take any more water in.

This is like the violet flame of consciousness that is coming onto the planet. There is only so much that you can absorb at one time. That is why we will be streaming information over a period of time.

[Voice sounds and humming] Thoth would like to speak to you. Thank you and please meet with us again three to four times next week.

Thoth: Hi, dear one, it is I, Thoth, that is moving more into the forefront. It is a very symbiotic and natural resonance that you and I have. It is a strong connection, and now that you are where you are, it will begin to nourish your body in a way that will feel quite good to you.

We will rotate whom you are connected to because the Council's energy is where you are going, it is not where you are, and in a way I, Thoth, am where you have been and where you are going. There will be during this transition period a handing of the mantle, so to speak. Just

---

*The Energy Support Program is a daily program offered by Danielle that supports the individual to move into and maintain a higher vibration. Please refer to the resources section at the back of the book for more details.

know that we will work in a very concentrated way and it will nourish your body.

The Council of Light: Now it is the Council that is moving more into the foreground, so you can begin to identify the different signature energies. We would ask you to continue your groups monthly and to offer a variety of Council of Light topics based on the consciousness, guidance, and information you translate from us. Thank you and we will be working with you in your dreams. We look forward to that which is coming.

COUNCIL OF LIGHT MISSION:
JOY WISDOM

The following was taken from a later personal meditation with the Council of Light.

Hello dearest one, it is the Council of Light that is coming forward at this time. In a sense we are an intergalactic council. We have representatives from all different star systems and beyond. That is why it has been a process for you to be able to connect to us and why so few have attempted it in the past—because there is quite a range of consciousness among us.

As you know, each person, as a part of their soul's lineage, has different experiences with different galactic energy. Every being in the Council of Light will not have a resonance with every person's soul lineage. That is why each person who comes into contact with us will have their own Council of Light. Our intent so perfectly aligns with your intent that there is a pure, loving, and joyous connection. Yet some of the physical sensations that you have been experiencing have been a result of widening your bandwidth, widening your range so to speak, and this will diminish with practice. We are glad to see that you are back again and that you are here for the fun of it, for the joy of it, and for the experience of blending with us and connecting to us.

If there was a mission statement that we have, our main purpose is to spread wisdom that results in joy. You could say that we are joy wisdom. Yet if you would break each part of that mission statement down, our purpose is to share wisdom that brings and creates joy. Within this mission there is a sharing, a receiving, an application, and a result. There is a cause and an effect and a very applicable aspect to the wisdom.

What are the things that create joy in human beings? Well, they are the things that all of you have been desiring for eons. There's nothing unique about this time and space and what you want is really not that drastically different than what people wanted a thousand years before. However, the mechanism and wisdom for achieving joy is particular to this time and space.

As we have said earlier at the first meeting we had with you, this particular time that we have come into connection with you is due to the unfolding of the energy on planet Earth. The unfolding of the expression of planet Earth is a very deliberate and potent time. As we have said the result of joy in one's life spans across time. It is not really anything new on that side of the equation; however, the wisdom that we share is very particular to this time and space. Not to say that the wisdom wouldn't have worked in the denser energy of two thousand years ago; however, it would not have been as fruitful.

There is a wisdom that is available collectively and it is awakening within the consciousness that is very particular to the now on your planet. This is why we can share with you the Rays of Light. These Rays of Light can be a process that you can entertain to create joy in your life. This is why we can share with you the beliefs that will open your ability to receive. This is why we can speak to you of the fact that all physicality is pure divine love, is neutral, and that the physicality around you is creating health, wealth, and happiness.

These are values that those among you in this planetary time have and hold and make sense to you. There is an awareness that the planet is made up of vibrations and what you might call subtle energies. These vibrations and subtle energies of thoughts, beliefs, feelings, emotions, vibrations, and visualizations have increased in their application leading to results.

There are scientific as well as collective consciousness reasons for this, but we feel that you agree with the concepts, and so it is not necessary to go into the details. You know within yourself that this time feels very different. Because it feels different there is a trust that you have that what we are saying and the wisdom that we are sharing can be applied in a very timely manner to create long-standing results that people have desired throughout time and space.

WORKING WITH THE COUNCIL OF LIGHT

Guidelines and Energetic Preparations

This is the Council of Light that is moving more to the forefront of this now moment. It is with great joy and appreciation that we are communicating with you in this way. We very much look forward to the delight and the joy that this continued conversation will generate for you in the words, pages, and chapters to come. There is much that we will share with one another.

INTERACTIVE COMMUNICATION

We would like to begin by explaining that this communication is one that is interactive even though at first glance it may seem as if you are reading text that has already been transmitted and that it is a one-way conversation. That is not the case because the words are simply placeholders for vibrational communication. We are vibrating with you from the place of unity, wholeness, and joy, and you are vibrating with us as well from your wholeness and from your multidimensionality. All of that transcends time and space.

It is just as it would be if you were having a conversation with a dear friend. That conversation might be happening in person, across continents, on the telephone, on email, or in other various forms. Conversations, communications, and energy exchanges can happen and do happen all of the time beyond time and space. You have had experiences of this already in your life. This is an adventure together and one in which you are getting to know us; it is something that is organic and beyond the pages in this book. As we are with you through the words and through the vibrations, and as you choose to create a direct relationship with us, we are also with you as light beings, as your Council of Light, in this space and the dimensions that you are in.

FOLLOWING YOUR INNER GUIDANCE

One of the many enhancements and benefits from this material is that you become clear about what is best for you; it is recommended that you follow your inner guidance and interact with us as if we are with you, because we are with you. If you have a question as you are going through the material or you are wondering about something, then just ask a question and allow yourself to receive guidance from yourself or from us. Or if you need to adjust the vibration to be slower or faster to assimilate the material with total ease you can ask for this, and this is also something that we are watching for as we are with you. There is a sense of the transmission being orchestrated and yet it is something that you can guide, lead, and direct.

PARTNERSHIP
AND EMPOWERMENT

We want to convey that we are entering into this conversation from a place of equality, partnership, and from a place of a back-and-forth interaction. A part of that equality is also you being empowered and you taking the reins and being the one that directs the process, because ultimately this material has been brought in response to what it is you have been calling forth on an individual scale, a global scale, as well as a universal scale.

CHOOSING TO BE PART OF THE VIBRATIONAL SHIFT IN CONSCIOUSNESS

The other invitation is to recognize that this is not a new relationship between us, because there is really a remembering that is happening; it is a choice that we each have made to come together at this time and to be a part of this vibrational shift in consciousness. Because this consciousness has been divinely transmitted it has been transmitted in wholeness and in a multidimensional unity consciousness fashion. As you are interfacing with the consciousness and the words and the exercises it is such that you can connect from your wholeness, your soul, and your multidimensionality.

We would like to speak for a few more moments about the transition that is happening on the Earth plane. In the Egyptian Book of the Dead, which is also referred to as "Coming Forth by Day," there are the hieroglyphs that create the Pyramid Texts. The Pyramid Texts are a sequence of symbols that describe how a human becomes a star and how a star becomes a human. There is an ascension and descension process. This is one way to look at the awakening. Some call it the Aquarian Age—moving from the third chakra into the fourth chakra. Some do not know what to call it but they feel different than they did last year and the year before. Some speak of it as an acceleration of frequency or vibration. Some call it the Golden Age.

The key to this change and the way to navigate the change with the most ease and grace is very simple and is not anything that you do not already know. We are encouraging you to be as happy as you can be and to be you as full-on as possible. If you are you and connected to you living from the inside out you will be less likely to fall into other things. Being you will be the thread that takes you from one way of being into another.

You are bridge people; you have decided to be here at this particular time to assist in this process and to be a part of this process. It is exciting. It is simpler than many are making it out to be. Allow it to be as simple as coming together and sharing community and sharing joy. Allow it to be as simple as expressing yourself.

BEING PRESENT AND OPEN FROM YOUR WHOLENESS

We invite you to be open to being with the material, the consciousness, the energies, and the vibrations from the place of all of you.

Your intellect has a part in this process, and yet it is not the only way to comingle with this material. Your emotions have a part in this process, and yet to only be with this material on an emotional level wouldn't include enough of you—just as going through it only with your intellect wouldn't include enough of you. Approach this process with the choice and the intention to allow all of you to be present; this is part of what's required, and you can do so by simply having that be your choice. When you invite all of you to be present as you're reading each chapter and as you're doing the exercises then you have an incredible advantage, because you're already setting the stage to come from wholeness and to include the parts of you that are moving at a slower vibration. Those may also be your doubts, your fears, or your negative emotions as well as those parts of you that are moving at a higher vibration—your soul, your energy, and your consciousness—and that by having all of you present then you are coming from that place of wholeness.

It is suggested that before proceeding in each aspect of the book you take some deep breaths and choose to be you and only you and include all of you in the process. Then as much as possible be present with your mind, your heart, your emotions, your body, your soul, and your wholeness through this process, which brings us to the further explanation of what a divine transmission is.

WHAT IS A DIVINE TRANSMISSION?

A divine transmission is a broadcast of frequencies from Source. It is an extension of consciousness from Source that is gifted, that is transmitted, and that is broadcasted. You are also a divine transmitter and receiver; you are constantly broadcasting and receiving and that's why this is also interactive—because as you are connecting with the divine transmissions in this body of work you are also receiving them.

You are transmitting what you need, you're transmitting what would be beneficial for you, and you're transmitting what isn't quite clicking. This divine transmission is pure frequency—it is vibration, it is consciousness, and it is energy—and that's why it is exactly the prime matter, the juice that allows you to actualize the deepest desires of your soul. It allows you to manifest the deepest desires of your soul because all of that is happening on a vibrational level and in that space in the universe everything is vibration.

From our perspective something that has been overlooked in a lot of the approaches to transformation and evolution is that if you are addressing only one part of something, only the logical mind or the logical aspect of something, and you're not including the energy of the intuition or vice versa, then it's only accessing one part of the whole. Yet because this is a direct transmission of consciousness, energy, and frequency, and you are frequency and consciousness, there is always a choice of what you're receiving and what you're not. That's why we suggested to you to come from the place of equality and empowerment and recognize that you're guiding this process, you're in charge of this process, and that nothing is being done to you. This is always one choice after another after another. The only way that it works is because we are equals. You are we and we are you.

LIGHT LANGUAGE

From the place of equality and of recognizing that you are also a light being, then from our perspective, we're speaking the most profound language. It is the language of what we would call light: the language of energy, the language of frequency. You may be familiar with thinking of yourself as a body, as a personality, or as different roles that you have. Yet you are a broadcast of light, you are an embodiment of frequency, and you are an embodiment of the essence of your soul.

To have a conversation that is based in light, energy, and consciousness, as you are light, energy, frequency, and consciousness, is the most direct, accelerated, and phenomenal way to provide you with the offering and the choice to realize what it is that you're here to realize in this lifetime. That realization is personal and individual to you and yet it is also global to you. That this material has found its way into your life, that you have transmitted a request for it and received the response to that request, also indicates that you are a part of this shift in consciousness.

HOW EACH CHAPTER WORKS

You know within you that there is an easier way to manifest; that there is a way that includes your infinite nature, your soul, your multidimensionality, and also includes the parts of yourself that you don't like. A direct application of consciousness, which we're calling the Rays of Light, is like taking a laser and specifically opening something. That laser can be focused, pinpointed, and clear, and the application of frequency is such that it has a ripple effect—it has a process in which it expands out and out and out. That's why we're meeting you peer-to-peer, eye-to-eye, divine-to-divine, from this place of us being energy and you being energy, and we're having this energetic conversation.

The structure of these conversations is such that each one is whole in and of itself. You can go through this material like it is a symphony. In a symphony each movement has a beginning, middle, and an end, and each theme with its unique tempo has its own story to tell and its own beauty to express.

Or you can see each chapter in this book like a beautiful painting.

Each painting is rich and vibrant and has so much to give; yet each painting just happens to be in an entire art gallery. When individual paintings are collected together in a gallery or individual movements or themes are collected together in one symphony each part stands on its own. It's whole in and of itself and yet by having them in a collection and having them together the consciousness increases exponentially.

Just as you would have two parts of a play with an intermission in the middle, there are also two parts of this conversation. Part one focuses on the Rays of Light. Part two discusses how you can use these rays to increase your health, wealth, and happiness.

THE RAYS OF LIGHT

The Rays of Light are like the vocabulary to tell a story; they are your tools to manifest your soul's deepest desires. The Rays of Light provide something very unique and potent for your evolution, for your increased happiness, for enhanced health, for your enhanced purpose, and for whatever your deepest desires are. They create incredible acceleration. Then as you go through the rays and bring them together they create a larger repertoire of tools, a larger recipe, a larger system in which, step by step, you can manifest the deepest desires of your soul. You can just use one or you can use them all together.

It's like being a carpenter, being somebody who builds houses: you have a hammer, a drill, nails, and different tools that you use for different parts of building the foundation. Each tool has a different purpose. That's the same with the Rays of Light. Each Ray of Light is a divine transmission of consciousness, but with a very refined energy and vibration and a specific purpose. You use this tool just by calling on it; it's like turning on a light switch. The light is just there and then it's applied. It's similar in some ways to what you might know about energy healing or meditation or journaling or anything like that. It is applied but it's applied as energy and consciousness to energy and consciousness, and that's why it works.

All of the Rays of Light accelerate vibration and energy by including everything into the oneness, into the wholeness, and also returning everything back to its natural state. Because really what's stopping you from manifesting what you want is you. You're the only one that's powerful enough to do that and the way you are doing that is through overlaying a vibration or a frequency or an energy on top of your natural state. Once that energy gets transformed, alchemized, and transmuted, then your natural state restores.

A SCRIBED TEXT LAYERED
WITH CONSCIOUSNESS

Because this is a scribed and transmitted text, it is layered with consciousness, encoded with vibration, interspersed with various access points to light and divine knowledge to the Akashic Records, to divinity codes, to sacred geometry, and light and various energy and consciousness. Each time you go through the material you're different and each time you go through the material you're accessing a different facet of it. It's like a painting made up of a canvas and different colors of paint and lines and shapes. If you just look at the line or the shape or the colors you don't get the whole picture—you don't get the sentiment that it's sharing, the story that it has to tell, the entirety of the beauty that's there.

It's the same with a divine transmission. If you only look at the words from the lens of one aspect of yourself then the whole story isn't quite accessed. It's also important to state here that there's no way to get it wrong. We're just inviting you to recognize that this is an ensouled text. It is a being and a consciousness in and of itself—and as such you are accessing the multiple layers of that. In English there are the letters and individual syllables, but when placed together in a sentence with the tonality added in they transmit and emit something beyond just a, b, c, d, or beyond just the individualized words. Then if it's scribed text, which this is, it also includes the wholeness of that energy and vibration.

THE CREATION OF
MULTIPLE ACCESS POINTS

Each chapter is presented in such a way that it's not so much linear as it is spherical, it is a spiral, it is a lock and key. This energy, once you have been with it, gives you more access to the energy and gives you more awareness of the energy that you were in before. That then opens up another passageway into something that you hadn't accessed before, and so on and so forth.

It is a vibrating, alive, organic, dynamic, multidimensional, encoded, scribed conversation of energy and consciousness that's transmitted from a place of divine wholeness and is being received by you from a place of divine wholeness. You're transmitting from this place of divine wholeness and the material moves back and forth, an invitation to include more of you, to include more of your infinite nature, to include more of your soul and to be more of all that you are. That is truly where the magic of bringing vibration into form is realized.

This "bringing vibration into form," this manifestation, is simply energy crossing the threshold from an idea into form. The threshold that gets crossed is the idea that you're separate: everything gets absorbed back into the wholeness, back into the oneness. You can also imagine that each spiral part of this conversation is also like a possibility or an invitation for a thorough scrub of overlays, distortions, projections, separations, or illusions that you had chosen consciously or unconsciously to entertain at some time.

THE APPLICATION OF THE RAYS OF LIGHT

Once you have the Rays of Light through part one, you're well-positioned to enter into part two, which is the discussion about important topics such as health, wealth, and happiness. Each of these discussions goes into more depth about a particular topic to provide examples and to provide practical ways to implement this energy and consciousness into your life because it may or may not be a new language, a new dictionary, a new art form for you. There are spoken exercises, written exercises, and meditative exercises to support you in manifesting the deepest desires of your soul. It is very much an experiential text.

AN ORGANIC PROCESS

We have shared multiple layers of consciousness about how to be with this material and that truly is the essence of it. We invite you to just be in it, to have fun with it, to be light with it, and also to use your guidance as you journey through it. There isn't a specific guideline such as sitting with one chapter a day for a series of days or to work with one Ray of Light for thirty days. It completely depends on your awareness and what you're perceiving. Some that come into contact with this material will stay up all night reading it from front to back and will feel like it's so familiar and that it's one long story or picture. It's received in wholeness in a short amount of time.

For others it will be more like a buffet and you're just going to have the first course and then you'll have the second course, and then you'll have the third course. Then you're not going to be hungry for another few days or another few hours, but when you're ready you'll continue with the material. If there was a specific structure that we thought would be of benefit for you we would offer it, and yet what we have shared will help you get the most momentum out of this material. It is more about how you're being with the material than how quickly or how slowly you go through it. It is an experience, it is a conversation, it is something to be enjoyed—to be savored—and remember that you can always ask for the energy and consciousness to be adjusted if that's something that you require.

YOUR INNATE CAPACITY FOR DIVINE
COMMUNICATION

One more train of thought: you may have in the past thought you needed to be somebody special in order to have conversations with light beings, with the Divine, and with your soul. You might have thought that you would need to be psychic, clairvoyant, a priest, or a healer, among other things. What is being underscored is that you already have these innate gifts within you, and that to be able to have a direct communication with the Divine within and without is normal; that is a given. Approach it from the knowing that you are already doing it in your own way. Completely allow it to be and look like whatever that way is for you. It may not be the way that it is here: it may come in pictures, it may come in feelings, it may come in knowing, it may come in different ways, and yet it is happening. You can awaken even further your capacity for this dynamic, organic conversation and your understanding that you have tons of help in the energetic realms—in the divine realms—knowing that we always are interacting with you in accordance with your free will and your conscious choice. That is what guides the process. We will place this energy and consciousness on the altar, and yet it is truly up to you to take it from the altar. That's just part of the divine order of the universe.

EXPERIENCING JOY WITH THE COUNCIL OF LIGHT

Meditations and Exercises

There is so much that we could share and so much that we will share, but we would like to provide a way for you to connect to us on your own. This way you can continue to receive the nuances of what would be appropriate for you in your life on a deeper level now, and also after this time together. We will begin with a "Tuning In" meditation, a process to meet your unique Council of Light members. After that, we have provided three exercises for you to use when you want to feel better (move from a sense of duality to unity) or increase your vibration and clarity:

Exercise 1. Work with the energy of polarity by quickly moving back and forth between the opposites to create a hologram of unity.
Exercise 2. Raise your vibration by shaking or vibrating love to allow the energy of love to shine through you.
Exercise 3. Ask us a question that you would like to receive guidance on and then decide how you would like to receive the answer.

We look forward to co-creating this conversation and these experiences with you.

TUNING IN
. . . .
Connecting Directly with the Council of Light

Have a sense of our energy becoming stronger in the space in and around you. You may connect directly to us as a council or group or you may connect to a certain member of our galactic, intergalactic team that then connects you to all of us. Although we can come in as a whole, as a unified field, you are calling a particular connector point to us. The way you connect to us is unique to you. In whatever way it's manifesting for you, your awareness of us, your connection to us, allow your sensations and ask for an understanding of our signature energy, of our essence. Like a fingerprint is a unique pattern, you are connecting to the signature energy, the unique pattern of us, which is unique to you.

Notice the sensations or feelings from our signature energy. What are the qualities of this Council of Light as you are experiencing us? Ask for a symbol, a word, or color in which you can connect to us in the future; notice your sensations and allow yourself to receive. Take all the time that you would like with this process and when you feel complete take three deep breaths to anchor this experience. Then take a few minutes to write about your experience in your journal.

. . . .

We have connected to you. You have created an understanding of our signature energy and you have received consciously or unconsciously a way to connect to us in the future. This imprint, this introduction, this initiation, this calibration has been made so that you can directly access this consciousness that we have to offer. We have explained our purpose, we have introduced ourselves to you, and we have created a way for you to continue to connect to us directly on your own.

HOLOGRAM OF
WHOLENESS AND NEUTRALITY

Now we will move into some of the wisdom that we have been talking about. In your experience of your life there are moments where you feel happy, there are moments where you feel less happy, there are moments where you feel healthy, there are moments where you feel less healthy, there are moments where you feel wealthy, there are moments where you feel less wealthy, there are moments where you feel unified with the Divine, and there are moments where you feel less unified with the Divine.

Have a sense of all of the moments of this lifetime where you have had a fluctuation in your being or a fluctuation in the things that we have just described: your health, wealth, happiness, and your connection to the Divine. To get the most out of the following exercise, it is recommended that you read it aloud.

SPOKEN EXERCISE
Working with the Energy of Polarity

Begin to flip and flop between the polarity of these experiences: healthy, unhealthy; wealthy, unwealthy; happy, unhappy; connected, disconnected; happy, unhappy; wealthy, unwealthy; healthy, unhealthy; happy, unhappy; connected, disconnected; and go back and forth fast, fast, fast, fast. It is like you are flipping a coin back and forth until the polarities speed up so much that it creates a hologram of wholeness. Rather than seeing a coin of heads and tails, healthy and unhealthy, as you flip back and forth it creates a hologram—a multidimensional aspect of the coin of healthy.

To clarify this further, let's identify one aspect. You have this multidimensional coin of healthy that happened because you flip-flopped back and forth through your intention until it sped up so quickly that you created the hologram. Is all contained in the hologram? Yes. Are there the healthy and the unhealthy? Yes, it all exists within the hologram; however, it is the wholeness that is expressed. It is not the imbalance or the unhealthy that is manifest. It is not the healthy that is manifest. It is the wholeness, the beyond, the ascended aspect that is manifest. We could speak of this as neutral; there is positive and there is negative—neutral holds the positive and the negative. They become equal and then they are neutral.

This concept of wisdom is one that is particular to the time on the planet right now. As the energy of the Earth accelerates and you accelerate there is a calling to move from polarity or duality into oneness—to move into the neutral pole, to move into the inclusion of all there is. This flip-flop exercise is one that you can do while you are experiencing the polarity.

As you are in your life and you are having a negative moment, consciously bring your awareness to a memory of something that you have experienced that was positive—in particular around one subject like health, wealth, happiness, or feeling connected to the Divine—and in your mind switch back and forth. You have a cold, for instance, and you acknowledge, "I have a cold." Then the next second you say, "Last week I felt vital. I have a cold. When I was a kid I had energy. I have a cold. I've been well. I have a cold. I have been well. I have a cold. I have been well. . . ." You say it so fast back and forth and back and forth again that the negative and the positive poles can no longer be distinguished; they merge into unity, into oneness.

This is an exercise we would invite you to do and to practice. We would say that when the negative and positive become one then you will have an experience that you would actually call positive. Inherent in the neutral, inherent in the wholeness, inherent in the unity is what you notice or call the positive aspects. As you go back and forth between these you move from healthy to unhealthy and you create the hologram of neutrality and then you experience health.

It seems a little counterintuitive but the difference is there's greater neutrality that occurs. There's a greater enlightenment or detachment that happens where you can still see that healthy and unhealthy are the same thing, it's just one is manifest and the other is unmanifest.

When the duality comes back into unity then you have the experience of something that is far greater than a momentary state of health and a momentary state of unhealth. There is the eternal nature, the broader perspective, the knowingness that all that exists is well-being, all that exists is health, all that exists is unity, and all that exists is joy.

THE ENERGY OF LOVE

We are taking a collective survey of the higher selves of those beings who are calling forth this information and who are reading it (or will read it) to see which morsel of wisdom to share next, which nugget, and what is most important for you as a whole. The cumulative request was around the energy of love. Love is the closest word that you have that implies the pure frequency, the high frequency that is in some ways— although it is not linear—the end result of the transformation where your planet is headed. Where you are headed is to know love, to experience love, to experience that high frequency, to align with the heart center and with the energy of compassion and the energy of the Divine. Love is the high frequency energy that the planet is moving toward.

You have use of the word love to describe everything from "you love carrots," to loving your spouse, to your desire to love yourself more than you ever have before, to this high frequency, liquid energy that we are speaking of that is love: pure vibration, pure ecstasy, pure heart energy, pure exuberance, and pure unity. There is a spectrum of the word love, and we are not speaking about the actual word, we are speaking about the essence of this energy. The way you can experience more love in all of its forms is to move into and hold a higher vibration. What you are longing for, what you are choosing to create, is in that vibration of love.

But how is it that you can consistently hold and align with the energy of love? Well, the answer to this is so simple that it is challenging to describe. You do not need to go anywhere or become anything or change anything to achieve a higher vibration or to achieve love, for it is a part of your being, your matrix, your nature, and your essence. It is more about how do you allow, shine through, or align with that which is already within you.

We will take you through a simple exercise to assist in this process. You can do this energetically (by visualizing the energy of love) or if you feel like moving your body you can do this physically.

ENERGETIC EXERCISE
Allow the Energy of Love to Shine Through

Begin with the intention of allowing the energy of love to shine through you. Allow yourself to align with the higher vibration of love and begin to vibrate love at the level of your cells. If you're adding physical movement to this, gently rock back and forth, back and forth, back and forth, using small shaking movements. Or you could do this in your field or through your intention, intending to vibrate, hum, and to make these small movements in your energy body.

As you vibrate it acts a little like separating the egg yolk from the egg white, but in actuality it creates a scramble: the slower and the higher vibration end up being merged. Using the analogy of separating, you're shaking the lower vibration out and you're allowing the love to become more predominant. As we said, this is not actually the function that happens, but conceptually you can begin to feel the slower vibrations speeding up and the love vibration becoming more prominent. You can make these small movements and intend to accelerate your vibration anytime you would like. As you do so the love energy and the high vibration shines forward and the slower vibration is included into the energy of love, back into the high vibrational field of oneness.

Spend as long as you would like vibrating love until all of you is shining through brilliantly.

To describe the result of this process in a tangible way, let's say you have a flashlight and this flashlight is covered in mud. You turn on the flashlight but at first you cannot see the light. You gently begin to shake the flashlight and as you do the mud and the dirt begin to flake off and more and more of the light shines through; you shake it so much that the dirt or the mud that was on there is gone. Or think about a penny that was tarnished that then gets cleaned and polished, allowing it to glow. This is not to say that you are not shining to begin with. If there are any illusions or any feelings that are covering up your essence, beauty, or your true nature, this opportunity supports you to allow them to be absorbed or integrated back into wholeness and oneness.

CONNECTING WITH YOUR GUIDANCE

We are here for you and with you, uniquely, individually. We are available to support you in accessing your inner guidance, to answer the specific questions that you have about your life. One question might be at the forefront of your mind. As the third exercise in this segment we would invite you to write down this question. If you need more time you can pause a few moments here to tune in, or if you'd like to repeat this process in the future you could go through all the steps like we have outlined here where you come into a higher state of resonance.

SUPPORT EXERCISE
What Would You Really Like to Know?

We invite you to develop a question or to allow a question to come into your mind, something that you would like to be informed about or receive more guidance about. What is it that you would really like to know?

Now use your breath to move into a higher state of resonance. Breathe and connect to us through your word or symbol. If you don't have a question in mind already, ask for your question to become clear to you. Once you have a question, ask the question and then it is up to you to decide what your way of receiving the answer will be. For example, you could ask to receive it in your dream state; or through automatic writing; or go into a meditation, form a connection to us, and receive visual cues. You may also receive a direct knowing-ness; you may hear your answer; or you may simply know. Allow all of your sensations to experience the information that comes to you. There are many ways.

Or you could speak to us and have a verbal conversation where you go back and forth between you and us. You may wonder in the beginning what's you and what's us, but you will begin to identify or distinguish between you or us as time goes on, and tap into a broader stream of consciousness.

We have provided in this introduction a process where you come into a higher state of resonance and then call upon us individually or as a blend, ask your question, and receive your answer. This practice of direct access to your divinity and higher states of wisdom is in align-ment with this particular time on the planet. It is a time on the planet that each person is empowered as the Divine creator being that they are, that each person has access to the infinite knowledge, that each person is able to discern their guidance. Rather than depending upon others—although it is fun, enjoyable, and helpful to elicit the support of others—you have a methodology and a way to receive the guidance yourself.

Remember that you are in charge of this process and that you can guide it at the speed that is appropriate for you. You can ask that it is with ease and grace for your system as you are developing the method of deepening your connection to Spirit. You may notice some adjustments in your body and in your life. If things are ever moving too quickly or too slowly you can ask for this to be adjusted and it will unfold perfectly.

We would like to thank you for calling us forth, for we are the answer to your call, and for showing up and saying yes to your whole life, to having it all, and to your spiritual connection. This concludes this segment; however, you may call upon us whenever you wish. We are with you.

An Application and

PART ONE

The Rays of Light

A Spectrum of Higher Consciousness

1

LIGHT

An Application and Transmission of Frequency

▲

Light: A transmission of frequency that houses all of the Rays of
Light simultaneously. It provides a practical application of light as a
tool to transcend consciousness and support yourself and others.

Welcome to this divine transmission with the Council of Light on the
subject of light. As much as possible bring your attention into the now
moment and to each now moment as it happens.

THE NOW MOMENT

This process is about transcending the non-now consciousness. What
that means is if you are sitting in a room at a hotel in Seattle, or in your
car, your home, in New Orleans or Oregon, wherever you are, that you
are present there. Whatever is happening in that moment gets your full
attention and focus.

There are many times that you are playing thoughts, scenarios, or
experiences in your mind that have already happened or have not yet happened that give the perception that they are happening in the now. This
is something that can happen with a negative experience, a story that you

have about yourself or about your life: you can keep it alive in the now moment even though it is not truly existing in the now moment.

TUNING IN
Entering into the Now Moment

Through your intention enter into this now moment as much as you can. There are various ways you can do this: You can breathe into your body, feel your heart beating, or anything else that brings your attention to the present.

From the now, put out your call to connect to the Council of Light. In this moment allow your sensations to be completely open and present. Notice your particular individual council. It may feel like a group of separate beings, a blend of consciousness, or you may not have a conscious awareness of us but just a knowing that we are here. You may have a sense of a light grid in and around your being. In these moments of silence this light grid, your blueprint, your Source energy, your inner matrix, is being strengthened and your inner communication enhanced. What that means is that if part of you is less connected to another aspect of you this is being strengthened or bridges are being made.

Spend a few moments anchoring and enhancing this connection, and when you are ready take a couple of deep breaths and gently return to the present moment.

LIGHT:
A TRANSMISSION OF FREQUENCY

Light has many definitions, yet what we mean by light in this particular way is a transmission of frequency. The sun travels in rays of light. Light can be applied to different environments; for example in light therapy, where you shine a light through a color and it is applied to the body's systems. Light also refracts on the water and reflects.

In the examples that we just mentioned you can see what direction light is pointing in or where it is being applied. Light as a tool of transmission, of frequency, of consciousness, is something that you may not physically see, though. To help you understand the concept of this definition, imagine that you can see light and that you are applying a certain consciousness or frequency to an environment.

APPLYING THE MODALITY OF LIGHT

At the end of this segment you will have a hands-on tool that you can apply and use. You may have taken classes in Reiki, reflexology, coaching, or sound healing, and they are tools in your toolbox. Now you have an additional tool that is being added to your toolbox: light, the application of frequency.

In what situations would you want to apply a frequency and to what environment? Primarily in the beginning you may choose to apply this frequency within your own life and your own being. However, you can also use it with other people, whether they are friends, family members, or clients.

Just like the words "radiate," or "radiant," there is something about light that emits, shines, and is different from water. Water flows, streams, and projects. Light is a form of radiance. One of the reasons why the tool of light is such a practical one is that you can utilize it in any moment without having to put your hands on someone, without having to speak a word, or really doing anything. You can use the tool of light in any situation and that makes it very easy to apply and call upon often.

In what instances would you be called to use it? One of the reasons that we, the Council of Light, are present on the Earth plane at this time is that we are here for the threshold, the transition, and the change in consciousness that is happening on the planet. You experience this in your own life where it seems like this minute is so much different than the next or even a week ago. From our perspective we feel that you are feeling and wanting to ride the wave into the new consciousness or the next evolution of humanity, divinity, and expansion. The tools of light will help in this transition.

Reiki

Your tools of Reiki, counseling, and whatever modalities exist on the planet right now are in some ways oriented toward a certain period of time.

For instance, with Reiki there were not many practitioners before the 1980s. It was kept secret; the information was only passed down orally, training was expensive, it was hard to find someone who practiced Reiki, and there was a major commitment in order to learn it. After the 1980s it spread like wildfire and it became more accessible, easier to get training, and less expensive. In some instances or some parts of the world it became an everyday word.

Presence

From 1980 until 2009 Reiki had a big role in the transformation. Yet as we are moving from 2009 to about 2030, light is becoming widespread. Light is transmitted through your presence.

You may have felt that when you are in the presence of certain people you feel uplifted, or when you are in the presence of other people you feel bogged down or confused. This type of presence that we're speaking of is the type of presence that is uplifting. However, that doesn't mean that everyone will like it, they'll want to have it, or they'll want to be around you.

A Self-Selecting Process

In some ways there is a self-selecting process that is happening more than ever on the planet. Some people are self-selecting to hold on to the old grid as much as possible and others are self-selecting to jump into the greater yet-to-be of the consciousness grid in the now moment. Some are somewhere in-between and vacillate back and forth.

We want to mention this because sometimes there's the thought that if you have a gift to share and you have a tool that could bring health, happiness, soul fulfillment, abundance, peace, joy, neutrality, expansion, and enlightenment, then there's an assumption that everyone on the planet would want it. But you have had experiences in your own life, have met people, have had clients that no matter what they don't want to change. There's no judgment around that from our perspective. It's their choice. We want to spell this out because it can be an assumption that when someone comes to you for a session, a class, or calls you for advice that they are looking for a change or a solution; however, they may be looking to have a sympathetic ear to continue the story as is.

We also want to say that when you decide to evolve, expand, work on yourself, be committed to your soul and to your spiritual path to living the best life that you can, it doesn't mean that everyone is going to be totally delighted or excited about that or want that for themselves.

You can self-select this tool of light and how much of it you want to carry. It can be assimilated over a period of time so you don't feel like you have to get it all in this one moment. But sometimes when you are applying the frequency of light or you're working with this tool it has the potential to act as a catalyst for other people. In your presence they may feel more of their own unresolved stuff coming to the surface.

Does that mean that this application of light hasn't worked? No, it doesn't mean that. It means that a part of the process of becoming lighter, of becoming more expanded, of becoming more unified or aligned with the self, is a sifting and transcending. If you look in nature there's a time when a pond turns over and all the gook comes to the surface. If you look at the pond when it is totally muddy you could say, "That doesn't look like it's getting cleaner." Yet that's a part of nature and it is a part of the cleansing process.

There is a part of the old consciousness that wants everyone to have as much happiness, health, fulfillment, and peace as possible. There is a level of mastery to be present with people and meet them where they are as stuff is coming up. This may be an area that you get more and more comfortable with as time goes on, because there's the recognition that everyone is exactly where they need to be no matter how it looks.

If you can be a catalyst for them to turn their pond over more quickly, for those that actually want that, then in the long run it's a great deal of service.

Light has an acceleration component to it and is like sifting flour; it changes in the density. As you sift flour it changes its texture and this is one of the many things that is happening in your own life. That is part of why it can feel so intense; the flour, as it gets sifted, probably feels like, "What's happening? Am I going to make it through this sifting?" It is a process and it is not something that happens overnight.

CONSCIOUSNESS: AN APPLICATION OF THE RAYS OF LIGHT

If you are painting your bedroom, the color you use changes the atmosphere and the environment of the room. In a sense as you are applying this tool of light you are applying consciousness.

What is consciousness? In this instance we are talking about particular particles of light that imbue a feeling, knowing, or sensation. We are talking about light and the application of light in a similar way as you would see the unlimited life-force energy of Reiki or Akasha; it holds everything, whereas a particular Reiki symbol holds a certain vibration or frequency. Each element—earth, air, water, or fire—is a certain type of frequency. The Rays of Light—the Love Ray, the Joy Ray, the Solar Ray, the Emerald Ray, the Forgiveness Ray, and the other various Rays of Light—have particular vibrations or frequencies for different purposes. Each of the other chapters in part one will explore an individual ray in more detail.

For instance, if someone was having trouble staying present in the now we would recommend the application of the Solar Ray of Light (see chapter 4). Because the Solar Ray is the Now Ray, it is a frequency that is encoded with a certain application of consciousness that when applied creates an alignment with the now.

ALIGNMENT AND THE FREQUENCY OF LIGHT

Let's say you are not exactly sure what type of ray to use in a certain situation, and you don't remember or don't know these individual Rays of Light. In some situations you may not know what you need to get unstuck or what another person needs to get to that next level. How would you call upon light and apply light as a frequency or a consciousness to a situation?

There are many different things that are going on simultaneously with a person. They have their thoughts, beliefs, emotions, physiology, and various levels of stress or conditioning among other things. One of the beauties about this tool of light is that inherent within it is an alignment faculty and ability so that when you apply the light it has inherent within it everything that a person would need. If what's really getting someone out of balance is their belief system, then inherent within the light would be the frequency that would help loosen their hold on their belief systems.

Or let's say they have a repetitive pattern or a soul learning that's really causing them trouble. Applying the frequency of light would create some freedom, some movement within that soul lesson or that repetitive pattern. Or perhaps it is an emotion or something that has gotten rooted in the physical and their physiology. Maybe it's a little bit of each one of those, and so as you apply the light it's like the one-size-fits-all frequency. It's then up to the person to be able to integrate it and receive it.

One thing that's different about using the tool of light for yourself or for someone else, as opposed to using other healing modalities, is that once light encompasses the person, they decide what to do with it. They may take it in or not.

It's like if you were a chef; it would be up to you to provide all of the nourishing nutrient aspects of a meal that would give someone everything that they would need to optimally function. You would make the meal and you would place it on the table and then you would leave. Then the person would come to the table and they would eat the food and then their system would assimilate it in a way that they can pull from it the nourishment. There are some types of food that are easier to digest, more flavorful, and more attractive; the person would have a better time with digesting and getting the nutrients from them. It is the same with the light. The light in this analogy would be like super blue green algae: something that is packed with nutrition and easy for the person to digest.

Sometimes when someone is stuck and you just say, "Oh, here's this thing that's going to help you but it's up to you to come to the table, to take the bites of the food, to digest the food, and to get the nutrients out of it," that person might feel too overwhelmed or not sure how to get to it. It seems like too big of a jump. The light and the application of this frequency provides a very easy shift; it already helps the person move into alignment.

Of course, not everyone's going to want to change. But for those people who do, it is a super-charged super food: a wonderful tool to have.

ENERGETIC EXERCISE
Radiating Light

Bring your awareness back to your Council of Light group. We will spend a few moments in silence allowing this light to come in so you can have a conscious experience of how it feels to you.

After you have a sense of what this tool of light feels like, begin to imagine that your inner being is emanating this light. This light is within your DNA, within your subatomic particles, within the minutest aspects of your being and the smallest infinitesimal particles of your being. Imagine that this light is shining from this very tiny place within you and that it creates trillions of little particles of light that all begin to hum together, stream together, emanate and shine from within your own body.

As this happens there is an alignment process occurring. You may have a sense of feeling like you are in right relationship with all there is. Allow these particles of light in your awareness to string together to create one big orb of light so that it is within every particle of your body. Spend a few moments turning up the dimmer switch of light in certain areas of your body that don't feel as if they're as "on" with this light as other parts. You may have a sense within your own body of "Wow, those light particles aren't shining as brightly or they're not strung together as much." Set your intention that the light in that one area, or multiple areas, of your body becomes stronger.

Especially focus on your neck, head, and shoulder area. Spend some time in the back of the neck, turning on the light and letting it shine through until it begins to get so strong that in a way it creates a halo around your head: an arch line and what the yogis would call the radiant body. The arch line goes from one ear to the next ear, and all the way from one shoulder to the next shoulder. This is really important. There is an aspect behind the head, neck, and the top of the shoulders that is a part of the energy system that is waking up. It will feel like having support where there wasn't support before. It is like you are being held or you can lean into something. It feels as if it is not hard to hold up the ten pounds that your head weighs. You feel held and supported in this area of your body. Continue to keep the light concentrated in your body.

Imagine that your body is like the sun and it has a certain physical location. Imagine that the rays of the sun are shining outward but the concentration of the sun's light remains within its own borders and physical dimension. You're not diluting the light from your own body in order to expand it out. You're keeping the light concentrated within your own body and then it begins to radiate, shine, and send out Rays of Light.

When you feel ready, take a couple of deep breaths and gently bring your awareness back to your body, moving or stretching your body in any direction you choose and coming back to this time and space.

UTILIZING THE TOOL OF LIGHT

You may be wondering, "Okay, now I have this tool, how do I apply it? How do I get the paint from the bucket onto the wall?" It's a process of shining, radiating, emitting, and glowing. In a way it's inherent; it's not something that you have to do. It's a natural process. If you turn on the light it glows. If you have a candle or a fire it has a natural halo or glow around it.

Let's say you want to practice carrying this within your own being. This could be a meditation practice that you have. But then let us say you don't only want to have it as your presence, you also want to apply it more focused than that. You want to utilize it in a conscious way. How would you apply the light to a certain area?

Suppose you want to bring the tool of light and the frequency of consciousness into your home to create a harmonic resonance that's good for everyone: pets, people, plants, and anyone that you may have in your home. You could direct this light through Rays of Light almost like a laser, although the process is less active than a laser. It's more relaxed than that.

ENERGETIC EXERCISE
Shining the Frequency of Light

Visualize an area of your house or wherever you live where you spend a lot of time. Maybe it's your bed, your side of the bed, a sitting area, office, or a chair that you sit in all the time. Imagine that this light is shining so brightly from within your being in the here and now that it's sending a Ray of Light to this chair, your side of the bed, or whatever you are choosing. There is a very inactive aspect to this. It's not something you really have to try to do. It just happens. You just glow and shine but you're consciously applying the light to your home. You may want to spend time doing this process to your entire home, shining the light.

Focus on a relationship that you have. Maybe it's a friend, a co-worker, a partner, or someone that you work with. Imagine that you are not doing anything to them but shining so brightly that the Ray of Light becomes present, and you're applying the color of frequency and consciousness to your connection to that person or those people. You maybe even want to choose someone that you're having a little bit of difficulty with, because then it could be like a test case. Try it and see what happens.

Focus on your finances and emanate this Ray of Light into your finances, applying the frequency of light and consciousness to your finances. You may visualize your purse, wallet, checkbook, bank accounts, and whatever else you may have. If you have them, focus on your credit cards, a mortgage, a trust fund, stocks, a retirement plan, or anything to do with finances. Maybe it's a debt. Shine this Ray of Light into everything to do with your finances. Maybe you're shining it on the sources of your finances and the ways that you make money: that could be your sessions with clients, your job, classes, or however it is that you make money. Shine it on the modality, on your mailbox, the way that you receive your money, the phone or your email.

We have practiced on a physical environment, a person, and finances, so for the last round of practice let's focus on your soul's purpose, your soul's fulfillment, and that which you feel is connecting you to what it is that you are here to experience.

Imagine that you can apply the frequency of light to your soul's journey. As we are applying this light to the soul's journey think of it as a spiral rather than a Ray of Light. It spirals in and around you as well as in and around your past, present, future, multidimensionality, past lives, future lives, and this life. There is an infinite spiral of light that's enhancing your signature energy, your essence, and your soul's journey.

Spend some time with this spiral of light, and when you are ready take a couple of deep breaths, move and stretch your body, and gently return to this time and space.

THE RAPID GROWTH CYCLE

We want to talk about the concept of rapid growth. Let's say that you wanted to do, be, or have something. There was often a time delay or a process between asking or having the desire and it showing up. Because of the time delay and the process there was an ease to it in some ways. There was also, and we mean this in the most respectful of ways, a naiveté around certain things that you wanted and what that would mean.

Suppose you have an intention to become more enlightened, more openhearted, or you want to become someone who has an expanded consciousness. In some ways those are abstract terms. You want to live your soul's purpose. These are words and yet when those things actually begin to happen more and more they may feel different or more plumped out than your idea of them.

In the process of becoming enlightened one of the steps is becoming lighter. In this step there is a transcendence of the density or a shedding of old identities; you may not have thought of this when you were asking for enlightenment. It's about shifting from being attached to the things that you care about to moving into a different orientation.

Let's say that you want to live your soul's purpose. It's not if you will or when you will or how much you will; you are living your soul's purpose no matter what. But if you want to really amp it up and align with what it is that you're here to do, in the past paradigm that would be a process that would take some time.

Or in the course of that process something that has been predominant in your life such as a relationship, a job, or the place that you live ends. Afterward there is a period of the unknown. After this period something new comes along. If that's spread out over the concept of time, which doesn't really exist anyhow, there's some space and a process to it.

Part of what happens and what is happening—in the future now—is that the acceleration is collapsing time; as it's collapsing time and you're applying the tool of light, things will happen much more quickly. It will be a rapid growth cycle. This is exactly what you've been asking for in some ways, and yet the experience of it can be intense and it can feel like you are not centered or grounded, or do not have your bearings in the same way as if it were happening over the illusion of linear time.

If you find that you are moving through something quickly the best way to do it is to stay connected to yourself. It's as if you are on a roller coaster. You can be holding on very tight and screaming in fear or you can have your arms up in the air and be exhilarated.

Another example is if you are on a fast river. You can think it's fun or you can try to slow it down. It can be exhausting. Or if you're riding a bike and you're going down the hill and it's going really fast and you feel a little bit out of control. You could try to put the brakes on but you could also just trust and go through it.

We are mentioning this because it provides a context for what you are experiencing as the Earth's vibration changes, regardless of working with this tool of light, and it will also be a component of working with this tool of light with yourself and with others. That's exciting because this rapid growth can create the transcendence and the transformation that you are wanting.

We are not suggesting that you hold back or that this tool needs a warning to it. We want to invite you to be mindful because sometimes if you ask for eight things at once—such as a new career, relationship, or a new home—and they happen all at once it could be an intense or stressful time. But maybe that's exactly what you want and that would be the best way for it to happen. Just keep that in mind as you're asking for things.

One of the ways you can play with this is to see if things show up more quickly than they used to. We would like for you to do some test case scenarios and focus on certain areas of your life, maybe even taking a few minutes to write down what are the most important areas that you want to focus on, and then applying this light to them.

SUMMARY

To utilize this tool the first thing that you do is to bring yourself into the present, in the now, as much as you can. Focus completely on the now. Ways that will assist you in doing this are to focus on your body, your breath, breathing into parts of your body; calling back your thoughts from past people, places, and times; and getting as current as possible. After this process, activate—from the subatomic level—small particles of your body, the light within you, letting it build, seeing these small dots of light stringing together and shining outward. Then you can focus on a certain area, place, or part of your life and imagine shining this light out into that area. Remember it will feel easy and light. It won't feel like heavy lifting. There's not a lot of doing to it. And then just see what happens. Notice what you notice.

The rest of part one will explore the characteristics and uses of the individual Rays of Light. You can call on those particular rays when the situation calls for it. However, you can still call upon the light for yourself—or someone else—without naming a specific ray. All the rays are all contained within the light as a whole, so you don't have to know about the particular stream. You can also call upon your particular Council of Light members to assist you.

2

THE LOVE RAY

The Unity Consciousness Ray

▲

One of the highest and purest vibrations available on the planet at
this time. Provides an opportunity to entrain to a higher frequency
and include any vibrations that are moving more slowly back into
oneness or wholeness.

TUNING IN
. . . .
Love Ray Activation

*This is the Council of Light that's moving more into the forefront of this now
moment. As we are acclimating to your system there are a few indications of this
acclimation process that you may begin to identify. You may have an awareness
of a deeper sense of calm in your mind. Your mind becomes still and very
focused on a quality and an energy of peace. This energy of peace also creates
the invitation for your body to relax even more deeply into the energy and the
consciousness of you.*

*The Love Ray is moving more into the forefront of this now moment to
transmit the pure consciousness of this illuminated energy. Simply allow yourself
to drop into this peaceful state in your mind, the relaxed state in your body,
and have an awareness of the Love Ray. To first tune in to the Love Ray bring
your awareness to your heart and to the beat of your heart. Feel the sensation
or perception that your heart is like a compass and that it is a compass of your*

soul. Feel the sensation that this compass is pointing you toward the true north of your soul, the path of your soul, the direction of your soul.

Spend a few moments in the heartbeat: the beat and the pause. Both are equally significant. As you are with the beat of your heart have the awareness of the dynamic flow of the beat and then the absence of the beat. Both the beat and the absence of the beat are very active states of the heart.

Now tune in to your pituitary gland in the center of your head and imagine that in your pituitary gland there is a similar pulse as the heartbeat: there is this pulsation and then a silence, pause, or a stillness, and then there's another pulsation and a silence, pause, or a stillness. Feel the pulse of your pituitary gland.

Then bring your awareness from the head, down through the heart, past the navel center to the base of the spine and feel a similar energetic pulse, a heartbeat at the base of your spine. Head, heart, sacrum. Now that you have been with these three places and the energy pulse that exists within these three places, choose to activate the Love Ray at the head, the heart, and the base of the spine. This energy already exists within your system; it has been dormant and awaiting this moment of your choice. The Love Ray is a high vibrational frequency of oneness. It is a vibration that creates harmony. Take a moment to go within and allow your awareness to guide you in accessing more and more of the Love Ray. When this initial process feels complete continue reading.

. . . .

THE LOVE RAY AS
UNITS OF CONSCIOUSNESS

The Love Ray is units of consciousness that are in a state of oneness, in a state of harmonic resonance, and in a state of high vibrational frequency. The Love Ray is a vibration and is not an emotion, yet the word "love" is very indicative of the Love Ray. The emotion of love when you feel love, when you fall in love, is an indication of what is present within the Love Ray. Yet the emotion of love is only one small facet of what's possible with the Love Ray.

To further explore what the Love Ray is and how you can use it, we will begin by having you connect to it as a vibration and as a frequency of oneness. If you think of it as units of consciousness, drops of energy or drops of frequency, then as you apply drops of the Love Ray to your system, as you apply drops of the Love Ray to your plants, as you apply drops of the Love Ray to your home, your body, your finances and to your relationships, then it brings a field of oneness and harmony to those things. It creates a vibrational invitation for that which was in a place of chaos or disharmony to organize into divine order and into a place of harmony.

Harmony, if you think of it in terms of sound, is really not that everything becomes the same—it's just that there's a resonance between the uniqueness of everything. Everything is meant to have a distinct vibration and a distinct purpose. Part of how that harmony is created is that the overlays and the distortions that have been placed upon that which would naturally be in harmonic resonance get included back into the wholeness. It gets entrained into a higher vibration and it gets acclimated into the vibration of oneness.

Let's say you have a hundred people and they are each sitting in a chair, and in between the chairs are cubicles or partitions that are blocking each person from being able to communicate or connect to the rest of the people. Then you apply the Love Ray and the Love Ray dissolves the partitions. They are then able to gift and receive that which is meant to be gifted and received within the community of these hundred people. That's a conceptual view of what the Love Ray does, because the Love Ray also opens up the natural connection or oneness. Oneness connects to the interconnectedness of all things so that that interconnectedness can be free flowing. It can be free flowing in such a way that there is a natural circulation and vibration and wholeness that is there. The Love Ray is the high vibrational frequency.

As you apply drops of food coloring to water the water becomes the color of the food coloring. As you apply drops of the Love Ray, units of consciousness of the Love Ray, to yourself, to your money, or to your health, then these areas of your life are imbued with harmony and high vibrational frequency. That which you desire, that which you would like to actualize, that which you would like to manifest, is moving at a higher vibration. It is a matter of you taking down the partitions between you and everything that you are choosing to actualize.

ENERGETIC EXERCISE
The Love Ray as a Fountain

If you choose, activate the Love Ray within your pituitary gland, within your heart, and within the base of your spine. Then allow the Love Ray to build. It builds like a fountain in each of these three areas. It builds like a fountain at the base of the spine as it accesses more and more and more of the Love Ray. This Love Ray fills up and circulates up the channel of the central column, the center of your spine, to meet the Love Ray at the heart that then circulates throughout the entire circulatory system. This Love Ray is awakened within the entire circulatory system and this fountain rises up through the throat to meet at the pituitary gland. It almost tickles the pituitary gland and awakens the pituitary gland.

Continuing on its journey, the Love Ray descends once again from the pituitary gland down through the throat, down through the heart to the base of the spine. Then it ascends again, and this time as it ascends you may have an awareness of a spiral staircase like DNA. This spiral staircase circulates around the spinal column, and as it does your energy rises in frequency and it comes into a greater state of oneness and harmony. This Love Ray vibration calls to it anything that has been forgotten or been in a space of exile. The Love Ray, this high vibration, invites anything that's moving at a slower vibration to entrain to it. It does so with ease and with grace. It simply is a call to move up to a higher vibration.

You may think of this like in an Olympic race. They have a pace setter: the runner who is out in front setting the pace for the other runners to entrain to or to follow. The Love Ray is setting the pace of the frequency of your system that can easily be brought into oneness through the harmony and the high vibration of the Love Ray. It is consciousness, it is light, it is frequency, and it is vibration that is including all there is. Breathe and allow this to be.

DISSOLVING ILLUSIONS
AND MOVING INTO HARMONY

You are in a cubicle and the money, the joy, the health, the happiness, the career, the relationships, the connection to your soul and your consciousness, the home, the car, whatever it is that you would like, are all within different cubicles, divided by partitions. The partitions and the cubicles are illusions. They only seem to be there. When you are sitting in your cubicle, when you are sitting in your partitioned-off area, you can't see or touch that which is outside of it. As you involve yourself with each Ray of Light they dissolve the illusion of what you feel keeps you separate from what you would choose.

The illusions may sound like your negative beliefs, they may sound like being super attached to the outcome, they may sound like or look like feelings of unworthiness, or you can't have what you want, or if you have what you want you'll be in danger. There are a hundred different forms of whatever that illusion is, and yet the Love Ray, as you apply the drops of consciousness, absorbs and brings back into harmony this discordant vibration, these overlays, projections, separations, untruths, and chaotic energy that are masking the unique vibration of each signature energy.

EVERYTHING HAS ITS OWN
UNIQUE SIGNATURE ENERGY

This concept applies to the body. A disease somewhere in the body is an overlay that's been placed upon the optimal functioning of that part. If you take it even one step deeper and look at the vibration of the liver, for example, and the vibration of the bones and the vibration of the ears, we can see that they aren't all vibrating exactly the same when they're in their optimal frequency. The bone has a unique signature energy, the ear and its capacity to hear has its unique signature energy, and the liver has a unique signature energy. If the liver gets stressed then there's an overlay of stress on top of the liver. When you apply the Love Ray the liver can just be the liver again. It absorbs the stress of the liver and it absorbs the pattern that the liver has taken on that isn't actually its pattern.

THE LOVE RAY IS RESTORATIVE

A way to look at the Love Ray and its purpose is to see that it restores things to what they actually are. That is why we are connecting with you, because your natural state is resonating with the vibration of joy. It already resonates with the high frequency.

Imagine that you are applying units of consciousness of the Love Ray to the partitions around you. As you are applying the Love Ray the illusion that's separating you and the idea that you are even separate dissolves and the interconnectedness, the communion, begins to flow again. The energy flow begins and your projections—let's say about money because money often has a lot of projections on top of it— dissolve so that you can be interconnected to the energy of money.

YOU ALREADY KNOW THE
DEEPEST DESIRES OF YOUR SOUL

You may choose to drop some units of Love Ray consciousness onto the illusion that you don't know your soul's deepest desires. You are always getting information from within you and from within your life: messages, guidance, instinct, intuition, and knowing as to what it is that you would really like. A sense that we have about you is that you've come to this material from a place of readiness, from a place of wanting to spend what you would think of as units of time, the rest of your incarnation in this body, in ways that are deeply meaningful and deeply satisfying for you on a soul level. There is an urgency within you to spend your time doing what really matters to you, to get on with what it is that you're here for, and be liberated from anything that seems to be blocking you from that. The Love Ray is available for that as well. The Love Ray is allowing the energy and the harmony within yourself to be you.

ENERGETIC EXERCISE
The Spiral of the Love Ray

Spend some moments in silence with the spiral of this Love Ray moving up and down the spine from the base of the spine to the heart to the pituitary gland and then from the pituitary gland to the heart to the base of the spine. The Love Ray can be a pathway that the other rays are more easily assimilated in. It's like how you can add herbs to water. Water is a carrier of other substances, just like the Love Ray can be.

Now have an awareness of this spiral ray building in consciousness. It is a gradual process because you are remembering the Love Ray directly from within your own cellular memory, from within your DNA, and from within your own Akashic Records. This awareness, this consciousness, is building in momentum; it's building in consciousness and the longer that you're steeping in the Love Ray the more you are realizing the evolution of your soul. The evolution of your soul is such that as you raise your vibration, as you increase the speed in which your cells are moving, you have access to more of your infinite nature and to your soul. Through the Love Ray, if you choose, begin to open the pathways of communication with your soul. As you're opening up the pathways of communication with your soul you can recognize or perceive that the Love Ray is flowing and spiraling within the consciousness of your soul as well. The Love Ray within your body and the Love Ray that's flowing within your soul create a oneness with body and soul.

As the Love Ray is a ray of harmony and it is a ray of high vibrational energy and it is a ray of oneness, feel a greater assimilation with your energy and consciousness as a multidimensional being, as a divine being. The Love Ray also provides an opening to expand your awareness to include that which may be unknown to you about you. This initiation is also awakening, if you choose it, your capacity to manifest, your capacity as a creator being, and your capacity to access your innate capacities to feel joy, to resonate with health, to resonate with wealth, and to be in oneness with the deepest desires of your soul.

Knowing that the energy of the Love Ray will continue to build as we continue our conversation about the Love Ray, gently bring your awareness back to an awake and aware consciousness. You may gently feel inclined to stretch your fingers or your toes or rub the palms of your hands together or even clap a few times. This clapping works directly with the heart center as a beautiful way to assimilate more of the energies.

COMBINING RAYS OF LIGHT

You may, as you move forward into the Rays of Light, begin to see the potent combinations when you use certain rays together. For example, when the Love Ray is connected to the Emerald Ray, which is the You Ray, together they help you authentically be you. There is a tendency to want to get rid of that which you would call negative and to avoid those experiences that are less preferred or less desirable. We agree that it is not beneficial to stay in any polarity for an extended length of time. Allowing and integrating these thoughts, feelings, attributes, and experiences will assist you in coming into wholeness. Similarly, integrating your positive gifts allows room for less developed aspects of yourself to shine forth. The combination of the Love Ray and the Emerald Ray assists you to pulsate with your essence, your signature energy in a state of harmony, creating this exquisite quantum effect.

SUPPORT EXERCISE
Integrating Back into Wholeness

You might have a running dialogue in your mind of negative self-talk or things about yourself that you may not like. Allow those thoughts and any sensations associated with them to come into your awareness. Perhaps it is a habit, a body part, or some quality about yourself that you do not like. Allow it to come to the surface.

Rather than trying to get rid of this part of you that you may not like as much as other parts, we invite you to allow it, thank it, bless it, and to include it back into the wholeness. That we began with your heart center and the back of your heart center at the start of this segment, and connecting to the energy of love, was on purpose. The love vibration is inclusive. Love and having an open heart is neutral. It is large enough to include the positive and the negative. It includes the wholeness.

Include back into the wholeness any aspects of you that you may not have preferred as much as others. This is trapped energy and is energy that you can be utilizing. It creates a fragmented frequency. It is like having interference on your radio station when you are in between stations. There is not a clear signal that is being transmitted. Intend to integrate this aspect back into the oneness and the expansiveness of the heart and love energy. It is like recycling and melting a bottle back into its preformed state. It is alchemy. Even if your conscious mind does not know how to do this, a part of you does.

Think about a gift, talent, or an attribute of yourself that you like, find wonderful, that you lean on or lead with. Thank and bless this part and bring it back into the wholeness, into your heart space and into love so that it creates an opportunity to move into areas of you that have been underexplored or underdeveloped. It is not that this gift, talent, and attribute goes away. It is so strongly a part of you that it will remain a part of you, but it allows another aspect of you to come forward more.

We invite you to think on the soul level, the level of intuition and the aspect of your spirit, what is it that you feel is an essential part of you that has not been explored fully. This may be a whisper, a dream, a thought, something that you experienced as a child, something that you think you would enjoy doing, or a part of you that you know is there but for some reason, whatever the reason is, it has not been expressed fully. Invite this part, whether you consciously are connecting to it right now or not, to come on line, to be a part of the wholeness, to be a part of your expression, to be part of the you that you are transmitting, that you are projecting, and that you are bringing into the presence of your life. Invite this part to be integrated back into the wholeness, allowing you to have greater access and a deeper connection to it.

Spend some time with this process, and when you feel ready take some deep breaths, gently move and stretch your body, and return to this time and space.

We are presenting the Rays of Light as individual bands of consciousness, and yet just like a rainbow is a spectrum of consciousness, so are the Rays of Light. As you bring one Ray of Light into proximity with another Ray of Light then something unique is generated and cultivated. These Rays of Light may merge together like blue and red become purple, and they may also act together like a candy cane or a stripe where they're next to each other, like a prism reflects light.

THE DESIRE TO BE IN LOVING COMMUNICATION AND CONNECTION

Because the Love Ray is so associated with the word and emotion of love we recognize that one of the deepest desires of your soul is to be in loving communion with others and to be in connection. You may want to manifest a person to share your love with or you may want to manifest a better connection with your family or your friends. The Love Ray can induce a state of harmony and a state of vibration within you that then creates an invitation for those that want to be in communion with you. Yet we feel that if you were to associate the Love Ray solely with relationships that would actually limit what's possible with it. Can you apply the Love Ray to relationships? Yes, and yet to only use it for that would be tapping into a small, small vibration of what is possible with it. As you see that it enhances oneness or interconnectedness with all there is, you can also see that attribute is one of the keys to manifestation.

APPLYING THE LOVE RAY TO THE BODY

The Love Ray could also be applied physiologically to the body when there is something that has been lost—like in a stroke when you've lost part of your capacity to move. Applying the units of consciousness of the Love Ray can help reopen the connections to that part of the body. Or if there's part of the body that's gone numb the Love Ray could be one that would create the interconnectedness to the body. This also works for relationships; let's say there are aspects of your relationship that have gone numb or you don't have a direct connection to them—maybe these are affection, laughter, sensuality or sexuality, communication, tenderness, or gentleness. Applying the Love Ray to the relationship can help awaken those connections once again.

APPLYING THE LOVE RAY TO OTHER ASPECTS OF YOUR LIFE

If your creativity has been dormant, or if you have not had access to your creativity, after applying the Love Ray it would be enhanced. It is the same with your money and your finances. If you apply the Love Ray to your money and your finances then any interconnectedness that's been missing can be reawakened. Sometimes when it comes to money people may have a sort of amnesia or a numbing out or a shutting down. One of the coping mechanisms that some people adopt with money is to try to ignore it, not opening the bills, not having an awareness of how much your expenses are, and having an ostrich-in-the-sand approach to money. If you apply the Love Ray to your money relationship then it creates an open-eyed experience.

UTILIZING THE LOVE RAY IN STAGES

One aspect of the Love Ray is that it can be utilized in stages. It's like when you're putting a pot of water on the stove to boil and the water is cold. If the cold water is a slow vibration (which it isn't, but for the purpose of this analogy we will call it so) and the boiling water is a faster frequency, there is a gradual change in frequency—there is steam. The water doesn't boil instantly. It's a process.

That's the same with the Love Ray. As you apply the Love Ray you don't instantly snap into this high vibration. It could work that way and yet it's not the way that you have been used to having it work. Utilizing the Love Ray in stages or as a process also allows you to be with it in ways that are with grace for all levels of your system. It's like a time-released vitamin; you eat the vitamin and yet the benefit of the vitamin keeps going and going. It's not only what you can uptake in the moment that you can utilize. That's the process of oneness, that's the process of disintegrating the cubicles, the illusions, the partitions.

WRITTEN EXERCISE
Exploration of the Deepest Desires of the Soul

We would like to complete this segment with a writing exercise. What is it that you would like to connect to in this moment that would totally realize the deepest desires of your soul?

Once you have your paper, pen, or computer and keyboard ready, call upon the Love Ray. You may do the same exercise that we did in the beginning of connecting to your heartbeat, connecting to your pituitary gland, connecting to the base of your spine, calling upon the Love Ray and letting it build a pathway and the spiral of ascension and descension. Call upon the Love Ray; when you feel that you've connected and you have an awareness that you feel a greater sense of harmony or a greater sense of peace, ask to connect to your soul and to communicate with your soul. The Love Ray is creating a deeper interconnectedness, a oneness to your soul and the consciousness that your soul has. Then ask, "What are the deepest desires of my soul?"

Spend a few moments writing about the deepest desires of your soul. Maybe this is in longhand or maybe it comes out as a list. Spend about ten minutes with this, and in the last couple of minutes, if you can, create a list or a sentence that really embodies for you the deepest desires of your soul.

The reason that we're recommending that you don't spend tons of time on this is because when you're in this interconnectedness with the soul it just comes quickly; you can trust that what comes through is what you're wanting to know at this time. Once you have your written form you may want to put it on a different piece of paper. Then imagine that you are calling upon the Love Ray and that you're dropping units of the Love Ray onto this piece of paper, and that that is a process of manifestation. It's disintegrating anything that is creating a lack of connection between you and what it is that you're choosing to have in your life, and that it is also amplifying your vibration to be in the high vibration of that which you would choose.

The Love Ray has been transmitted completely. It is one that is available to you, and we've shared many ways that you can apply it directly to your life. Enjoy the Love Ray.

3

THE JOY RAY

The Portal to Greater Health, Wealth, and Happiness

▲

Enhances the vibration of joy and supports you to see the joy that already exists right here and now. It helps you entrain to the high vibration of joy, to take an energetic journey into a higher state of awareness and frequency. This alignment with joy is fundamental to enhancing health, wealth, and happiness, because joy is in vibrational proximity to these qualities.

TUNING IN
. . . .
Open to Receive This Divine Transmission

To assist your system in receiving this divine transmission, please find a comfortable position in which you can relax and begin to focus on your breathing. Notice your breath coming in and going out of your body. Allow your breath to slow down naturally and to deepen. As you are breathing begin to focus on your feet. Feel your feet and breathe into your feet. Allow the act of breathing into your feet to represent the energizing of your path and your walk in life.

Bring your attention to the space above your head and breathe into your higher self, which exists about an arm's length above your head. Focusing on and breathing into your higher self energizes the part of you that knows—the part of you that is intuitive.

Having breathed into your feet and your higher self now begin to focus on your heart center. Breathe into your heart. As you are breathing into your heart and energizing your heart, focus on the emotion of gratitude. Notice what you are grateful for and what you appreciate in your life. The energy of gratitude and appreciation helps open your system to receive this divine transmission. Feel your heart open wide.

To complete this process of preparing to receive, inhale from your higher self above your head and focus on this breath going all the way down through your heart and down toward your feet. Now exhale from your feet up to your heart and up to your higher self. Practice bringing the breath up and down and then down and up again.

. . . .

INCREASING JOY IN YOUR LIFE

Our purpose is to assist you in increasing joy and through that increased joy to increase the amount of happiness, health, and abundance that you experience in your life. We are doing this through these words but mostly through the vibration of this divine transmission of frequency and energy. This is a freewill universe, so you are in charge of your experience. You are in charge of how much benefit you get from our encounter. You are in charge of how much benefit you get from our interaction.

A CHOOSING EXERCISE
The Willingness to Live an Exquisite Life

Allow yourself to feel, hear, know, see, taste, and sense the energy transfer that is happening in this moment. With your free will ask yourself this very important question, "Are you willing to experience more joy in your life?" This seems like the simplest of questions and you may rush to answer: "Yes." You may desire to be happier, to have more joy, and to have more fun. These things may be what you have been longing for. On the surface it is easy to answer yes, and that is actually all that is necessary. Yet on a deeper level are you actually willing to be happy, to be at peace, to see life as a joyous and fun experience? Are you willing to move beyond what you know of separation consciousness or lack? Are you willing to move beyond the lack of happiness, health, joy, money, time, peace, vitality, and energy? Are you willing to own that you know everything that there is to know about not having enough, about not being enough, and are you willing to step into the unknown of consistent moment-to-moment joy, bliss, and unity?

From our perspective we feel that you have learned everything there is to learn from your repetitive patterns, from your sense of feeling unfulfilled, and that there would be more to learn from living an exquisite life. Take a moment through your intention to preserve the conscious and unconscious learning from your life up until this point.

If it is your choice, say out loud, "I am willing to have an exquisite life." By simply having made this choice, this decision, and having set your intention to experience more joy, your entire being is able to receive more consciousness. Focus on the cells in your body and allow this transmission of energy to be received from the level of your cells. Take all the time that you would like to bask in the enhanced energy of your cells. When you feel complete, stretch your body and gently open your eyes.

We have mentioned that we are a council of intergalactic beings. This sounds stranger than it actually is, yet it is one way for you to perceive us. At our base we are made of the same thing as you are. This divine substance is your heritage and is our vibrational makeup. The questions and the longing that people have on the planet at this time have called us forth. It is not that this wisdom is something that you lack or is something that is outside of you. It is a process of remembering.

ENERGETIC EXERCISE
Remember and Awaken Joy

We will spend a few moments in silence transmitting energy to assist you to come into a greater resonance of joy. At this time we are transmitting the Joy Ray to assist the transmission and the receiving of this joy frequency.

Focus on a time where you felt joyful, where you felt bliss, fun, ecstasy, and laughter. As this memory of joy is coming into your awareness, have a sense of your cells dancing, have a sense of the energy within your body beginning to bubble like effervescence, like bubbles in champagne. By simply remembering this time of joy, something within you is awakening; something ancient and deep, familiar, and fun is awakening within you. Allow this joy to erupt within you, to activate within you, to awaken. It is your divine birthright to be joyous. Spend a few more moments of concentration remembering and activating this Joy Ray. Notice if it has a certain color for you or a certain word associated with it. Ask for a symbol in which you can connect to it in the future. Knowing that you can call upon the Joy Ray whenever you would like, gently bring your focus back to feeling your body and noticing your breath.

Remembering and awakening the joy inside you opens a door in your life. Once opened, the paths to joy are countless—so long as you are willing to recognize them. The next exercise will help you connect with the energy of these joyous opportunities.

SUPPORT EXERCISE
Create a Joy List and Connect Daily to the Joy Ray

We would invite you to create a joy list; a list of activities that make you feel joyous when you do them. Place this list close to you where you can see it. You may even contemplate putting activities on your list that you have never done, but the idea of them brings joy.

We would also recommend that you call upon the Joy Ray for five minutes a day. You can begin this segment of your day by stating out loud, "I am willing to have an exquisite life. I call upon the Joy Ray." Then focus on your symbol, your word, or your memory to activate this Joy Ray. Then just allow yourself to be in the energy of the Joy Ray for the next five minutes of the exercise. During the exercise you can also imagine that you are doing the activities on your list. Spending five minutes a day consciously connecting to the energy of joy in its purest state will increase the joy in your life.

THE VIBRATION OF JOY

You may think about joy as an emotion. This is partially true. In actuality it is a vibration; it is energy. In its purest form it elicits a very harmonic resonance and a very peaceful state. As you are connecting to this energy, to this frequency of joy, it encourages your body, mind, emotions, and spirit to align with oneness: to come into a state of unity, into a state of harmony. From this state of harmony you are able to connect to the deepest parts of you: to your spirit, your soul, and to your heart's desire. All of you functions as one unit.

One of the main reasons that you may feel discontent in your life is the splitting of your energy. Your mind thinks one thing, your emotions feel another, your body is in tune with something else, your spirit is singing an entirely different tune, and you may feel confused, scattered, or not present. By introducing the Ray of Joy, the energy of joy, into this incoherent vibration there is a unifying effect. You are so much more than you can see, touch, and feel. Your essence is actually timeless; it is eternal.

SUPPORT EXERCISE
Immerse Yourself in Joy

We invite you to think of something that brings you a lot of joy; it could be a memory, thought, person, place, or a color. As you are thinking about and connecting to this energy and memory of joy, allow it to spark the natural rhythm of joy within you. Immerse yourself in this feeling of joy and allow it to permeate every aspect of your being.

When you are ready take a couple of deep breaths, stretch your body, move your fingers and toes, and return to this time and space.

CHOOSING JOY

You may have a habit of putting most of your attention on what you can think about and what you can see. Yet our hope for you is that you begin to put more attention on your essence, on your eternal nature, and on your multidimensional self. As your body, mind, emotions, and spirit come into resonance then your eternal nature, your divine nature, and your essence are able to communicate with you more fully.

There is also the thought that your external environment is what is dictating your feeling of happiness in your life. If there is something in your life that is not to your liking then you feel negative, unhappy, or discontent. If there is something that is to your liking you feel happy and at peace. From our perspective this is one of the main reasons why people feel unhappy. It is a no-win situation to allow your inner state and your inner feelings to be dictated by your external environment. The amount of time that you are perfectly the right temperature, have the perfect amount of rest, the perfect amount of nourishment, and all of your conditions are perfect is a small window. Your environment is always changing. If you shift your focus from allowing your external environment to elicit a state of joy or a feeling of joy and you consciously decide to be joyous regardless of any situation, then you will have a joyful life. If you choose joy moment to moment then you will have a life of joy.

When you are connected to your expanded self, you are in tune with the larger picture of your life: of your soul's evolution, of your past experiences, having purpose, and of everything that has happened in your life being the best thing that could have ever happened. It is this expanded state that allows you to be neutral enough to decide that everything in your life is good and is a reason for joy.

ENERGY

We initially stated that our purpose is to enhance joy so that you can have more happiness, health, and abundance in your life. You may be wondering: What does one have to do with the other? How does experiencing joy on a regular basis enhance your health, wealth, and happiness? They are intricately connected, and there is actually a shift that is happening in the consciousness of the planet and those that inhabit it. Because of this shift the connection is even more accessible and even more true. It is common knowledge that everything is at its base made up of energy. This energy is moving at different frequencies and vibrations, and depending on the speed and the density of the energy it creates different forms of physical matter. The density of a chair is different than the density of water in the ocean, yet down at their base they are all made of the same matter.

You are also made of energy and your body is made up of an infinitesimal amount of different frequencies that have optimal frequencies to create optimal functioning. Your liver is vibrating at a different level than your skin. The frequency of your heart is different than the frequency of your thumbnail. The way that all of these energies move together in an innate wisdom to create harmony and health is beyond what your mind can comprehend. In actuality you do not need to think in order to digest your food or to breathe. These are automatic parts of your autonomic nervous system.

ENTRAINING TO THE
HIGHER FREQUENCY OF JOY

We were talking about vibration being the basis of matter and how your intellect, your mind, is not responsible for the optimal functioning of your body. These two premises, these two reasons, are also true for why joy creates health, happiness, and wealth. Joy is a high frequency energy. In the laboratory when you have two heart cells next to each other the one that is moving more quickly will entrain the one that is moving more slowly to it. This is the process that is also occurring through this divine transmission. You are entraining to the higher frequency energy of joy. That which you desire in your life is also moving at a high vibration or a faster resonance than that which you do not prefer. Disease has a higher density than health does; it is a lower vibration. As more of your energy moves from your mind into the rest of your being, you are able to experience greater levels of synchronicity, greater levels of unification, of oneness, and of wholeness.

As you are resonating in harmony you are in tune with your intuition and your inner guidance. The chatter of your mind and the distraction of your emotions are unified into the whole; it is one sound. In this one sound you are able to move through your life more effortlessly and function at a very supreme level. To be informed from your essence, from your soul, about what actions to take enhances the return on your efforts.

SYNCHRONICITY

For example, you may desire a new home. You could look through the newspaper or the Internet listings for a new home. You could hire a real estate agent and go out weekends and evenings looking for your new home. This is an example of how you may have approached the goal of having a new home in the past.

There is an easier way. If you tune in to the Joy Ray and you allow yourself to come into wholeness and connect to your inner wisdom, your inner guidance, and your intuition, then you can ask what would be the most optimal action to take. How can you achieve your goal of a new home with ease and grace? You may see in your mind an old friend that you have not seen for ten years, yet you are guided to call this old friend. As you do, you discover this friend happens to be living in a home that is for sale that is the exact specifications that you desire in your life. Through this one small action your goal of finding a new home is achieved. This is an example of the way in which the energies on the planet are changing and the way in which you are being invited to change how you are living your life. Inspired action, unified action, and divine action are shortcuts to where you want to go.

MOVING TO A HIGHER LEVEL
OF AWARENESS AND BEING

One of the reasons why we are here at this time offering this wisdom that increases joy is that it is a very unique time on the Earth. In some ways it is like living at a time when there is not the technology of the telephone. You try to explain what the telephone is, and the capacity to understand the technology is challenging. The idea that you can pick up a physical object and talk into it and talk to somebody who is on the other side of the world is a concept that—for those people who lived before the telephone—is a challenge to believe and to understand.

Once people have seen the changes of a hundred years and have used a telephone, at some point its use becomes automatic. Yet between the time before the telephone was created to the time when a person has the phone and uses it every day, there is a shift in awareness and a shift in consciousness that has to happen.

This is similar to what is happening on the planet at this time. Communicating through telegraph, through letters in the mail, through telegrams, and in person are remnants of another time. Now you can connect to anybody around the world through the Internet. This is another concept that people had to get used to. Now it is automatic. It was the same with electricity; before there was electricity the concept of electricity would probably seem crazy, yet now you flip the switch and you trust that the light will go on.

We have been beaconed forth at this time by those of you who are seeking information about where you are headed and about the new ways of living and communicating. They are based somewhat in where you have been. It is a natural evolution. People were talking to one another long before the phone was created. The things that you will be doing and the ways that you will be doing them will be based on the foundation of where you have been. You have had the goal of having a new home but the way of achieving the goal changes.

DESIRE AND CREATION

This is the type of information that we are here to share. One of the challenges that we have is that the consciousness is so steeped in what it knows that in order to open up to what is yet to be there takes a level of trust, a level of desire, and a level of willingness. But it is the natural evolution and we know that if it feels good to you then you will have a higher likelihood of trying it. If it makes sense to you and it fulfills a need that you have then you will want to evolve, you will want to move forward. It is the desire that you already had that called forth the creation of the telephone. It is the desire that you already have that calls forth the ways of living your life with enhanced ease and grace, joy, and fulfillment.

The timing of us being here and speaking with you in this way is intentional. There is a critical mass of needs and an expansion in consciousness that will fulfill those needs more easily. We have come full circle from where we began; we will complete by encouraging you to spend five minutes a day with this joy energy and begin to ask for divine inspiration. Follow your instincts and make a conscious decision to experience more joy.

4

THE SOLAR RAY

The Now Ray

▲

Supports you to be energetically focused in the now. It allows
you to be present and to see and gravitate toward the good that
already exists in the now moment. This is a key shift to being in
unity consciousness, for it transcends the distorted illusion of focusing on the past or future.

TUNING IN
. . . .
The Eternal Nectar of the Pineal Gland

*We begin our time together on the subject of the Solar Ray. Take a moment to
connect to your pineal gland in the center of your head. Allow the eternal nectar
of the pineal gland to overflow, to expand, and to become more moist and juicy.
Imagine your pineal gland is a chalice overflowing with this eternal nectar and
saturating your entire body. As your pineal gland is overflowing you become more
moist, more supple, more flexible, more receptive, and more relaxed. As this
nectar is traveling and filling your whole body, focus on your adrenal glands and
imagine that there is a wellspring of divine nectar saturating your adrenal glands.
Feel this divine nectar feeding, nourishing, and refilling your adrenal glands.*

    *All there is exists in each moment, in each memory, and in each particle of
your being. There is an unlimited life-force energy that exists within you. Within
this universal life-force energy everything exists. Good exists in every moment,*

every particle, and in every aspect of your life. It is a matter of choosing to find it, choosing to illuminate it, and allowing your awareness to gravitate toward it.

Imagine there is a star like a disco ball in the center of the room you are in, and it contains a refraction, a reflection, a ray of energy, the Solar Ray. Connect to your pineal gland and stimulate the memory to be able to see the good in any moment and the innate ability to gravitate toward the good. You are activating your innate sense and instinct to discover the good in each moment. Spend a few minutes allowing the Solar Ray to activate within you your capacity to access the good in any moment.

. . . .

The Solar Ray is the Now Ray. The Solar Ray is like the sun and is ever present. This one ray, this one band of consciousness, can completely enhance the good that is in your life already. The concept and illusion of the past, present, and future, the sense of separation and longing, the sense of searching, seeking, doing, and striving, has created a distortion. It has created a warp in time, a split almost like a tear in the fabric of creation. The Solar Ray fills in that tear.

Distrust is part of the reason people resist the Solar Ray, or the ever-present nature of the Divine or the now. This distrust is founded in the old paradigm. If you choose to move into a higher consciousness or into happiness you will move beyond distrust and into your own knowing. For it is not really distrust or trust, it is simply a knowing. This connection to your own knowing will allow you to be much more comfortable with spending time in and connecting to the present moment. You will find yourself connecting to the now moment and the next now moment and the next and the next now moment. You will wake up and will spend less time focusing on the things of the future.

YOU HAVE ALL THAT YOU NEED

You have all that you need in each and every moment. You have enough energy for this moment, you have enough time for this moment, you have enough finances for this moment, you have enough for each moment of now. Fear, anxiety, and the sense of scarcity happen when you think about needing resources for every now that has ever been and will ever be, and this creates a sense of scarcity and a sense of lack. The necessity of what you need is the attraction that draws to you that which you need. In each moment you are putting out a signal to call forth the meeting of that desire.

UNSTRINGING TIME

Allow yourself to unstring time. You may know that time does not exist, that it is an illusion, that there is no past, present, or future, and that all time exists now. If it feels like something you would desire, unstring your need for everything from all time. Let us say you need 500 pounds of food for the next amount of time, which does not exist. You do not need all 500 pounds of food right now. You could not eat all 500 pounds of food. It would not be fresh, it would rot, and it would not be necessary. What we are asking you to do by asking you to unstring the pearls around food or nourishment throughout time and space is to allow yourself to, in this moment, have the pound of food that you need for this moment.

One question that is frequently asked about meditation—and we believe your entire life is a walking meditation—is how can I still my thoughts? How can I be present? How can I quiet my mind? Here is an exercise that you can do to bring yourself into the now moment.

PHYSICAL EXERCISE
Being in the Now by Tuning In to the Solar Ray

To begin gently place your index finger on top of your thumb and tap your index finger to your thumb. You may have the desire to move the thumb toward the index finger, but that is a different motion. Just tap the index finger to the thumb and connect to the now, connect to the

Solar Ray. As you are doing this tapping say, "Now, now, now, now, now, now, now, now, now."

Keep tapping, and if you find yourself late at night in your bed thinking about the future or being stuck in a thought process that is taking you into the past or the future, do this tapping exercise for five or ten minutes. Tap the index finger onto the thumb and it will bring you into the now. Every time you tap say, "Now, now, now, I have a body, I have a body, I have a body."

You can also alternate the tapping by creating a formula such as tapping for three minutes simultaneously with both hands and then tapping two minutes alternating hands, varying your pace—fast then slow. Then hold the fingers together for one minute and go into a deep silence and the infinite experience of the Solar Ray, feeling the energy in your hands.

This is something that you can do at any time that will allow you to reweave into the moment of now. As you feel the kinesthetic sensation of your fingers touching have the mantra of now in your mind. This brings you out of the distortion and into the now.

Why does being in the now enhance the good that is there? It is because there is abundance in the now, and as you are focused in the now it unites you with unity consciousness. You have enough energy, vitality, abundance, and resources. You are connected to your Source.

UNIFYING YOUR ENERGY IN THE NOW

Another aspect of what is happening during this transmission is non-verbal and allows your system to embrace a more unified way of running energy. You have a predominant way of running energy just like you may be right-handed or left-handed. Parts of your system are very strong and parts of your system may be underutilized or underdeveloped. Just like the bodies an Olympic athlete and a couch potato have the potential to be used the same. Both the body of an Olympic athlete and the body of somebody who is not using their muscles have the innate wisdom to run a marathon or jump over a bar. Even if you have a tendency to utilize or underutilize your energy in one way or another it does not mean that the body is lacking the ability to run the energy in the way that it is meant to.

We will work with you verbally and nonverbally, and as we are doing this it is our request that as much as possible you stay in a meditative and relaxed state. Imagine that you are on a meditation retreat right now and that you are practicing focusing on your breath, quieting your mind, and focusing on the nectar running through your body.

ENERGETIC EXERCISE
Divine Nectar

As part of the preparation to reengage fully with the Solar Ray, encourage your system to stimulate your pineal gland and moisten your system. It is like going from a raisin to a grape. Allow yourself to become plump and juicy with this moisture. Feel this divine nectar lubricating your entire system.

Focus on your brain and create connections between the left and the right and the middle aspects of the brain. The brain has different functions and different parts are in charge of different things, yet it is all brain. Rather than being in different parts of the brain we are inviting you to be in the entire brain. Focus on this chalice, this cup of eternal nectar overflowing into your brain and bringing life back to parts of the brain that have been dormant or inactive.

Visualize yourself on a stage and that on the stage there are various actors and actresses. The different actors and actresses have unique parts, contributions, dialogue, and songs. Some of these actors may have a sad scene and some of them may have a happy scene. Some of them may be falling in love, dying, enjoying company, and some of them may be lonely. As if you are the director of this play, give permission to each of the actors and actresses to thoroughly enjoy their part, to play their part perfectly, and to enjoy thoroughly whatever it is. Through your choice to direct them to enjoy every part thoroughly you are bringing the joy to the sad scene, to the happy scene, to the death scene, and to the falling-in-love scene. There is joy and the enjoyment of all aspects of life. Life is not only experiences that you may feel are like utopia; utopia exists in each moment. We are inviting you to give yourself permission to enjoy every part of your life.

Imagine a spider, the weaver, and the hologram of your system of light. Focus on all of this light being woven into a beautiful mandala, a beautiful symbol, and allow the spider energy to fill in areas of the web that had been torn, that had been weakened, and that had been overlooked. You may think about these tears as parts of yourself that you may have kept hidden or underdeveloped. Feel the Solar Ray bringing everything into the now. Take the time that you would like to be in this energy, and when you are ready take some deep breaths to complete this process.

GIVING YOURSELF PERMISSION TO BE HAPPY

Give yourself permission to be happy despite what anybody else is feeling or thinking. It is a funny thing from our perspective that you would choose to minimize your joy or your happiness from the idea that you do not want to rub it in somebody else's face, you do not want to shine if somebody else is not shining. It does not really work like this. If you are who you are in each moment—whether it is shining or not—there is a level of authenticity and a level of permission that gives someone else permission to be who they are. There is some part of the tribal nature of the human race that is built into trying to be a match and to be accepted when in reality each person and each moment is rich and is the full spectrum of the colors. It is a palate, it is a landscape. If you were meant to be a cookie cutter then you would be a cookie cutter. You are meant to be you.

We invite you to have a party for yourself. What we mean by that is whether you are in the car or in your home do something like putting on the music and dancing and singing or something that would be fun for you. Really express yourself to the loudest degree possible. Suppose your normal energy on a regular day is a certain type of energy, and you are by yourself outside. It is quiet and you hear the sounds of nature. This environment has one type of feel. Now imagine walking into a disco and you feel the bass of the music in your body. You see people dancing and sweat pouring off their bodies and there is a different vibration, a different octave of expression, and a different chemistry to the scene in the disco versus the scene in nature. We are inviting you to use your energy like a kaleidoscope and to have a party, whatever that means to you, so that you are shifting your energy from nature to that expanded energy. Notice the Solar Ray, notice the energy of the Solar Ray, and notice the energy of the Council of Light.

FOCUSING ON THE GOOD IN EACH MOMENT

Choose to illuminate within you the aspect of your system that is focusing on what is already good in each moment in your life. Part of your nervous system has the hypervigilance to create safety and is focused on keeping you safe by looking for potential danger. This is not a mechanism that needs to be anticipated. Anticipatory anxiety, worrying, thinking about what may happen, what the worst case scenario is, are actually a bleeding over of a part of you that is instantaneously able to identify a sense of danger. If there is something that you need to be aware of you will be aware of it. If you need to move away from a truck that is driving straight toward you there is a part of your system that will be able to do it. The habit or conditioning of looking for what disaster may be there, or what may not work, or what danger lurks in the shadows is not actually necessary. It can happen unconsciously, it can happen instantaneously, and it becomes conscious as it needs to.

There is nothing wrong with this aspect. It is a skill that is developed and is something that we would invite you to include in your being. Yet for the hypervigilance to be the main mode of operation, or for anticipatory anxiety or worry to be the main aspect of operation, is outdated and is part of the old paradigm. As you are moving into your greater yet-to-be, the energies that are available on the planet are inviting you to be completely different in ways that you can't even imagine.

This is the opportunity to ignite your ability to naturally be drawn to the good, to naturally focus on the good, to look for the good, and to look for the thing that you can appreciate in each moment. You are awakening an instinct and training yourself to look for that which is good and enhance that which is already working. It is a discipline, it is a practice, and it is a conscious decision, the benefits of which are great.

This universe is a law-of-attraction universe; what you focus on increases, so consciously choose to focus on good and focus on joy in each moment. It does not mean that you do not feel the feelings of a sad time, of a death, or of a change, but you feel the joy that is present. You enjoy that moment. You are focused on the good of that moment.

We are asking you this question, "Would you like to turn on, awaken, and remember your ability to look at what is good?" As you are deciding we are assisting you in doing this, so just notice your sensations as this is happening.

THE SOLAR RAY AND THE JOY RAY

It is through the Solar Ray, the Ray of Now, that you can tap more deeply into the Joy Ray, which was explored in the previous chapter. As you are living in the Solar Ray, as you are connected to the One, and as you are in the now there is a tremendous capacity for living a rich, fulfilled, vibrant, engaged, juicy, and aligned life. As you string together the now moments of liquid love, juiciness, and delight you then have a loving, juicy, and delightful life.

BECOMING A BUTTERFLY

There has been much discussion about this particular time on the planet. There has been much prophecy and many projections. One of the ways we would look at it, if we were you, is that this time is like the process of becoming a butterfly. You have been in a cocoon, in your own juices, transforming into something that was there all along but then takes on a completely different form. It is up to you, just like a baby chick cracks her own egg, to decide when you are ready to become that butterfly, when it is your time to leave the cocoon or to leave the shell of the egg. If a chick were to leave the egg before it was ready it would not be beneficial. Do not feel as if you need to rush to get where you are going. You will get where you are going. Just notice as you feel ready that there is a launching off place, a place where you decide to become that which you have been becoming.

The Solar Ray is an energy that can assist you in walking through the doorway of the consciousness that you have grown up with and have known, down through the doorway and into the hall and into the other energy of what you are becoming. Think about the Solar Ray as a portal, as a map, as a way that you will get from where you are to where you are going. It is only through the now and through the focus of the good that you will enhance your journey.

THE GALACTIC HUMAN

What is a galactic human? In the Egyptian scripture the Pyramid Texts, there is the initiation of a human becoming a star and of a star becoming a human. We as the Council of Light are assisting you in connecting to the stellar consciousness. It is as Thoth says so perfectly in the Emerald Tablets, "As above, so below; as within, so without." You are corporeal at this time; you are physical at this time. You are on the Earth and in gravity; you can see the physicality and the Earth. You can look within you and see the within.

We are assisting in illuminating your connection to the above. It is a mirror image, it is pattern upon pattern, and it is heaven on Earth. You can go up to go down, you can go down to go up. It does not matter. But bringing your awareness equally to what we would call above or the stellar consciousness or the galactic aspect of your humanness is very helpful at this time. You do not need to go out of your body to do it; it is within you. The stardust is within you. Yet it may not be as big of a practice to notice this consciousness. The magic of the moment exists in the now. You are a seeker looking for that magic, looking for what you know to be there even if you cannot see it all the time. You believe in fairies, you believe in stardust, you believe in magic, you believe in healing, and you are the ones that can see it for others until they are able to see it for themselves.

FINDING THE GOOD IN DUALITY

We have much more to share yet all we have is the now to do it within. We would invite you to call us in to build a direct relationship with this consciousness and to practice the meditation of tapping the index finger and the thumb and connecting to the now, to the Solar Ray, and to build a practice of focusing on the good. You may have this question in your mind, "What is good now? Where is the good in the now?" The practice of appreciation, the practice of a gratitude journal, the practice of a success journal would assist you in focusing on the good.

There are things that we feel are missing in some of these practices, though, in that they only focus on that which you would categorize as positive. You know that there has been much fertility that has come from what you would classify as the worst times in your life. You could have a success because you got angrier than you ever have in your entire life, or that you were sick for a week. It is not that we are asking you to focus on the sickness but to focus on the good and the value in even the most challenging times. There is success and things that can be appreciated in every moment.

You can illuminate the aspect of each moment that you want to focus on. You have been given the glasses of the Solar Ray so that you can see your life and enhance the good that is already there. You may also practice this skill by calling upon the Solar Ray and spending a few moments going through and focusing on the things in your life that are good and then imagine turning up the volume on them—enhancing them and making them even brighter. This is a practice in neurolinguistic programming where you turn up the brightness on something that may be dim. Even if it is a small bit of good, still find it in each and every moment.

5

THE EMERALD RAY

The You Ray

▲

Provides an energetic alignment with your authentic and multidimensional self, inviting you to be you full out. This Ray and way of being is an essential key to navigating the changing times, for as you are tuned in to who you are from the inside out you are naturally in the right place at the right time and in a state of joy. You are empowered and happy, for you are expressing your unique brilliance.

TUNING IN
....
Observe Your Physical, Emotional, Mental, and Spiritual Bodies

To begin our session with the Council of Light and the Emerald Ray—the You Ray—focus on your body. Imagine that it is the first time that you have noticed your body; it is the first time that you have noticed the tangible aspect of yourself. Imagine that you are getting to know yourself from the place of the observer. Just notice your body, your hands, your feet, your hair, your coloring almost as if you are a writer and you are describing your physical attributes. Notice that you are a woman or a man, that you are a certain height and have a particular color of hair. Notice all the things that describe your physical being. Just spend a few moments connecting to these things.

70

Even though you are not your body it is connected to you; it is an aspect of you. Now shift your focus to your emotional body, like you are an observer noticing your emotional body. Constitutionally what types of emotions do you tend to feel? Are you a very light person? Are you a very introspective person? Are you a very deep person emotionally? Do you gravitate toward one type of emotion or one type of feeling? Just observe your emotional body and the multitude of facets in your emotional body.

Now focus on your mental body that constitutes your mind and your beliefs. What type of person are you? Witness your beliefs as if you are seeing them for the first time. Are you on the leading edge of thinking? Are you a person who is very traditional in your thoughts? Are you a person who is very intellectual and likes facts and history? Are you a person who believes that anything is possible? Just notice what types of beliefs live in your mental body. What subjects have you gravitated toward in your life? What you have learned, what you have stored in your mind? Allow this look at your mental body from this perspective to deepen your connection to an aspect of you. You are not your mind and yet your mind is an aspect of you.

Now connect to your spirit body, your soul body, the aspect of you that is eternal, that is infinite, and just spend some time getting to know that part of you. Perhaps this is the easiest part for you to connect to or perhaps this is the most challenging part of you to connect to. On a soul level what do you feel like your purpose is? What do you feel like you are here to do? What do you feel are the lessons that you have been learning or gravitating toward? What really touches you on a deep level and ignites your spirit and calls to your soul? What do you dream about on a soul level?

. . . .

THE EXPONENTIAL
AND MULTIDIMENSIONAL YOU

Now that you have connected these aspects of you from the place of the observer, forget everything that you have just observed. Forget everything that you know about yourself or you think that you know about yourself. This is a unique request, yet the Emerald Ray, the You Ray, is really about the exponential experience of self; the quantum experience of self. It is not one thing or a combination of aspects; it is beyond even the beyond. The saying "To thine own self be true" and the question of "Who am I?" have been a part of human consciousness since its inception yet how to know oneself seems as if it is a very ethereal experience.

You could also approach this by noticing what you are not. You could notice that you are not a man or a woman, that you are not a baby, that you are not these tangible things. After you spend a few moments or minutes or days or decades focusing on what you are not, we would invite you to also forget what you are not. There is something that is so automatic about being you, that is so unconscious about being you. The body's autonomic nervous system, the part of you that breathes, the part of you that digests, the part of your heart that beats, does not need your conscious awareness to function. There is an aspect of you that is there regardless of your conscious awareness of that part of you, and this is what we are inviting you to connect to. You can focus on your breath if you want to. You can feel your heart beating if you want to. You can perhaps less viscerally connect to your digestive tract. You can have a sense of these experiences that happen automatically even as the aspect of you that we are inviting you to connect to is so automatic. You can still have an experience of you.

The beginning of this transmission is not to provide a riddle but to open your mind, to open your awareness, to awaken within you the possibility that you can know yourself by not knowing yourself. You can simply connect to you and be you in a way that is a direct knowingness that may be automatic and unconscious. The aspect of you that we are inviting you to tune in to is actually larger, more expansive, and in the realm of your multidimensionality. Yes, you can imagine that you are light and that who you are is being expressed through this lifetime like a flashlight or a Ray of Light, yet it is more expansive than that. You are not only a flashlight. How would you describe the qualities of the particles of light? There is an aspect of turning on a light that you may not understand but you trust.

As we, the Council of Light, are moving into the Emerald Ray and inviting you to connect to the Emerald Ray, to the You Ray, we are asking that you expand your awareness to your multidimensional level of you and your you-ness. Think about your thumb and how your thumb has a unique print. Your thumbprint, your fingerprint, is completely unique. As you look at your thumb you do not see all of the individual lines that make up your fingerprint, but if you were to put your thumb in some ink and then put it on paper you could see the individual lines. This is an example of your life. Your life is the ink; your life is the paper that illuminates and makes visible your unique essence and who you are. You could look at yourself and see your thumb in isolation, yet it is through the living of your life and the reflection of your experiences that you truly identify and express the nuances of you. They illuminate the nuances of you.

The most potent thing that you can do during the changing times on the Earth is to simply be you. This tool is the most important tool to apply at this time. Yet we are saying that being you is a complex thing. It is not necessarily something that you can consciously identify, yet you being you is available from the lines of your multidimensional awareness. There is an aspect of you that knows you. We invite you to tune in to that part of you that knows, to tune in to that larger aspect of you, the light that comes through the light, the flashlight, and ask the part of you that knows to allow more of who you are to shine through into your awareness on every level of your being. Ask that part of you to shine through not just in your conscious awareness but also through all of your subtle senses and beyond.

We are asking the part of you that knows to illuminate, to turn on, to amplify who you are. This process is a hookup to your own energy and to your own essence in a way that is expanded. You may feel a richness, a plumping up, an expansion, a fullness of who you are almost like a dimmer switch that has been turned from low to bright, or a balloon that was empty but now is filled and expanded, taking up its full space. Part of what is happening is that there are aspects of you that are coming forward at this time to be more pronounced and shared in your life and on the Earth plane. You may think of it as one line in your thumbprint that is taking more of your attention or becoming more prominent and expanded in some way.

YOU ARE UNIQUE

"Who am I?" is one of the most classically pondered questions. "Why am I here? Who are you? Why are you here?" These questions can be maddening to attempt to answer. They can also be exhilarating to attempt to answer, yet for now, rather than focusing on the understanding of who you are, and the expression of that in a purpose, we are boosting or amping up your essence, your signature energy, in relation to where you come from.

If you are a snowflake, we are plumping up this snowflake and making it larger. If you are a beautiful flower, it is opening more. It does not matter who you are or why you are here in this moment, the innate wisdom of your essence is within you. There is something that is so unique about you that it is easily recognizable to others. They feel your presence in a very powerful and potent way.

ENERGETIC EXERCISE
Amplify Your Signature Energy

We will spend a few moments in silence and invite you to connect to the Emerald Ray and in your own way expand your unique you-ness, your essence, and your signature energy. Allow. Breathe. Feel yourself immersed in the supportive, powerful, and loving energy of the Emerald Ray.

Now we would like you to visualize that you are sitting on a set of bleachers and that you are in the seat in the row of bleachers that indicates your age. If you are thirty years old, then there are twenty-nine empty rows in front of you. If you look behind you there are more empty rows of bleachers as place holders representing your future.

Imagine symbolically that the energy of your conception is on the first bleacher and your one-year-old essence is on the first bleacher. The first bleacher is one, the second bleacher is two, then three, four, five, six, seven, eight, nine, and so it is that the chronological ages of your past are on the other bleachers up until the row where you are now.

The reason for doing it this way is because sometimes there are aspects from childhood that are not fully integrated in relation to essence or signature energy. We are not speaking about trauma, pain, or things related to that. It is only your essence as a one-year-old, your essence as a two-year-old, your essence as a three-year-old, your essence as four-year-old, your essence as a five-year-old, your essence as a six-year-old, and seven, and seven to ten, and ten to twenty, and twenty to thirty, and thirty to forty, and forty to fifty, and so on that you are connecting to.

You can also integrate with the future essence of you. One of the beauties of being you for a longer period of time is that in some cases you have the opportunity to express more of who you are or to show underexpressed areas even more fully. Allow through your intention the power of the essence of you throughout all time and space to be connected, unified, to come into harmony, a state of peace and alignment. Align with you throughout all time and space.

There could also be bleachers for past lives, yet we are specifically focusing on you in this lifetime—your personality, your being, and your experiences—because this is the life that you are living now. Past lives are interesting, they have connection, they are touchstones, and they are part of you and your origin. Yet what is important in this moment and for the purpose of our intention together is this particular lifetime and the unique expression of your essence.

Imagine now that the bleacher is a spiral and that you are in the center of it. See all of these expressions of your essence in a spiral in and around you in a fluid way. You are not static; you are organic and you are moving. You may be expressing one aspect of you more in one moment than in another moment.

In this next segment set your intention to amp up you, your essence, and your signature energy even more. Take ten seconds to do this and set your intention to turn on your essence, your unique energy, and your signature energy as much as comfortably possible.

You can move with it. You can turn it on all the way now and adjust it if you desire or need to. Take the next ten seconds to do that: one, you are becoming more of you, three, even more you, five, seven, nine, ten. Stabilizing, stabilizing, stabilizing, stabilizing, stabilizing.

As we are stabilizing this turned-on, full-on, vibrating you, think about something that you are passionate about. Think about something that really excites you, that really gets your juices flowing, and you find incredibly yummy. As you are focusing on that which brings you passion, that which you are passionate about, that which turns you on, that which amplifies the natural juiciness of your system, notice how that expands your essence and your signature energy. It is like fuel for your being-ness.

As we are continuing this, we will speak for a moment about the aura or the electromagnetic field and the energy body in terms of your personal space and your territory. As you have been connecting the Emerald Ray and turning your essence up, you have expanded into a larger territory; you have gotten bigger. Allow your aura, electromagnetic field, personal energy, and territory that you occupy to become bigger and to correspond with the you that you are expressing now.

Take all the time you would like expanding your aura to be current with the full expression of you. When you feel complete with this process take a couple of deep breaths, move and stretch your body, and when you feel ready gently return to this time and space.

THE AURIC FIELD

In some yogic traditions there is the thought that when you are healthy and radiant your aura is nine feet in all directions. This means that when you are with others you are sitting within each other's auras, yet this is not so literal. Let us say that before this exercise you started with your aura at three feet. Imagine that the space that you occupy is now four feet around you in all directions, or six feet around you in all directions, or nine feet around you in all directions.

We know that some people can go way out into blocks, countries, or galaxies, but we ask as you expand your territory that you do so in a very consolidated way—in a way that is not diluting your essence but is just the right size for you. This may mean that you feel the need to expand or you may feel called to consolidate your energy rather than spreading it out. Do whatever feels the most comfortable for you where you are not diluting your essence.

When you are occupying your space, territory, body, mind, emotions, spirit, your multidimensional wholeness, and your heart there is an exquisite radiance that happens. There is shininess, sparkle, opulence, luminosity, and brightness. The purpose is to unhook or to integrate back into the wholeness the tendency or the compulsion to contract when someone else is contracted or to contract out of a desire for approval or for any reason besides consolidating. There may be or has been the desire to play small, hide, or not shine who you are.

ENERGETIC EXERCISE
Amplify You to Enhance Your Vitality and Health

Feel the quality of energy that is in and around you at this time. You are being invited to go into an alpha state, into a deeper state of consciousness. You may feel the energy as palpable and very strong. The fun thing about the energy that you are feeling is that it is not so much about the energy that is being transmitted through these words that you are feeling, it is your own energy that is being felt. Spend a few moments in silence as this connection to you strengthens on a very deep and core level. And if there are any, notice your sensations.

As your connection to the you of you expands we will share how to amplify being yourself and how to access more of who you are. We would invite you to stay connected to your own energy and to stay connected to your inner resonance. Focus on the back of your sacrum and breathe life into that area. Imagine that it is like a room that has been closed and you are opening the doorways to this room and letting in light and air. This is a great exercise to identify if there are any parts within you that have been closed down. It is a way to open up. You are dusting off the cobwebs of you, dusting off the aspects, and breathing life and light into parts of you. Focus on this area of your sacrum and in particular the relationship between self-permission to have pleasure and your root chakra, which is related to your security, your survival, and being in the body. We are inviting you to embody a consciousness of wholeness that you not only have permission to experience pleasure, but it is also an intrinsic part of your safety, thriving, and your survival. The old belief would be that if you experience a lot of pleasure, if you give yourself permission to have what you want and to live the way you want to, then it jeopardizes your safety; it is a life or death decision. The consciousness that you are moving into, the wholeness that already exists within you, supports the concept that giving yourself permission to experience pleasure enhances your security and your safety.

There are parts of you that are a part of your autonomic nervous system on a physiological level that you do not have to focus on but they are there. This is also true about your multidimensional self. There are aspects of you that exist within you but you may not have the awareness that they are functioning or that they are there. That being said, the consciousness that is most supportive for you at this time already exists within you. It is not that you need to create something new or find something new or affirm your way into a new belief. It is like taking a moment to focus on your heartbeat and feeling your breath going in and out. Right now we are encouraging you to focus on the aspects of you that not only give you permission to experience pleasure but to notice that it is your birthright. The more pleasure you experience the more grounded you are and the more safe you feel.

Now focus on your throat center, your thyroid, your pituitary gland, your adrenals, your endocrine system, and in particular the smaller glands in the body. Focus on a smaller gland rather than a larger organ. Then imagine this really yummy nectar, this juiciness, this vitality, this eternal nectar bubbling up from within these organs and infusing life, infusing vitality, infusing nourishment into these organs. Focus on this nectar for as long as you feel called.

YOUTHFULNESS OVERFLOWS FROM YOUR ETERNAL NATURE

From a yogic perspective it is said that as you age the pituitary gland gets smaller, yet if you meditate it can maintain its size or grow. Part of what you are connecting to in the above exercise and now is the youthfulness in these organs and their optimal functioning. This may come as a surprise but there is a part of you, and part of what you are here to illuminate within yourself, that we would call age-defying. In a more positive way it is the knowledge that health, youth, and vitality are available to anyone regardless of their current state. There are some people who are devoted to extending life, living until they are 120, looking like they are twenty when they are eighty, and it is not this aspect of youth and vitality that we are referring to. The aspect we are talking about is the one that says that—as you are tuned in to your eternal nature, the consciousness of you that feeds you, that nourishes you in a way that is beyond sleep and exercise and food—the body is designed to live much longer and healthier than it often does.

There is a belief that the older you get you decay, that you get sick, and then there is death and it is painful. Yet you can decide to simply, as you are ready to, walk out of a perfectly healthy body whether you are ninety or whether you are four. This is a possibility, and so just notice your beliefs about aging and notice your beliefs about spirituality, and then link up those beliefs in ways that support your continual vitality and health into time and space in the future.

Another way to support your vitality and health is to look at the direction or flow of chi in your body. Chi can move in one direction or another. Just like the natural pathway of chi while eating is that you swallow, the food goes into your body and you digest it, the opposite direction of that is vomiting. When you vomit there is a reversal in the flow of chi or energy that just switched back. This is also true of things such as nosebleeds. Just notice if there is any part of you that has a tendency to switch the directions of your energy to be the antithesis of what it is naturally. This could manifest in your life like drastic mood swings, or feeling like you are two different people in the same body, or that you can be as high as a kite one day and as low as the lowest the next day. Think about this not from a place of polarity but from a place of the direction of chi, the direction of energy; think that it can flow and then switch directions.

In actuality the thing that is most interesting about this is that there is heavenly and earthly chi flowing within you at all times. It comes from above down to your feet and it comes from below your feet up to your head and circulates and spirals within. Both directions are happening, and that is natural from an energetic perspective, but physiologically you do not want your energy going up with food or with blood, and similarly with some of your emotions. It is more optimal for you to have your energy flowing in your emotional body in a certain direction and pattern than in the opposite. Just ask the part of you that knows to be watching for your energy flow in the direction of your energy.

To continue the expansion of the Emerald Ray, focus on an aspect of you from when you were young, a joyous curiosity, and call this energy to be included back into the wholeness, back into the you. This joyous curiosity that is being reintegrated allows you to come back into greater states of play; play comes into the multidimensionality of who you are in the now. Each aspect of you is related to who you have always been throughout time and space, yet there are parts that are more prominent during certain developmental stages than other developmental stages. You are bringing parts of you that are appropriate for this time and space more into the forefront. This is part of the shift that the Emerald Ray offers and why being you is the best tool to access the new Earth energies. When you are being you, and there is that clear signal, then you have access to the planes of consciousness that are available and that are different than they might have been in the past. Being you in the now is the best of both worlds.

ENERGETIC EXERCISE
Regenerate and Renew by Being You

Focus on your skin and in particular the skin around your neck and your shoulders. Imagine the color of skin as it has decayed, like a gray color. Through your intention focus on bringing that gray color back into the pink rosy hue of flesh that is healthy and vibrant and vital. This exercise is one in which we are inviting you to take back some energy from things that have decayed—to regenerate like a lizard can regrow its tail. There could be a part of you that has fallen away that can be regenerated and is very important for your now in relation to the changes that you are making on the level of your vision, on the level of your being, on the level of your becoming. Practice this regeneration technique and you will be regenerating that which is optimal to regenerate. Joy and play may be aspects of you that are being regenerated at this time. Notice what other aspects of you are being regenerated.

While that is also happening focus on the center of your crown chakra and the center of your head. There is an acupuncture point here that is the gate to the heavens. In acupuncture when you put a needle in the center of your head, the soft spot in that one area, it opens up all the other energy centers. Just imagine that there is some stimulation in that area of your crown, like a needle or like acupressure or massage that is opening the gates to heaven. By heaven we just mean higher realms of consciousness and in particular your higher realms of consciousness. Your higher realm of consciousness is that part of you that does understand that which seems incomprehensible, that part of you that does know what is happening even if it seems impossible to understand and to know.

Now focus on the center of your wrists, where you would put perfume, and imagine that you are stimulating these pulse points with a really yummy shea butter or jojoba oil, rose oil, something that is really redolent for you, and just imagine that this part of your being, this part of your body, is opening up and purring and is really enjoying the luxury of this stimulation. Even though this is not a major energy center or a major chakra it is an important aspect of who you are. It is opening up an inner sanctuary, an inner access, a key to beauty, to light, to love, to the sensual experiences. Take the time that you would like enjoying this exercise. When you feel complete take some deep breaths anchoring that which you have experienced in this potent exercise.

PERSONAL POWER

One of the aspects of you that you are moving more into is your personal power. There is an aspect of power that encompasses vulnerability and is soft—this is important. This power is something that you carry, a wisdom that you carry, a teaching that you carry. Imagine that you have tuned in to the radio station of you, that you are vibrating power, and that you are allowing yourself to be current with who you have become. Imagine that your beliefs have launched you into a different phase or a different period in your life and that it is now time to live your life from this expanded perspective.

For example, let's say you were a person who had really long hair for a long time and that you used to braid your hair every single day. Your hair was all the way down to your waist, and so a part of your routine, a part of your identity, a part of your action every day, was to wash and to comb and to braid your hair. Then you get a haircut, a short bob, and it is just wash and go—easy and light and fluffy and there is no need to be operating as someone who has hair down to your waist that needs to be washed and combed and braided.

What we are inviting you to do is to completely own the new hairstyle, the new bob, as symbolic of owning the new you. The parts of the new hairstyle and the actions that the hairstyle requires are different than the ones from the old hairstyle. This seems like a superficial way to explain a deep concept, but we feel it is simple and one you can connect to. Part of what you are doing is catching up with who you have become, and to own that you are a leader in this experience of life— that you have something to share and to teach that is unique and that is expansive and beyond what you may have previously felt or experienced.

ACCESSING HIGHER REALMS OF CONSCIOUSNESS

There are different ways to access higher realms of consciousness. In the past it may have felt natural to you to go into your light body and energetically leave your physical body to tap into higher realms of consciousness. At this time on Earth, because it is a time of individualized unity, the more in your body you are the more easily you tap into higher realms of consciousness. The more you that you are, the more you can connect to your divine self. Therefore, although this may feel counterintuitive at first, we would like for you to explore going deep within your body as you meditate and access the cosmos this way.

ENERGETIC EXERCISE
The Light of the Emerald Ray

We are now going to make the Emerald Ray, the You Ray, available more consciously. Imagine that you are standing in a beam of light and that this beam of light is surrounding you. This beam of light is above you and below and around you and within you, and this beam of light is infusing the Emerald Ray, the You Ray, into each and every cell of your body, turning on the codes and the molecules and all aspects of your being to be in alignment and harmony. As the Emerald Ray saturates every cell of your body, have a sense of the exquisiteness that is you, the expanded you, the full-on you rising to the surface.

Welcome and embrace the Emerald Ray and welcome and embrace you. You are already fully realized, you are already all that you long to be; allow the Emerald Ray to illuminate your exquisiteness even more. Take three deep breaths to integrate the Emerald Ray as much as you possibly can, allow each breath to make space for you to allow in even more of the Emerald Ray awareness into your consciousness. On the third breath cycle invite your system to remember more of the Emerald Ray and continue to absorb, awaken, and align with the Emerald Ray. Take all the time that you would like with this process.

JOY AS A PATH TO MANIFESTATION
AND ENHANCING YOUR PURPOSE

We invite you to be you. Being you is a direct map, a code, to having more of what you desire. When you are being you, when you are turned on, when you are expressing yourself, when you are visible, when you are living your purpose, when you are sharing all of the intricacies of you—such as what you may like or not like or feel lukewarm about—there is a call that you put out to the universe. This call or intention lets it be known that you are here to experience more joy, more health, more vitality, more abundance, and more fulfillment. This call encourages you to express more of your purpose.

We would like to talk for a moment about you and the You Ray in relationship to your purpose, in relationship to your soul's journey, in relationship to the higher perspective and what brings you fulfillment. Part of being you in the now is an invitation to align with what turns you on, what lights your fire, and what you are drawn to do or called to do. This is not to say that you have been playing around up until this point, but we are encouraging you to allow this to become more of a priority and to bring this further into your experience and your conscious awareness so that you are moving into what it is that you are here to do. We feel that in a general way the purpose at this time on the planet is for you to experience more of that sense of alignment, more of that sense of inner resonance and harmony with who you are, and as such to move away from resisting who you are and what is happening in your life.

SHIFT FROM RESISTING THE NOW TO INFINITE ACCEPTANCE OF THE NOW

There is a lot of unnecessary energy that is put into resisting what is in your situation in the now. For instance, let us say you are in the now and you are hungry but you are resisting being hungry. Or you are in the now and you are cold and you are resisting being cold. Or you are in the now and you are having a fight with your partner. Or you are in the now and you are in a traffic jam, or you are in the now and you are experiencing fear, or you are in the now and you are experiencing something really wonderful. We are not just pointing out the things that may be uncomfortable but also something that creates more of a resistance.

The resistance of wanting things to be different is another way to describe this. You have this job or you have this relationship, you have this house, you have this body, you have this time, you want to be healthier, you have this whatever it is and yet you want more, you want this to be different, but you are focused on resisting what is in the now.

When you allow yourself to be you—and as a part of being you trusting yourself and knowing that as a creative being you have manifested the best thing that could possibly be in this moment—it is in alignment with supporting you on your path and with your purpose. Then you can free up energy from resisting that and just be with it, just move with it. Your life is your message. Everything is on purpose; everything that is happening is perfect and it is orchestrated by you. It may be a smaller, larger, or infinite aspect of you that you are not conscious of. It may be an aspect of your soul that is completing something from the past or it may be that it does not make sense, so you are then encouraged to focus on allowing yourself to be you and to shine and to be comfortable with what is in the now. And, yes, please want more and focus on having more and exploring more and becoming more, yet as you do this, do it from being you, do it from being comfortable in the now, do it from that place of infinite acceptance.

SPOKEN EXERCISE
Choosing to Be You

Focus once again on the Emerald Ray, the You Ray, and engage your free will. Are you willing to be you? If so, then say "Yes" to being you more fully than you ever have before.

A theme that sometimes arises around your willingness to be you and to be okay with who you are is a worry that not everybody is going to like it. You may be you and it may push other people's buttons and they may not like it. They may even tell you they do not like it. You may be you and what that means is that you are in some ways a part of a minority.

You can look at it this way: people originate from stars and each one comes from a different galaxy. Some of you come from the same origin, but some of you are of a minority origin. A part of you may have been trying to look more like the majority of those around you, and in the process you stop being you. Embrace the uniqueness of you as you move toward greater willingness to be you. A large percentage of the population may not be enthusiastic about your origin, your essence, or what you are expressing, but the good thing is that it is safe to be you and there is no reason to not be you. This time on Earth is celebrating your origin in a way that it has not previously.

In some ways it is your time. You have been on a lengthy journey; it is like you have been playing in a backup band forever, and perhaps have not even been that popular or that noticed. Now it is like, "Wow," because when you are yourself you do not have to care what other people think, and there is also a part of being you in the now that is going to be more attractive than it ever has been before. There will be a popularity and interest that you are the expert of the time, the leader of the time, the teacher of the time, someone to be modeled after and celebrated and enjoyed and revered and honored. Even though being you means that at times others might not like it, during this time and in the future now moments are going to be delightful for you. You are going to have this sense that this is what you have been waiting for. It is like trying to light a lighter and it just sparks but nothing catches fire, and then finally it lights and you can build your fire and warm your food and live your life in a way that is just amazing. Your time is now and your time to shine is now, and so with all that in mind—and we have already asked before but we will ask again—are you willing to be you? If so, say "Yes," knowing all that that entails. We invite you to celebrate your unique essence and celebrate what is rare about you and to allow that to show—allow that to shine.

6

THE RAINBOW RAY

The Ray of Wholeness

▲

Supports you in integrating all of you into one harmonic and resonant field of consciousness. The Wholeness Ray supports you in seeing all of the nuances and the whole picture in any given moment. Some of the benefits of connecting to the Rainbow Ray are to allow you to ascend beyond being stuck in a negative emotion or experience to the wholeness that exists in each and every moment.

TUNING IN
· · · · · · · · · · · · · · · · · ·
Letting Go of Your Belief Systems

Bring your awareness to the here and now. Allow yourself to let go of anything else but the here and now. Imagine that you are holding a rope that is taut and attached to the other end of it are your belief systems. Imagine that you are holding tightly to your belief systems, tighter and tighter, and that these beliefs are like a helium balloon that is floating away. As these beliefs are floating away notice that you are still holding on tightly. As much as you are able to give yourself permission, let go of this balloon. If it is challenging to conceptually let go of these, imagine that the balloon you are still holding on to tightly is hovering above your head. To give yourself some incentive to let go imagine that the belief systems are like rocks that will come crashing down on top of you. Engage your free will and decide if you are willing to let go of your belief systems, or if you prefer you can allow these rocks to fall onto your head. If you have chosen to let go of your belief systems let go of this imaginary rope and imagine them floating away back into wholeness, back into oneness. Feel a sense of getting lighter, of feeling freer and more whole.

Sense, see, feel, or imagine that we, the Council of Light, are moving more and more into your conscious awareness. Spend a few minutes communicating directly with your Council of Light about the Rainbow Ray. Feel yourself entraining to and remembering the Rainbow Ray. As you connect more and more with the Rainbow Ray, have a sense of your wholeness expanding, that you are including all of the parts of you into one harmonic resonance. When you feel complete bring your awareness back to your body, feeling lighter from letting go of your belief systems. Take three deep breaths to complete this process.

. . . .

INDIVIDUALIZED ONENESS

The concept that "We are all one" is expressed quite often. At the same time though, it is also the era of the individual. It may seem as if these two perspectives of oneness and individuality are in opposition to one another, and yet they strengthen each other. As each person fully occupies his of her life and expression of that life, it strengthens the whole, the oneness. The microcosm reflects the macrocosm and the macrocosm reflects the microcosm.

Wholeness or oneness is like a painting that is always changing depending on the configuration of each moment. If each person brings a different color, a different structure, a different part of the painting, then the stronger and more vibrant the individual is—the particular tree, the patch sky, the blade of grass—the more beautiful the whole picture will be. As people are called to express themselves fully as vibrant, unique individuals, the beauty of coming together is amplified.

You could also think of this in terms of music with each person as an instrument. When each instrument is finely tuned and is playing beautifully, the harmonic resonance of the collective sound is gorgeous. This can be an invitation for a person, if their instrument is not well tuned, to tune it in a way that is better than before. This is not because it is creating disharmony in the resonance of the oneness, but rather because the contrast is so large between feeling in tune and feeling out of tune. From our perspective whether someone is in tune or out of tune, whether someone is happy or not, it is all the same; it is all energy. It is what you decide as good or bad, what your preference is or is not, that leaves you feeling as if you are failing, succeeding, happy, or sad. You could go through the exact same experience two different times and feel the exact opposite about the same experience. The experience is still the experience, yet your perception of it is what changes.

NOTICING THE UNNOTICEABLE

Working with the Rainbow Ray allows you to be able to see the symphony in action. Within each individual there is a myriad of colors, textures, sounds, and instruments that are playing at all times. For instance, let us say you are feeling depressed, frustrated, or angry. In that moment that may translate as the color black or red and all you may see is that red or black color. Even though you may feel the emotion of depression, anger, or frustration, there are still many other things that are happening simultaneously. Your breath is moving in and out of your body, you are digesting your food, there is a part of you that is in the state of well-being, and there is part of you that is still connected to your resourcefulness.

An example of this would be if you were looking at one of those dotted pictures where, depending on what you are focusing on, you either see a blur of dots or you see a beautiful landscape or an eagle that takes form. It all depends on your focus. This is also true for anything in any moment. When you are connected to the Rainbow Ray it allows you to notice the unnoticeable. It allows you to see the presence of all there is in each moment and to see the broader perspective that supports you in seeing wholeness.

LETTING GO OF RESISTANCE

Imagine that in this moment you are angry and your anger is a painting. All you feel is anger and the anger looks like a black scratch. If you soften your focus, though, you can add an interesting texture to the depth of the whole painting. But if you are only in that one feeling of anger in the moment then it may seem like that is all there is. From our perspective one of the most beneficial things you can do on the planet at this time is to connect to a full-on acceptance of all of who and what you are. If there is an acceptance of what is going on and of what is being felt, things can remain in their right relationship, divine timing, and divine order. When there is resistance or an attempt to hold on, then things get dragged through time and space beyond their original purpose.

If you feel the feeling and allow it to move through you and move on, then it has its right relationship to the rest of the painting, to the rest of the symphony. But if you feel the feeling and you wonder why you feel the feeling and you wonder when it is going to end and where it came from, then it is no longer just a feeling and it becomes something larger.

AN INVITATION TO A FULLER PERSPECTIVE

We support you to allow the parts of you that feel as if they have become overdeveloped to the detriment of your wholeness to come back into a fuller perspective. Perhaps this is a part of you that you may or may not like, but you feel it reflects only one aspect of you and you desire that it be integrated back into wholeness. Maybe this aspect is about repetitive patterns that you have and you feel they are overshadowing the rest of what and who you are. This repetitive pattern is only an aspect. It's like the paintings you did as a child where you draw with bright crayons on a piece of paper, add black paint on top (which represents the repetitive pattern in this analogy), then use a penny to scratch a new design in the black, revealing the colors underneath. In a sense this is the opportunity that you have to allow the repetitive pattern to just be a part of the wholeness.

There is an energy healing technique from kundalini yoga called Sat Nam Rasayan where you allow each of your sensations to be present. Paying equal attention to each of your sensations allows your energy to flow freely. This is a wonderful technique to utilize when one sensation is feeling very loud or prominent and you want to get back into the flow of the wholeness that exists in each and every moment. For example, you allow yourself to feel frustrated, to feel your body in the chair, and to hear the sounds in the room. You just allow each one individually and with equal attention. After a few minutes of this you feel more and more relaxed. This is a similar process to what you are doing by coming back into wholeness. You free up the energy to be in all of the potentials and in all of you at once. It does not mean that you will not still tunnel in on a certain perspective or a certain way of being or that part of your personality will be stronger than other parts; that is natural.

We are not trying to make everything uniform or monotonous but rather to let things flow and to provide the whole perspective. As you have negative and positive—which are the same things at their base, as you have them in wholeness—then there is inclusiveness of all there is. There is oneness, there is unity, and there is neutrality. When you are in the positive or the negative then the wholeness perspective is lost. Spend some time being with all of you without trying to change anything—then the things that need to change will change.

GIVING YOURSELF PERMISSION TO LIVE MORE FULLY

You may feel as if you want to launch into living your life with ease, grace, and joy, and that you want to have fun and love every moment. There is this small part that feels like a splinter; it is aggravating or annoying and wants to be a part of the whole once again. This part wants to give you permission to live an exquisite life, to live a fabulous life. You living a fabulous life does not take anything away from anybody else, and it has no bearing on what another person chooses. You cannot help somebody who is sick by being sick yourself. You cannot give away your health to someone else. This concept also applies to money, happiness, and love. This is becoming more and more obvious and it is part of why relationships are breaking down right now. These are old ways and their time is over. Your life is yours to be lived in exactly the right way for you. Give yourself permission to allow your life to be as exquisite as it can be, knowing that you do not take anything away from anybody else by being happy.

EXPANDING WHO YOU ARE

Your purpose and how to express it does not really matter in the way you may have been conditioned to think it does. The universe is already whole and complete; no one and nothing need to be fixed. Therefore, you do not need to express your purpose in order to "save" the world; rather, it would satisfy you on a soul level and you would feel fulfilled if you moved into expressing your purpose. Taking on this perspective of sharing your purpose for the joy of it, rather than out of some problem that needs fixing, frees you up to live your purpose more fully. Through sharing your purpose, you would break through old fears and personality traits. One of the benefits of the human condition, of wanting to expand, is that on a soul level this is the person that you must become in order to have or to do something.

If you want to run a marathon the person that you must become has discipline, is physically fit, has endurance, focus, and commitment. As you become the person that is able to run the marathon there is an expansion of who you are. As you become a spiritual leader and teacher it is not so much about the class that you offer or the people that come, although they will get great benefit from what you do. It is more about who you must become in order to express this and ultimately the joy that you experience in your becoming.

ENJOYING THE RIDE

We want to assist you in turning up the Rainbow Ray and the positive flow that you are already connected to. Now is the harvest time for you, the time where all that you have done and all that you have worked for is coming into fruition and is paying off. It is like you have been pedaling uphill and now it is a time to coast. There is not really much you have to do but just enjoy the ride. To assist you in enjoying the ride we are amping up the positive flow and the energy that you are connecting to more than you ever have. Your job is to just have fun as you go down the hill.

We can take this analogy one step further: if you have just climbed a mountain or you have pedaled up the mountain and you are coming over the crest and you are about to go downhill in a nice, relaxed way and just coast, then you might be tempted to look over your shoulder. As you look over your shoulder and try to see the mountain you just climbed up it throws you off balance. It does not allow you to just enjoy the ride and the coasting. A way to help enhance your ability to enjoy the ride is to not look over your shoulder at where you have been. Just coast. You have already climbed the mountain; you have already been there. Now place your attention on coasting and enjoyment, and that will help you resolve what needs to be resolved more than if you were trying in a more direct way to connect to the old energy of the ride you already completed.

APPRECIATING THE COMPLEXITY
OF THE SYMPHONY

Focus on this Wholeness Ray, this Rainbow Ray, this energy of unity and harmony. When you listen to a song and within a song there are many instruments and a voice, you listen to the full spectrum of sound in its oneness, in its collaborative appeal. You are not thinking on an intellectual level, "Okay I am going to train myself to listen to the drum. I am going to try to hear the drum." Or, "I am going to try to hear the violin or the bass guitar." You just enjoy and listen to the whole song without picking it apart. This is what the Rainbow Ray can assist you with. The Rainbow Ray assists you in experiencing the complexity of all of the components that currently exist from this place of freshness, from this place of appeal. You can move in and out of your awareness of the solo guitar, of the vocals. Some may catch your attention more, but you are not blocking out the rest of the song. This is a good analogy to play with in relation to all of the parts of yourself; you can spend more time just allowing all the parts to create the song that is you, and from time to time move in and out of different solos or different aspects and highlight those.

HAPPY, ENGAGED, AND FULFILLED

If you were to do things with your hands such as playing the piano, giving a massage, grooming a horse, making food, or so on, this is something that has the potential to make you feel very happy and fulfilled. It is not so much that you make something with your hands but more that an experience happens.

If you play a song on the piano it does not mean that there is a physical thing that you have made. If you make a meal you eat the meal and the meal is gone. It is not so much about building things that are physical that last for a long time; it is more about using your hands in a purposeful way that does not necessarily lead to a permanent end result. It is about the process of being engaged with your life. As you are engaged with your life it will be a much more enjoyable life. Yes, there is purpose in everything and your action leads to a destination, yet if you focus on being engaged rather than on the outcome you can be happy and fulfilled.

IMPERMANENCE AND
THE ART OF LETTING GO

A sand painting takes hours to make and is beautiful, magnificent, and then it is just blown away or smeared over; this is the type of attitude that we would recommend you bring into your life more. It is not about the permanence of what it is that you are creating or experiencing. It is not about attachment. It is about the beauty of the creation. It is about the meditative aspect. It is about the joy of coming together in community. It is the weaving of the threads of each moment, and it is the detachment of letting go. It is not the final product but rather the act of creation and being detached to the outcome that is important.

As you look at your life right now in regards to what cycle you are in, what you are doing, what you are being, who you know, what you have, what you do not have, what you want or what you do not want, see if there is a way for you to let it flow together like a sand painting. Then if you love it or you hate it, imagine just blowing the sand painting away. Imagine, if it were a song, erasing the song. Imagine, if it were a piece of glass art, dropping it on the floor and the glass smashing on the ground. Allow yourself to begin anew.

One of the benefits of the Rainbow Ray is that because there is such an awareness of time and space and everything being connected, there is no need to be attached or to hold on to any one moment, experience, or occurrence. There is no need to be attached to any one moment of bliss or pain because there is the knowledge that more is on the way and more has already happened. It allows you to let things be in the time and space where they are meant to be.

Another benefit of the Rainbow Ray is that it allows you to be more current in each moment. Imagine that you have a rope around you that you are dragging with you from the past, and you have another rope tied around your ankle that you have thrown into the future. Then you have a whole mess of ropes, maybe fifty or 100, that are tied to past and present thoughts, beliefs, and experiences, and they are all jumbled together. Imagine that each one of these ropes is tied to a rock or a suitcase (representing the past or future experiences you are attached to) and you are bogged down and cannot move forward or backward. There is no space for you to be who it is that you have become, because you are dragging all of the past with you or projecting into the future.

Feeling confused or not knowing comes from these different ropes that get dragged along long after their time has happened.

EVERYTHING HAS ITS TIME

You have the opportunity to allow these ropes and these parts of yourself that are overdeveloped to be reintegrated back into wholeness. It is like recycling; everything has its time. A tree has a winter, spring, fall, and summer, and when the leaves fall off the tree in winter it is just a natural part of the process. The having, the letting go, the being, the becoming, birth, life, and death are all just a part of the process. As you are able to tune in to the frequency of the Rainbow Ray you tune in to the frequency of wholeness. When you do this you are able to be more streamlined and more in the moment.

We began this session with inviting you to allow your beliefs to be a balloon and to let them float away. This was the beginning of the practice of letting something go, of allowing it to be in the time that it existed. What is changing for you are your belief systems and the things that you thought you knew in the past and that you no longer know. This also applies to the things that you did not know you knew. Allow your belief systems to be like a sand painting that had its time and its place, but now it is time to make another painting. This will bring you much freedom and much joy.

SPANNING TWO BANDS OF CONSCIOUSNESS

It is a very interesting time to be on the planet because you are spanning two different bands of consciousness. You have lived during one era and you are living and will continue to live during another era; one is quite different from the other. If you are trying to live your life based on everything that you have known up until this point, which does not have anything to do with where you are going, it will feel like chaos. If you allow yourself to drop what you have known up until this point and see each moment as fresh and new and with a new perspective, then things will go much easier and you will be in the beauty and the harmony of the now.

It does not mean that the good and the bad—or what you feel is good or bad—ceases to exist, it is just that it is different. You are different than you were in your twenties. You are different than you were seven years ago. Physiologically your cells die every seven years. The idea of having a disease that you bring with you beyond seven years does not make sense from a physiological space unless it becomes a rope that you drag with you into the next new cell and into each new cell after that.

The point that we are trying to impart is that by allowing your wholeness and who you are in the now to be fluid, to be a combination of all these beautiful art forms, and to be detached with who you are moment to moment you will experience a great deal of beauty, joy, and fulfillment. One of the things about the Aquarian Age is the ability to see things from a cutting-edge, innovative perspective and in an expansive way. There is the ability to be open to a totally different concept that may be in complete contradiction to a concept that you held dear just a moment ago. This is one of the joys of this time. Nobody else can be you. You can only be you if you allow yourself to be who you are in the now. Not the you in the future, not the you in the past, but the you in the now.

INTEGRATING BACK INTO THE WHOLENESS

As we are completing this segment we would just add that if you find yourself in an extreme behavioral pattern, an extreme thinking pattern, or you are obsessing about something that you are doing, be aware that this can be a natural process of integrating an issue into your wholeness. Once you have explored the issue in the extreme then it is a part of you. If you find yourself getting zealous about a certain thing just allow it to run its course and know that you are just integrating that part of you into the wholeness.

ALLOWING THINGS TO RUN THEIR COURSE

There is such fear around addiction and obsessive compulsiveness, but sometimes what happens on a soul level is that there is a perception that the soul has scurvy and it needs fruit. The perception is that the soul cannot get enough of the fruit, and the fear is that if the fruit is taken in excess it is going to be harmful for the whole being.

We are not talking about going on different escapades that would not be beneficial, but if you find yourself monofocused on something in an extreme way and you allow it to run its course, then it is like quenching a deep thirst. If you try to truncate it, do so in moderation. Again this is not a blanket statement, but you will know it when it happens. You will just say, "Oh, wow, I cannot get enough of this one thing. It is all I want to do, it is all I want to focus on, I cannot get enough of it. I better stop." Just allow it to run its course and it will move through more easily and more quickly.

There is much available during this time. Allow yourself to be open to it. One of the purposes that we, the Council of Light, have is that we are available directly. Call upon us, build a relationship with us, and ask us for help in deepening your connection to the Rainbow Ray or with any area of your life.

7

THE FORGIVENESS RAY

The Freedom Ray

▲

Allows you to be you and others to be them from a place of mu-
tual respect and equanimity. The Forgiveness Ray encourages you
to pay attention to you and your life with a fierceness so you can
be current with who you are. The Forgiveness Ray is evolutionary,
for it transcends the illusion of power differentials in relationships
and the idea that motives or negative aspects of self are hidden.
The Forgiveness Ray encourages each person to be who they are
fully and to know that as you are being you it is beneficial for everyone (whether they like it or not).

TUNING IN
. . . .
Embodiment

*As we begin this divine transmission of the Forgiveness Ray, bring your focus
to your feet. Breathe into your feet and focus on moving your awareness and
consciousness into your feet. Move your awareness into your ankles and feel your
ankles. Bring your awareness into your shins and calves. Move your awareness
into your knees and notice what you feel from your knees down to your toes.
Consciously be in your feet and lower legs. How does it feel to consciously
be aware of your feet? Imagine that this is your first conscious awareness of
occupying your body through your attention and awareness.*

Move your awareness into your thighs, into your hamstrings, and into your quadriceps. Be aware of both of your legs. See if there is any area in your lower body from the legs down that feels like more time and attention are needed for your awareness to move into it. Maybe there has been an injury in this area or this is a place that you do not usually focus on.

Focus on the base of your spine at the perineum right between your legs and move your awareness into your entire pelvis, occupying your pelvis and moving into the root chakra, the grounded foundational aspect of your body. Bring your awareness to the lower half of your body and move your attention into your abdomen, your lower back, your intestines, and your organs. As you occupy these spaces you feel relaxed. You feel an increased alertness and vitality. You may even feel that you are being reintroduced to these parts of yourself.

Move your awareness into your lower ribs, liver, spleen, navel, spine, and your entire back. Be aware of and feel the entire space below your heart center down to your feet. Bring your awareness to the front, back, and sides of your body. Pay attention to the column of your body. Notice if you feel your body more in the front, back, or the sides, or if it feels the same all the way around.

Bring a focused attention on the space right in the center of your back, behind your breastbone and the heart chakra. Imagine that there is one vertebra there—in the midsection between your shoulder blades—that begins to hum, light up, and vibrate. Feel this one vertebra humming, vibrating, and lighting up. It may feel as if there is more energy on the back of this vertebra than in the middle or in the front, or vice versa. Focus on the middle, back, and the front of this vertebra and see and feel it light up. As it illuminates, as you occupy this vertebra, notice your sensations. If this vertebra were related to something, what would it be related to? Allow the answer to unfold consciously and unconsciously.

Begin to occupy your shoulders, your chest, the lower part of your clavicle, the front of your neck, and the anterior muscles in your neck. There is something very important about the clavicle and the frontal muscles related to this segment on freedom and the Forgiveness Ray. These places are like the toggle point of holding your head up. Without these muscles and structure your head would just fall back. There is tension and strength in holding your head high that is related to these muscles.

Occupy your shoulders, your arms, elbows, wrists, and your hands; feel your consciousness, your signature energy, your vibration, your unique essence, down through the inside of your elbows, through the softness underneath your arm, and to the tips of your fingers. Feel from the neck down that you are completely and consciously occupying your body.

Move your awareness up your neck into your head, into your eyes, ears, nose, forehead, the back and sides of your head, and up toward the top of your head. Stay in your body and focus your awareness on grounding your consciousness from the tips of your toes to the tips of your fingers, and to the top of your head, so that you are feeling all of your sensations at once. Say to yourself, "I am occupying my toes, my ankles, my knees, my elbows, my wrists, my joints, and now I am simultaneously occupying my entire body." In this exercise you are occupying one part at a time and then you are simultaneously occupying the whole body. This sensation may feel like becoming aware of the individual teeth on a zipper (each part of the body) and then zipping the zipper together (feeling all parts at one time, simultaneously). Spend a few moments continuing this process of occupying your body.

....

PAYING ATTENTION TO YOUR LIFE

We want to begin this segment by encouraging you to occupy your physical body and to bring your awareness to your entire body. Notice that it took a certain amount of attention and focus to be in and have awareness of your body as you did the meditation. This is the same level of attention and focus that is really needed for you to pay attention to your own life, your own unfolding, your purpose, and your evolution.

You still have a purpose whether you are focused on it or not. You still are interacting with your body whether you are occupying or focused on it or not. Your foot is still there even if you are not consciously in it. Imagine how much more vitality and vibrancy is available to you if you are conscious and awake in your own body and in your own life.

One of the reasons we began with anchoring your consciousness in your body was to get you grounded enough for the galactic energies that are coming through. We also want to show you what the Forgiveness Ray has to offer and to outline how important it is for you to pay attention to yourself and to begin to become a finely tuned being with your own sensations, feelings, intuition, guidance, and body.

HABITS AND CONDITIONING

Much of your conditioning includes habits and routines that actually numb your awareness of your inner sensations. You have trillions of cells in your body, and there is much going on that you do not need to be consciously attentive to. We are not suggesting that you have to be hypervigilant about everything. However, what we are saying is that when you are awake, when you are conscious, when you are focused on what is yours to be focused on, there is an incredible sense of freedom, ease, grace, and joy.

You are able to feel unencumbered and to be in the moment when you know that you are hungry, thirsty, tired, or that you want to exercise, work, or sleep. Imagine what it would be like if you were to conceptually let go of all the arbitrary systems that you have in place around food, money, sleep, relationships, work, and every way that you are spending your time; instead, be fully guided by the now. "Now I am sleepy, now I am tired, now I am hungry, now I feel active." In doing this there would be a level of alignment with your own inner guidance that would relate to the senses and transport you into another dimension of being.

We do feel that some habits and routines are important, helpful, and beneficial because you do not need to be spending every moment deciding consciously and being completely focused on whether you are hungry, tired, or getting an intuition. Some of the habits and routines that you have are creating vitality and some of them are decreasing vitality. The ones that decrease vitality are what we are here to speak of, especially those regarding how you relate to yourself and others. Some of these habits are due to conditioning and others are part of the collective consciousness.

THE FREEDOM OF TRANSPARENCY

One way to begin to interact with people is to do the exercise of occupying your own body and your own space. You can listen to and connect with another while at the same time feeling connected to yourself. One of the things that is becoming more evident as the illusion is falling away with the old consciousness is the heightened awareness of what another person is feeling, seeing, and saying in the privacy of their own mind and their motivations. All of that is now becoming uncloaked. Even people who do not consider themselves psychic, intuitive, or aware of the subtle senses are beginning to be able to perceive from other people at a very deep and profound level what they are thinking and feeling, without the person having to reveal it to them.

Hiding, pleasing others, and doing something because you feel like you have to are becoming transparent. As they become transparent, one of the realizations is that it is no longer necessary to live your life for someone else's expectations, thoughts, and feelings, because they are beginning to know that is exactly what you are doing. In the past you may have been able to ignore your intuition about doing something for another person even though it was going against your inner knowing. The other person did not know that you were going against your own intuition and inner guidance. Now they will know. As a result it frees time; all of the things that people do around pleasing, acceptance, thinking they can save the world and the tribal consciousness, are falling away and are becoming transparent.

As people are awakening, even if they do not want to, the awareness of the other is becoming heightened. If you are empathic, knowing or sensing what another is sensing without them telling you, this will come as a relief. It will also in some ways take a level of commitment to stay and be with yourself as you are seeing or watching what someone else is going through or what is going on with them. When you do this while fully occupying your body there is an entirely different level of awareness, consciousness, self-love, and acceptance that can lead to beautiful, clear, life-enhancing, life-enriching experiences, relationships, and knowledge.

Staying in Your Own Yard

Imagine that you have your own house and your own yard. Everyone else that you know also has his or her own house and yard. You are in your own yard and then you go into another person's yard to talk to her, and you are seeing and feeling what is in her yard: her plants, weeds, clutter, cobwebs, beauty, abundance, and joy. There is a comparison that happens. You are in your yard and you compare yourself to her yard, or you judge her yard while leaving your own yard completely unoccupied. When the universe finds a vacuum it fills it. Therefore, when you are in someone else's yard, yours is unattended and other people's energy, thoughts, and stuff can take residence in your yard.

Many times empaths try to go into another's yard to anticipate how they can keep themselves safe so that the other person does not get angry or upset. They may also do this so as not to take on the other person's energy. They are anticipating these kinds of things happening, and that is exactly the thing that leaves them open to taking on other people's energy and taking responsibility for things that are not theirs.

The best vantage point for you, if you are choosing to live in this new energy and in this way, is to be in your own yard and pay attention to your own yard. Connect to the other people's yards without leaving yourself unattended or unfocused.

SELFISHNESS

In some ways it is the era of selfishness. Other people may tell you that you are being selfish and that being selfish is something bad. In reality when someone is saying that you are being selfish, what they are really saying is that you are not making their life the most important thing in your life.

There is some confusion around the idea of selfishness that we want to clarify. Each person chooses to come onto the planet at this time for their own journey. It is all about them and when they pay attention to everything about them—you may agree with this or not—they are in the best position to be a loving and nourishing presence in other people's lives.

LETTING GO OF PITY

The idea that it would be helpful to another if you are poor, sick, tired, confused, unfocused, or weak does not make sense on a conscious level. But this is how people approach someone who is poor. They feel bad if someone is poor, suffering, dying, or hurt. There is the belief that if they are living such a wonderful life and if they do not feel sorry for this person somehow they are being cold, aloof, not caring, and not being a humanitarian.

Yet one of the most beneficial things that anyone can do for another person is to see this other person's divine self, to see their soul, to see their situation, to respect the decisions that they have made consciously or unconsciously to be exactly where they are. This can be one of the most beneficial things because when you do this you are seeing through the illusion of their life for them. You see through the illusion of the poverty or the illness. You see that they are eternal and that they are abundant. As you hold that belief for them, that unity consciousness and awareness, then it is actually more of a support to them than pitying them or trying to save them.

We have shared a great deal of information about how things are becoming more transparent. Most importantly, though, we encourage you to be involved in your own life with a fierceness that is beyond anything that you have experienced before. If your number one priority is you and your life and you pay attention to that with a fierceness that is singularly focused, then that would be an example of the benefit of the Forgiveness Ray. There is no such thing as an imbalance of power in a relationship unless you create it in your mind.

CREATING NEW CONNECTIONS

You have heard the saying "You cannot see the forest for the trees." What we are referring to here is that sometimes you get lost within your own forest. Or sometimes you get caught in a spider web of your own making.

SUPPORT EXERCISE
Opening Up New Pathways

Imagine that you are in your own maze and that we, the Council of Light, are with you, connecting to your multidimensional self. Your multidimensional self is the part of you that is beyond space and time. It may be described as your soul, but it also includes your body, mind, emotions, higher self, and your divine self. This is the part of you that is plugged in and knows all there is to know. It is the part of you that knows that from a higher wisdom place you are creating new pathways.

Ask your multidimensional self to create connections that were not previously there. If you think of a maze you could imagine that you are cutting down parts of the trees so that dead ends are now pathways to something else. If you use the cobweb analogy, imagine the spider web is being cleared away so that you can walk through without being caught in your own web.

Feel that we are working with you directly. We are in the maze with you and are offering the full potency of the Forgiveness Ray, which takes you out of your own trappings and opens up new pathways. It allows you to focus fully on your own life with fierceness, passion, and vitality beyond anything that you have experienced. Your own life becomes the most exciting, exhilarating ride and your maze turns from a trap or a game to an amazing and beautiful garden that is always fun, always a joy, and always a pleasure.

While this integration process is happening we will return our focus to the vertebra in the middle of the spine at the back of the heart chakra. Bring your awareness to that vertebra once again and know that this is the home of the zest for life. As you are in this place it is like every moment is the most exhilarating moment that you could ever experience. It allows you to really be turned on in your life; to be passionate, excited, and on fire about your life. Even if what you are on fire about is lying on the couch and watching TV and doing nothing, you do it in a way where you are so on fire and passionate it is as if you are riding a rocket to the moon. It does not matter what you are doing because you see everything with a fresh eye. Feel this vertebra and the Forgiveness Ray solidifying the new connections you have made within yourself and anchoring your zest for life.

As this meditation is coming to a place of completion, tune in to the Forgiveness Ray and allow your sensations to flow. Notice how this ray feels, what color it is, what sensations you feel as you are steeping in it. Take all the time that you would like to explore the Forgiveness Ray and receive its benefits.

SEEING THINGS WITH NEW EYES

How can you see things with new eyes? Suppose you were to teach someone something they have never done before but you have already done a hundred times. If you teach a friend to drive you would pay attention to how you put gas in the car, how you turn the car on, and how you turn the signals on. You would pay attention to where you look while you are backing up, how you get on the freeway, and how much space you have between you and another car. You would see all of these things as if it were the first time you had seen them, even though you drive everyday.

This is the kind of focus we are speaking about when you begin with a presence and a fierceness to pay attention to each moment and each aspect of your life with excitement and exhilaration.

RELATIONSHIPS AND PRESENCE

From our perspective you make your relationships much more complicated than they need to be. We could say this nicely or differently; however, from our perspective relationships are much simpler than you make them out to be.

Everyone that you come into contact with is there on purpose. It is no accident who is bagging your groceries, who you are married to, who your child is, who you are walking down the street with, or who is in the car next to you. If you approach your life as if there were no accidents, then everything has synchronicity, is in divine order and divine flow, which simplifies many of your relationships.

Be present with the person who is bagging your groceries to the same degree as you would be present with your lover, present with the person who brings your mail, and present with yourself. Allow each person to play the role that they have. Someone brings your mail, someone is your mom, and someone is your grocery bagger. These are job titles, yet in reality if you were to think about each person playing their role perfectly it would simplify things so much.

RELATIONSHIPS, FORGIVENESS, AND BOUNDARIES

If someone is in your life and they are making you angry, they are bringing up your issues, or you just feel frustrated, then you have a reason to forgive them. Know that they are playing their role perfectly—as are you—and if you follow what you are feeling inside then things become crystal clear. It is when you try to base things on assumptions, guesses, and how you think things should be that relationships get messy. If you were to say that anything to do with anyone else is not yours, this creates boundaries and parameters in relationships.

Let us say the general parameter in every relationship is that anything that has to do with you is yours and anything that has to do with anyone else is his or hers. This includes their opinion of you and your opinion of them. If you came from that premise and simply said those are the parameters in every single relationship, it would simplify things immeasurably. It creates an exponential opening within the relationship.

We would like you to maintain your awareness on your direct relationship with us and also with the Forgiveness Ray as you read this. What we have described to you is similar to the unlearning of everything that you have assimilated. One of the most important things as the energies on the planet are changing is for you pay attention to yourself, to embody your own being, and to be present within yourself.

MOTHERING YOURSELF

We would ask you to take on the energy of the archetypal mother in relationship to self-mothering, and we invite you to mother yourself in the way that Isis would mother you and in the way that the divine mother of all mothers would mother you.

Imagine that there is a pure unconditional love to this mothering and that you are taking impeccable care of yourself as if you were the most precious child on the planet. You are nurturing yourself, you love yourself, and you are accepting you for who you are. You see the Divine and the expansiveness, and you are open to and accepting of who you are. You are cultivating your signature energy, your greater yet-to-be, and your soul's purpose. You are mothering yourself.

BEING VISIBLE

A practical application of the Forgiveness Ray is to be 100 percent visible as a unique, sensual, spiritual, playful, and powerful being. You may be worried that this could create a ripple in your relationships but in reality it can add to the juiciness and depth of your relationships. The important thing is that you give yourself permission to be entirely seen and in the act of being seen you see all of yourself.

When there is something that you feel guilty about, it is probably happening during times when you actually are pulling back, not being seen, or not allowing yourself to see yourself. Our encouragement for you to utilize the Forgiveness Ray is to see yourself fully and be all of who you are in your relationships. It does not matter if anyone notices or says anything. There is not an attachment to any response; you are doing it for you.

WRITTEN EXERCISE
A Ritual of Completion

There is a specific ritual that is a practical application of the Forgiveness Ray. For this ritual you take five pieces of paper and write down five experiences or situations in your life that you feel are incomplete or unresolved. An example would be to include things related to an old job and the people there on the first piece of paper. Things that happened in your childhood that were unfair would be on the second piece of paper, and so on. You can write these things in invisible ink so that you are not feeling guarded about this.

After you have done this put the pieces of paper in a Mason jar and call upon the Forgiveness Ray to saturate the pieces of paper and situations written on them. When this process feels complete bury the jar in your backyard. If you wish you could even put a stone on top of the place you bury the jar. In this way it is like a death ritual. This process gives you permission to allow the experiences in your past to be dead, or to come to a place of completion. This will allow you to move on and beyond.

Alternately, you could write on these pieces of paper and burn them and that could be your death ritual. However, if you bury a Mason jar in your backyard you are going to remember that it is there, and you are going to remember the act of it and your decision to let go of these past experiences by bringing them vibrationally into the resonance of the Forgiveness Ray.

YOU ARE LOVABLE AND WORTHY

There is a thought in the human consciousness that has to do with being worthy, lovable, and cherished. There is a question about whether or not these things are true; a part of you is constantly trying to prove it over and over again. You ask yourself, "Am I lovable? Am I worthy? Am I deserving of being cherished?"

We invite you on all levels of your being to drink in now and for eternity the absolute knowingness that you are in an undeniable way lovable, precious, and cherished. The question of your worth is not a question. There is no such thing as worthy or unworthy. As you begin to act from the place of knowing that you are lovable, precious, and worthy, and you know this on all the levels of your being, you do not need to play that out with anyone ever again.

This is a decision and you can call upon it whenever you need to. Remember that you are lovable and you are worthy. When you unlock this door with the key of remembering, the love and clarity that you have desired will be there.

DIRECT KNOWING

There are those who have direct knowing; through their senses and intuition they are able to know in the moment what is happening. We recommend that you accept your own knowingness and not second guess it, tone it down, or try make it be nice for someone else. You know what is right for you on your path. Allow yourself to apply that knowledge and know that the more times you do that from the vantage point of your own yard, the more ease you will feel.

Here is a situation that we would like you to consider. You have your own happiness on one hand and the happiness of someone that you know on the other hand. A situation comes up and you know that if you do a certain thing you would not be happy, but there is a possibility that the other person might be happy. Which would you do?

This is what we feel you are choosing by saying, "I am following my knowingness but it does not feel good to me because I know that that person does not like it and they want me to be doing something else." But that has everything to do with them. We want you to ponder the concept that it is going to feel worse if you go against your knowing than if you follow it and someone else does not like it. In actuality it is all based on assumptions and perceptions. It is all about them.

FEELING JOY IN ANY SITUATION

Do you know the feeling that you have while you are doing something that you love? Perhaps it is sailing or being in nature. We suggest that you conjure up this sensation while you are in different situations. Imagine that you are carrying a heavy box up the stairs and you feel how heavy and uncomfortable it is and how tired you are. Rather than paying attention to the heaviness and how uncomfortable it is, occupy your body and be present in every moment as you would if you were feeling the glory and freedom while you are sailing. In that way each moment is filled with freedom, joy, zest, and the love of life.

We are inviting you to awaken or to call upon a muscle memory and an experience that will bring up a feeling and a sensation that you can have on demand. It is like On Demand television. You can watch any show you want to because it is on demand. That is the same concept that we encourage you to use. Feel in your body the feeling of the thing that brings you the most joy, and call it up on demand. The more that you do this, especially in situations where previously you would have been uncomfortable, upset, or angry, the more it will transform the energy to joy. Make a decision that you are going to feel joy in any given moment.

ALLOW YOUR BRILLIANT STAR
TO SHINE THROUGH

We invite you to imagine that you are the most brilliant glowing star that there is in the entire galaxy. There is a light bursting out of your chest and you glow all the time. You radiate and shine this brilliant stardust and everyone around you gets covered in it. It is like a laser light show gone wild.

To return to an analogy from the Rainbow Ray chapter (An Invitation to a Fuller Perspective), consider the scratch drawings children make with bright colors underneath black paint, which is then scraped off. You are a star and you are taking a penny and scraping off the black so that you can see the brilliant colors that are shining through. It is not even that you have to actively scrape off the black though; it is more that the light just shines through. It does not have to get rid of the darkness; there is no turning off the darkness. You just turn on the light. Allow the star, the brilliant star, to shine through.

YOUR NEW BEGINNING CAN START NOW

You have created a habit of slowly becoming that which you want, which is lovely. There is nothing wrong with that, yet this is the time in your life when you are being called to just do it. Let us say in the past you would think about something for two or three years before doing it, and then all of a sudden you would do it. Rather than thinking about it for a few years and getting comfortable with the idea, just act on it. You may not have everything figured out or have all the pieces together, but you take action, you get feedback, and you adjust as necessary. This is a shift in the sequence of "Ready, aim, fire" to "Ready, fire, aim." You learn from the process of being in motion and then you adjust as necessary.

There is some part of you that has been hesitating out of habit. The good thing about the hesitation is that you get to savor the becoming. Yet if you just allow yourself to move a little more quickly and trust that you will get the feedback you need, make an adjustment, and then move again, there will not seem to be as much distance between the new beginning and the old way of being. Your new beginning can start right now; it does not have to be fully thought out or every detail fully planned and organized. You can begin it and become it.

HAVING YOUR DESIRES

Your power lies in your continual decision to align and to take a leap in the remembering of who you are. The path is there and it is going to support you. With each step things become clearer. Your power to decide, reveal, and to remember who you are is something that you have in each moment. You can decide that you are a person who trusts, who is empowered, who feels good, who is following her or his bliss, who is abundant, joyous, healthy, who is in loving relationships, and who is free of negative habits. You can decide to be that person and act as if you are that person.

How would the person that has everything they desire act, feel, and be? You wake up in the morning and rather than feeling dread about something you have to do that day, or having a negative thought about yourself, ask yourself how would the person that I am, who has everything I choose to have in my life, feel in this moment? If I am in a state of radiant health, financial abundance, loving relationships, having the career that I want, being spiritually connected and awake, who would I be in this moment? Then take the next step toward being that in the moment. You do not have to walk the whole path at once; you can just start with that one step.

FOCUSING ON THE
FULL POTENCY OF THE FORGIVENESS RAY
AND THE COUNCIL OF LIGHT

To complete this segment we invite you to focus on a sensation where you felt the most freedom, happiness, joy, peace, and exhilaration during this divine transmission. Focus on feeling the full potency of the Forgiveness Ray and a strong connection to the Council of Light and to those members of the Council that are in the highest resonance with you. Hold your focus and attention and know that this process of transparency is going to be fun in time. It will be something that perhaps will take a little getting used to. Yet the underlying joy of this process is that nothing needs to be hidden.

There are parts of you that you hide and try not to show another person. All of a sudden everyone can see everything about you and nothing needs to be hidden and nothing needs to be forgiven. There is nothing that is wrong with you. You are not bad or dark. All of you is beautiful, perfect, and wonderful. In the transparency of that, in the absence of the pattern of trying to hide a part of you or trying to hate a part of who you are, there is a full-on acceptance and an alignment of wholeness.

Wholeness is the natural and integrated state of all the aspects of you that are in divine harmonic balance. If there is one part of you that is holding on to a negative perception of yourself and that negative perception is anchoring you and pulling you from the wholeness, it is like a hot air balloon trying to fly but not being able to. It has this one rope that is still holding it to the ground. As you let go of hiding the negative self-perception and give yourself permission to float into the unity of wholeness that is you, then there is integration, alignment, enlightenment, and a lightness that frees you.

The most important thing to understand about this segment is that at this moment—at this time on the planet—the more you are true to yourself the better everything is going to be for everyone. If it is good for you, it is good for everyone.

8

THE PEACE RAY

The Ray of Light

▲

Pierces through the illusion of separation. When the bubble of
Peace Ray is implemented you can anchor your thoughts, feelings,
and actions in unity consciousness. This Ray of Light is particularly
powerful for times when you feel overly empathic or connected
to what other people are thinking or feeling.

TUNING IN
....
An Awakening Process

*To begin this divine transmission with the Council of Light, focus on your spinal
column. Notice if one vertebra or one bone in particular calls to you and feels as
if it is lighting up. Once you locate this vertebra, imagine that you are bringing
more and more of your awareness into this spinal column bone.*

*One of the interesting things about the spinal column and the energy around
it is that it is a channel for earthly and heavenly chi. There is always energy from
above and from below flowing through your spinal column and the pranic tube,
or central column, which is the energetic space around your spinal column. This
area of your body is used to being simultaneously entrained to above and below;
it is always mixing and flowing and moving. As you are choosing one bone that
is in this river, one stone in this river of energy that is constantly flowing, you are
tapping into an ancient wisdom within your own being.*

Each and every person is a master of light and already has everything within them to transcend and connect to the soul and to the Divine. As you are becoming more aware of the river of divine energy in your central column and the vertebrae in your spinal column, know that this is a metaphor for an awakening process. Your bones hold inscriptions of energy. Your bones hold consciousness that is waiting to be read, illuminated, and awakened.

As you are ready imagine that more and more awareness is moving into this one vertebra, and that as you are touching it with your awareness it illuminates an ancient memory of the Peace Ray within you. This ancient memory creates a hologram of this Ray of Light around your entire body. This hologram is illusion-proof. It is a force field of light that surrounds you, brings clarity, awareness, and right relationship.

Dive more deeply into this vertebra by moving your awareness to the inside of the vertebra. Focus your intention to go deeper and deeper into the essence of this bone and notice an eternal nectar within you begin to bubble up, almost like a hot spring bubbles up from the earth. As this eternal nectar bubbles up notice that the memory of being a master of light becomes more accessible. Even though the source of this memory—this remembering process—is happening in one physical location it is being transmitted to your body, mind, emotions, spirit, and the multidimensional aspects of you.

You may have a sense that this remembering process is being broadcast through your system in the now moment. It is also moving backward and forward into all of your previous now moments as well as your future now moments. None of the wisdom and the learning that you have received from your previous experiences is taken away. However, by transmitting and encoding this consciousness into the past now moment it loosens the density and the weight of the anchoring of who it is that you were, allowing you to be who it is that you are now.

One of the desires that you have is to take a quantum leap into that which you feel is possible. Even though it does not matter what came before, you can, from one moment to the next, experience something incredible regardless of your past experiences. There is a familiarity, a habituation, and a connection to what has been. If you have been a person, for instance, who has had unfulfilling relationships, then it may be hard for you to imagine that in an instant you can be a person that has amazing communication, intimacy, and exquisite relationships with many people.

Or if you are a person who has had poor health or low energy in the past, because of the collective consciousness and the illusion of time, there is the thought that you cannot all of a sudden be in radiant health. Yet there is no reason why you cannot. This goes for career, enlightenment, prosperity, or whatever it is that you desire in your life. Even if you never had it before it can happen from one moment to the next. There is no reason why it cannot. Yet one common belief is that things need to take time, need to be a linear process, need to take a certain amount of effort and work in order to happen. This is not a process that is determined by those same rules. Continue to take a few more moments to focus on your spinal column. It just so happens that the new era is more conducive to your awakening than the energy of the past. This new era is encouraging you to remember. It is guiding you to be uplifted moment to moment and to acknowledge that anything is possible; there are infinite possibilities in each and every moment.

Be with this Ray of Light and peaceful energy for a few moments longer and when you are ready take a couple of deep breaths, move your fingers and your toes, and feel yourself come back into your body and back to this time and space.

....

A BUBBLE OF PEACE

You can call upon the Peace Ray when you feel stressed, anxious, fearful, or are having trouble sleeping. One of the primary benefits of doing this is that it creates a bubble in which the collective consciousness is not actively inundating you.

There is a line of tools that has been developed to help with all of the electromagnetic frequencies that are floating through the air from all of the different waves: radio waves, television waves, satellite waves, and microwaves. All of this electricity creates an energy that you cannot see but that is constantly surrounding you. When you have a salt lamp on or are wearing a necklace that counteracts the effects of the electricity, it helps to create a clear field around you. This is a concept that the Peace Ray models. It creates a bubble.

INDIVIDUATION AND ONENESS

One of the conundrums of this time of transcendence and transition on the planet is that there is more talk about being one. Yet at the same time there is an increased call to strengthen the individual essence, signature energy, personality, and ego. Even though some teachers are speaking about getting rid of the ego, the ego has its place. If you think about the concept of oneness like a chain, each link on the chain needs to be strong. Simultaneously there is a sense of the necessity of becoming who it is that you are, and to do so in a more visible, tangible, and unique way than ever.

At the same time there is a breakdown of the illusion of separation and an awareness of unification and unity consciousness. Oneness and individuation go together. It is like an electric plug and an outlet; each configuration fits into the other. You must be strong in your individuality and at the same time have the awareness of being one with all. Being all one does not mean merging with the collective consciousness. It does not mean taking on other people's belief systems. Within your own being you can see that you may have seemingly contradictory parts within you. Some people are also choosing to play out a completely different paradigm than the paradigm that you are choosing to play out. You do not need to plug into other people's paradigms.

EVERYTHING IS LIGHT

The Peace Ray allows you to stay in your own bubble of awareness where you know that at its base everything is the same. Everything is divine, everything is energy, and everything is light regardless of how that light is manifesting. It is all the same energy.

When you are in the bubble you can see a situation simply as light, whereas before you may have deemed it good or bad. You may see a person that pushes your buttons or a person that uplifts you as simply light. You do not get pulled into another person's vortex or the collective consciousness. This is important for many different reasons. One reason is that if you try to plug into things that are floating by during a transitional period they do not have the longevity, permanence, or sustainability that you are looking for. They are just something that is floating by.

An example of this would be the invention of the airplane or the computer. When there is an invention like this there are multiple prototypes that go into the process before the final one that actually works the way it is meant to work is available. If you were to purchase one of the prototypes it would not meet all of the requirements that it is supposed to meet. As each person is creating her own experience of reality there are many prototypes getting played out. There are many test drives that are being run. There are many different models of consciousness and awareness that are running simultaneously.

One of the benefits of the Peace Ray is that you are surrounded in a field where the illusion does not exist, because you are in a connected, awake, enlightened, and transcendent state. The Peace Ray embodies many of the qualities that are associated with those states of being.

A SENSE OF PEACE FOR THOSE WHO ARE EMPATHIC

The Peace Ray will create a sense of peace for you, especially if you are a person who is sensitive and empathic. It naturally sorts out what is yours and what is not. If you have tended to be reclusive or introverted, or get overwhelmed in large crowds, or by bright lights, noise, traffic, or family, then you will find that with the Peace Ray you are able to go into these situations and not feel the imprint and the impact of other people's energies. A good practice for you to develop before going into any of these situations would be to focus on one of the vertebra in your spine and illuminate the Peace Ray until it feels strong. It creates a bubble around you that is strong and peaceful.

ILLUSIONS AND SPIRITUAL EVOLUTION

We have alluded to illusion as being about the collective consciousness and the belief that struggle is necessary in order to have a drastic improvement in the areas of health, wealth, harmony, prosperity, and love. There are other collective illusions, such as time and space, and there are individual illusions as well. The Ray of Peace creates a bubble that is illusion free and illusion proof.

SUPPORT EXERCISE
Identifying Illusions

Spend a few moments in the Peace Ray without thinking and notice what illusions are holding you back from that which you desire. Pay particular attention to your spiritual evolution, your sense of enlightenment or transcendence, and become aware of any thoughtforms or beliefs that you might be carrying. Some of these thoughtforms might be, "Who am I to be an enlightened being? What is so special about me? How could I achieve something that generations have wanted to achieve? Only a small percentage of beings are truly enlightened." Allow whatever illusions come to your mind to be absorbed into the Peace Ray. Give yourself permission to move into greater alignment and remembering with your already-enlightened self. Take all the time that you would like with this process.

There is a belief that there is something particularly special about the people who are in a spiritually evolved state and that there are not many people who are. This is a part of the illusion, which, if dissected, could be based on the time-and-space continuum or on the historical fact of this lifetime. Yet if we were to look at civilizations such as ancient Egypt, Mu, Lemuria, or a particular part of the timing of Atlantis, those are examples where transcendence and enlightenment were experienced by many—not just a select few. This time on Earth is conducive for many people to awaken and to be in spiritual union, as it is the definition of this time to have a sense of unity consciousness.

There are some key components to getting to enlightenment, but the thought that you cannot be enlightened is a part of the illusion. The truth is that enlightenment is a memory that is within you. It is a part of your divine lineage and your being-ness. It is awakening and you are hearing the call and your inner desire to have that sense of union, expanded awareness, and awakened consciousness.

VARIOUS BLENDS OF SPIRITUAL EVOLUTION

There are different blends and types of spiritual evolution. In yoga there are some masters who are more traditional. They are celibate, eat a special diet, and do many hours of yoga and meditation. There are other forms of yoga, such as kundalini yoga, where the teachers and those that practice are householders; they are in relationships and have houses and families. You also see this in religions where some ministers or priests are celibate and others have families.

In the same way there are different brands of enlightenment or spiritual evolution. One is more traditional, such as the one associated with the Dalai Lama. The other brand is the householder spiritual being. This spiritual being is community based and is not contingent on having a life where she chooses not to have a relationship, not to have material wealth, not to eat certain foods, or not to participate in everyday kinds of activities. It is a generalized, accessible level of transcendence that is available in this new era.

Will there be some on the leading edge of awakening? Absolutely. Will there be some that will realize it before the general population? Yes, that is the way it works. Yet you do not need to change your lifestyle unless you want to. It could be that some habits that were not uplifting may fall away. Paradoxically these habits may also get stronger as you move into a higher vibration because it is a time of incorporating the lower vibration. That is the way that it has to be. The shadow or the dark comes to the surface to be integrated back into oneness just like the light and the heightened awareness is coming to the surface.

Would it be beneficial to meditate? Sure. Would it be beneficial to eat foods that you feel good eating? Yes. Would it be beneficial for you to be around people who are uplifting? Absolutely. Would it be beneficial for you to be spending your time doing what your soul calls you to do? Yes. All of these things are beneficial, yet they are not requirements or prerequisites. It is not the path that is important because, as we have been saying, you already are a master of light. It is a matter of becoming aware and realizing it. It is not something that has to be obtained or a mountain that needs to be climbed. It is more of an inner shift and an inner awareness. Being immersed in the Peace Ray on a regular basis will assist in this remembering process.

THE IMPORTANCE OF THE PEACE RAY

We have talked about various Rays of Light and how they have their own purposes. You may call upon the Emerald Ray, the Forgiveness Ray, the Joy Ray, or the Solar Ray in certain situations. Yet if there was one ray that you would have in your life on a regular basis it would be the Peace Ray, because it not only assists you in remembering that you are a spiritually evolved being of light, it also assists you in remembering who you are, your soul's connection, your divinity, and your inner guidance.

ENERGETIC EXERCISE
The Hologram of Light

You may now notice a shift in the energy of your individual Council of Light. Although we are here to help you we are not holding the Peace Ray for you in order to give you the opportunity to call upon it yourself.

Once again go into the process of finding a vertebra in your spine. It may be the same one as before or it may vary. Bring your awareness into this vertebra, touching it with your awareness, and as you touch it with your awareness have a sense of going deeper and deeper into the essence of the bone until you go to that space where there is only light and where you connect to the Peace Ray. As you connect to the Peace Ray it is like you are surrounded in a hologram of light. Have a sense of being surrounded in this hologram of light and feel it strengthen.

Spend a few moments in silence stabilizing your connection to the Peace Ray. Allow your awareness of it to get stronger. If it has a color, what color is it? If it has a feeling, what feeling is it? What texture is it? How do you recognize it?

TRAVERSING THE POLARITY

As you are immersing yourself in the Peace Ray we would like to talk about some keys that will help you traverse the transition. If you think about a global enlightenment program or a process where the masses are choosing to remember or to wake up, it is similar to being surrounded by a group of teenagers who are going through a developmental change on a hormonal level. If you are a teenager and you are going through your own changes with hormones and you are surrounded by other teenagers who are going through their own changes, then there are many hormonal energies that are flying around at once.

We bring up this example because there is the idea that as the new era becomes more grounded it will be utopic. This idea is correct because utopia exists in any moment. The more you can come from your essence, your signature energy, your soul, and living your life for you, the better off you will be in the transition. The more you can connect to the energy of neutrality, which is a benefit of the consciousness in the new era, then the easier it will be for you to traverse the polarity as it is coming up in various forms.

It is an interesting dichotomy because there has been such a tribal nature to the human race: the tribe, the family, the community, and the collective. The idea of "us and them" has been a part of this collective consciousness. Yet there is the awareness that it is not possible for everyone to be the same. It is not possible for everyone to like what everyone else is doing. That is not why people incarnate or why you come together. Being yourself, living from the energy of neutrality, and having fun will assist you in this process.

INDIVIDUALIZATION AND DISTRACTION

As you are continuing to deepen your connection to the Peace Ray there are a couple of components that we would like to share. One is about this sense of individualization, of keeping your eye on the prize, of keeping yourself focused on what is important to you. There is the possibility as the vibration on the planet continues to accelerate that you could get distracted. The distraction is a part of the collective consciousness. Many people want to be distracted and there are some good things about that. If someone is having a hard time and they watch a movie, they get distracted from their difficulties and that is good.

What we are talking about is a vibrational distraction, an unconscious falling into a groove that is not set by you. It is different from being busy. You can be busy and that is fine. We are talking about the issue of being distracted from what is important to you. Keep your focus and keep your intention. Ask yourself throughout the day, "What is important to me? Is this important to me? Am I focused on what is important to me?" If you find that you are living your life for other people or based on assumptions of what you think other people would like you to do, then bring yourself back to yourself. The more you are yourself the more joy you will have in your life.

LETTING GO OF JUDGMENT

The other kernel of wisdom that we would like to share is to encourage you as much as possible to let go of the energy of judgment. This will help you immensely. Spending time judging yourself or judging others is like trying to drive forward while looking at your rearview mirror; it just reverses the energy of where you are trying to go.

You will not be influenced by other's actions, beliefs, and thought-forms the more you engage the Peace Ray of Light. It does not really matter what other people are doing. It does not really matter what other people are saying. However many times a day you might be judging yourself, allow yourself to be in the now and keep your focus on what is important to you.

YOU GET TO DECIDE WHAT INGREDIENTS YOU PUT IN THE RECIPE OF YOUR LIFE

Imagine that you are going to the grocery store and you are getting ingredients to make your favorite broccoli soup. As you are in the produce section you simply select the ingredients you would like: broccoli, leeks, onions, potatoes, carrots. You may not like chili peppers and so you don't put those in your basket; the fact that they are in the produce section of the store does not bother you. You just walk on by them and focus on the ingredients that will make your favorite recipe come to life. You do not have to try to get rid of, judge, or eliminate the vast variety of ingredients in the grocery store that you don't prefer. You can just make your meal and your life and create your recipe with the ingredients that you want to put in it. If there is rage in the store of life, you don't have to put that emotion in your soup; if there is a food that you do not like in the store, it does not matter because you can stay focused and not be distracted by the other ingredients. In your particular recipe only put in those ingredients that you want.

SELF-JUDGMENT IS SELF-PRESERVATION

Why is it that self-judgment comes up? What is the purpose of self-judgment? At its base and purest level there is an element of self-preservation. If you are monitoring yourself then the thought is that you will be safe. Yet really the safest place for you to be is to be yourself and to love all aspects of yourself.

Let us say that you want to live a life of peace, joy, and soul fulfillment. You are radiating so much love and so much unity that as you are in that higher vibration other aspects that are moving more slowly begin to come to the surface—aspects that you might not like about yourself. Maybe it is that you judge other people. But as you include those aspects there may be only two units of the aspect of judgment and ninety-eight units of love and unity. Because of this the judgment seamlessly gets absorbed; it does not even matter and it is fuel for the whole.

Focus on aligning with what it is that you want to align with and embrace anything and everything that is you. Practice being in the Peace Ray and see how it changes you. Anything is possible; the potential is infinite and it can all happen now.

9

THE VENUS RAY

The Ray of Opulent Bliss

▲

Aligns your system with your birthrights of abundance, beauty, radiance, and bliss. The Venus Ray supports the understanding that opulence and bliss are the natural state of the universe and nourishes your system and all experiences that embody the Venus Ray to be in a state of overflowing.

TUNING IN
. . . .
Raise Your Vibration and Tune
In to the Council of Light

Welcome to this divine transmission with the Council of Light and the Venus Ray of Opulent Bliss. As we begin, focus on and call forth the full emanation of your heart center. Feel your vibration beginning to rise. Feel your vibration elevate, accelerate, and exponentiate.

When your vibration has exponentiated, tune in to the Council of Light. Your connection is unique to you. Take some time in silence and continue strengthening your connection to the Council of Light.

Keep in mind that each person has a different team, a different band of consciousness, that they connect to. You can compare this to feeling an affinity to a certain flavor, texture, or a way of life. You might like vanilla ice cream and another person might like chocolate. Or you might like jazz and another person likes classical music. As you connect to your particular team of the Divine it is similar in the sense that it is your preference to be in a certain vibrational field. It is your affinity to connect to certain levels of consciousness.

Set your intention to connect to a member of the Council of Light that is on your team: the Venus Ray. You may imagine the stellar location of Venus. Even though the origin of the Venus Ray is not Venus, Venus does filter and transmit an aspect of the Venus Ray. Travel back along the line of the Venus Ray and just take your time through your intention to connect to the strongest point you can. The Venus Ray is readily available to you. Everything that you desire is already within you, and so the Venus Ray is already within you. Spend as much time as you would like connecting to the Venus Ray and allowing your sensations to flow. What does the Venus Ray feel like? Does the Venus Ray have any information to share with you? When you feel like you are ready, take your time to come fully back.

. . . .

SHIFTING OLD PATTERNS
OF CONSCIOUSNESS TO NEW WAYS OF BEING

As you orient yourself to align and resonate with the Venus Ray, it cultivates a sense within you that you may not have fully relied on before. This can be likened to when a blind person begins to heighten his senses of sound, touch, and smell rather than focusing on what he can or cannot see. It is shifting your focus from one way of being that may have been very helpful, predominant, instinctive, and natural for one period of time to depending and building a relationship with other aspects of your being. It is a shift in consciousness. It is moving from a consciousness of lack, separation, or focusing on what is not present in your life to moving into a sense of contentment, wholeness, love, joy, abundance, contentment, unity, and fulfillment. It is a deprogramming from one way of being and aligning with another way.

ENERGETIC EXERCISE
Aligning with the Vibration of Love

This is the Council of Light that is moving more into the forefront of this now moment. As you are stabilized in your own vibration and frequency this is able to occur. We begin now with the full emanation of your heart space, for the heart is the nexus place of above and below. The heart is that space that is a portal to multidimensional vibrations and expressions. It is a portal in which you can enter into other dimensions and other time-and-space experiences.

As you are sitting in the emanation of your heart—and what we mean by emanation is the vibration, the bubble, and the manifestation of your heart—feel yourself surrounded by this vibration of love. Love is truly a vibration that is resonant with the alignment of soul and body, the alignment of Divine as Divine.

This divine transmission is occurring on multiple levels, and so we will be transmitting through the silence, through the language of light, through the divinity codes, through the DNA spiral, through the awakened spinal column, and through heavenly and earthly chi. Feel the vibration of love being fully awakened within you. Spend as much time as you would like basking in this love energy.

YOU ARE ALREADY
WHERE YOU DESIRE TO BE

We know that there is often a focus on getting somewhere. You want to move from where you are to where you would like to be. We would invite you to shift from this focus of getting somewhere to allowing and remembering that you are already there: there is here. For now just let go of the idea of needing to get somewhere or achieve something and resurrect within your own awareness the infinite possibilities of already being there. Imagine that you are already fully realized, you are already in a state of ecstatic bliss, you are already experiencing joy, and you are already awakened. By bringing in this vibration of already being there, of arriving and of remembering, it allows these things to be in the same location as you. It brings them into the present moment.

As we mentioned, our purpose is to enhance joy and through the enhancement of joy there is an enhancement of vitality, of vibration, and of vibrancy that rolls over into a sense of happiness, peace, and fulfillment. Opening up to the joy that you already are allows you to be in the same location as those things that you have been seeking or trying to find. Have a sense that you are already there. In this transmission you are becoming current with who you are. It is the concept of being in ease and grace that allows that which you have become to be in the same location as you.

Seeking, striving, and going after is like trying to grasp an inflatable beach ball that is floating on the surface in a pool or ocean; all the energy of trying to grasp it ends up pushing the ball further away. If you are in the energy of striving, in the energy of trying to get somewhere in your life, there is a pushing away of that which you are seeking. This is different than expanding into the now moment.

ENERGETIC EXERCISE
The Embodiment of Ecstatic Bliss

In this now moment you can imagine that you are in a pool, ocean, or beautiful lake and all that you have been seeking is now in the same energetic location as you. All those perfect people, places, and opportunities, represented by beach balls, are floating right next to you. You have access to the ball of fulfillment, the ball of peace, the ball of awakening, the ball of connection, the ball of community, the ball of love, and the ball of prosperity. The coherence of your vibrational matrix has aligned with what you are seeking and you are in the emanation of your heart and in this energy of joy.

This is the Venus Ray that is moving more into the now moment. Allow yourself to feel the vibration that is becoming accessible. Allow yourself to acknowledge the Venus Ray within you, the ray of bliss, the ray of ecstasy, the ray of opulence, this energetic tone of ecstatic bliss. You may have a sense of the Hathors present as well, for they have been stewards of ecstatic bliss for eons. As you are already there, allow yourself to be in alignment with this ecstatic bliss. It is as if this ecstatic bliss, this Venus Ray, this opulent bliss, were a fountain emanating from the portal of your heart center rising up through your throat, your third eye, and your crown, and showering in, through, and around you. This fountain is also rising up through your feet, your legs, your pelvis, your heart, and your crown. As you are in this shower of the opulent bliss, the ecstatic bliss, the joy, the Venus Ray that is in and through and around you, feel the birthright of joy unlocking from within your DNA spiral. Feel the birthright of joy emanating from the divinity codes within you, in the crystals of your blood, and in your bones. Feel the birthright of joy like stars glistening in the galaxy sparking within your bloodstream. Feel the birthright of joy circulating through your pranic tube, your central column, your spinal column, and the space around it. Feel the birthright of joy activating your pleasure centers, and by pleasure centers we mean all of you. You may think of your pleasure centers as related to the senses: your sense of taste, touch, smell, your sensuality, and your sexuality. The pleasure of sense is only one aspect of the pleasure centers that are your birthright. You are a multidimensional being and you have multidimensional pleasure centers. Allow the pleasure centers of your multidimensionality to be in the now moment and in an awakened state.

You are designed for bliss. When we speak of multidimensional bliss and multidimensional pleasure centers we are inviting you to feel into the pleasure centers of your soul, to feel into the pleasure centers of your divinity, and to feel into the pleasure centers of your brilliant system. Expand even further into the pleasure centers of your multidimensionality, feeling this fountain of the Venus Ray expanding and quadrupling. Enjoy this expansion of the Venus Ray, and when you feel a sense of overflowing, bring yourself fully back.

OPULENCE AS THE
DIVINE EXPRESSION OF CREATION

The invitation to be in the energy of bliss has been extended to the planet at this time, and some beings on the planet are choosing to take that invitation. As that is occurring you may be aware of more intergalactic activity, more communion with the heavenly energies within and without, and a more stardust quality of vibration. The Venus Ray, this opulent bliss, is a wave of consciousness from which you can garner much.

What calls forth the energy of beauty is this ecstatic bliss and opulence. The word opulence has an association with beauty—extraordinary beauty—and for some this may have a charge or an association with over indulgence, luxury, and hedonism, as well as the belief that it is for some and not for all. Yet by being at the place of opulence as a frequency and as a vibration of the ecstatic bliss of beauty you can feel into the boundless and infinite nature of creation. For why would you have something that would bring you joy or would bring you pleasure tied into the old paradigm of guilt or shame? Suppose it would be an experience of pleasure for you to x, y, or z, and then you held yourself separate from experiencing that pleasure. Opulence is the divine expression of creation. It is a vibration. Allow your consciousness to shift if you have or had any judgment around opulence or have a charge on that word to see it just for the beauty that it is. There is the opulence of the stars shining in the galaxy. There is the opulence of cherries blooming on a cherry tree. There is the opulence of an exquisite landscape. There is the opulence of the colors of fish in the universe. There is this outrageous beauty that exists in nature that is simply opulent. This is what we are inviting you to tune in to.

SELF-CREATED SUFFERING

It may seem ludicrous to think that anyone would want to create suffering, and yet there are times when your emotional body moves into a state of suffering and there is an imagined reason for the suffering rather than what is actually happening in the now experience. You may feel stressed, worried, or have a sense of struggle around how much you have to get done. Yet in the now moment there is only one thing that you need to do. It may be that this pattern of feeling overwhelmed happens right before you go to bed, when you start thinking about all the things that you need to do. This creates a sense of self-created suffering when really all there is for you to do in that moment is to rest, sleep, and rejuvenate. Whatever self-created suffering means to you, just decide within your own mind, within your own being-ness, whether you would like to continue to manifest suffering, or if you would choose to align with a sense of contentment, fulfillment, and peace.

There is something about suffering that is valued in the old paradigm of consciousness. It is valued to be seen as someone who has overcome obstacles, who works herself to the bone, and who has overcome all of the odds. There is value in being someone who achieves a great amount from action, from doing, and from stress. There is the idea that if your desires were to magically appear in your life then they would not be as valuable as if they were accomplished through hard work and suffering. There is a choice point or freewill moment where you have the opportunity to say, "Is that true for me? Do I believe that? Do I believe that it is valuable to experience joy, health, love, fulfillment, and prosperity with ease and grace? Or do I believe that it is more valuable if I suffer?" There are two different roads to the same destination—it is your choice which you take.

We want to reassure you that the things you desire come from a place within you that directly relates to expanding and aligning with what you desire. Having what you desire is not a "maybe," it is a given. Having what you desire is not a possibility; it is inevitable. That is easy for us to say from the sense that the soul is infinite. You might think that we are saying, "Well, you may not have health in this lifetime but you are going to have it in another." There is no way to disprove that what you desire is going to happen. Yet you prefer to enjoy your affinity for a particular thing in this life experience. Our point is to say it is not about doing it this way versus that way to get what you want. We are not talking about whether or not you are going to get what you want. The question we are asking is "What road do you want to take to be where it is that you are choosing to be?" There is one road called suffering and one road called alignment, resonance, ease, and grace. The Venus Ray transcends the energy of suffering. It is not the road of hard work. The Venus Ray is a subtle energy that is strong, profound, and aligns with the energy of ease and grace.

SUPPORT EXERCISE
The Desire Beneath the Desire

There is a magnetic pole to the Venus Ray that carries you forward to your destination. You may visualize it like a conveyer belt that is moving something that you desire toward you. Or you may see it like a moving sidewalk at the airport. There is a magnetism to the Venus Ray. In your mind's eye see the quickening of this magnetism. As the quickening of this magnetism is happening, see if you can go deep within yourself and identify what it is that you truly want: the desire beneath the desire. What is it that would bring you great joy? Perhaps it is a quality like freedom, trust, or joy. Perhaps this brings to mind a physical thing that you want or an experience that you want, like a home, a relationship, or a trip. This process is similar to a train that has been going on a certain track and then switches tracks; or a door that has been on a hinge and is taken off, freed. There is a sorting process that happens and teases out the thing that you desire from that which is underneath the thing that you desire.

Why does that make such a difference? It makes such a difference because when these are teased out you can have the experience of what you desire anytime and in any situation. You can experience what you want now and be content now. Once you have tuned in to that which is underneath the desire or that which you want, allow the Venus Ray and your intention to merge the consciousness of what you want and your now moment. Become the vibration that is freedom, abundance, trust, or whatever quality you have chosen. Breathe and anchor this sensation for as long as you would like. That which you desire and you are in the same location.

BELIEF AND CREATION

Have a sense of connecting to your mental body and your belief systems. Notice what beliefs would unravel if you were to believe that having what you want is a given. Think to yourself, "I have what I want, it is a given." You can create something in two ways. You can create something with a lot of effort or you can create something from your multidimensional body, from the yin manifestation, from the aspect of you that is the creator being. Just notice if there are any beliefs that you have that are coming to the surface that are perhaps out of resonance with creation through contentment, wholeness, and the Venus Ray.

Many times as we share information about the Rays of Light there are many examples, words, and detailed descriptions. In this instance the approach is more of an inception and a conception: you become fertile with the Venus Ray. You become pregnant with the Venus Ray or you do not. If you do there is a natural cycle to it and it has its own momentum. It does not need a lot of description.

You are a creator being with the natural instinctual awareness and expression of ever unfolding, infinite possibilities. That which you are seeking is seeking you. As you are connected more to the Venus Ray you can begin to imagine that it acts in a similar way to the Peace Ray, which created a bubble that you could be held inside and be free of illusion. When you are inside of the Venus Ray, when you are aligned with the Venus Ray, when you are radiating with the Venus Ray, it creates a bubble of consciousness in which you can feel the reality of your unrealized desire. Within that bubble of the Venus Ray there is an awareness that everything has already happened, your manifestation is complete, you are connected to it, you are aligned with it, and you have the experience of it. As you are connected to the Venus Ray, it shifts your orientation. It is an experience that is aligned with feeling as if what you desire is already here: "As I am aligned with the Venus Ray, I feel as if I have the experience of health. As I am aligned with the Venus Ray, I feel as if I have the relationship of my dreams. As I am aligned with the Venus Ray, I feel as if I am financially free."

You can continue to fill in the blanks and take out the words "feel as if" and instead use words that connect you more to the now moment: "I am financially free. I am healthy. I am fulfilled. I feel connected to unity consciousness." One way to tell if you are fully saturated in the Venus Ray is whether or not the words feel true. One of the illusions to which the Venus Ray provides a solution is the sense of not believing you have what you desire. If you state an affirmation that is not a part of your reality then it feels untrue. With the Venus Ray fully activated it is true and so it feels true.

In this transmission we spent time building the connection to the Venus Ray. If you continue to practice building your connection to the Venus Ray, it becomes more and more natural, more and more a part of your everyday experience. It becomes second nature. To practice working with the Venus Ray more consciously, choose a quality that you would like to feel within you. Maybe the quality is freedom, joy, fulfillment, or love. Maybe it is a sense of safety and security. Underneath the quality of safety and security there is the desire to feel like you have the right to be here, to shine your light, to be you, and to have what you want. There is this sense that it is safe to be you, you are safe to own your territory, and you are safe to be visible. This could be also be described as having self-permission and self-love.

ENERGETIC EXERCISE
Magnetizing the Quality of Your Desire

Identify a word or a feeling of the quality you want to magnetize within your system. As you are contemplating this quality, move back and forth between the word and the Venus Ray. In your mind imagine saying, "Self-love, Venus Ray, self-love, Venus Ray," or "Freedom, Venus Ray, freedom, Venus Ray," or "Passion, Venus Ray, passion, Venus Ray." Go back and forth between the quality and the Venus Ray so that it moves from feeling like a thought to having substance. When you have a sense of feeling imprinted with the quality you may switch to another one if you desire.

As the magnification of the quality gets stronger you can focus on the word or repeat the word. An example would be: "Abundance, abundance, abundance, Venus Ray, Venus Ray, Venus Ray," until they merge. The Venus Ray holds the quality and the quality holds the Venus Ray; they merge, they unify, they align, and they resonate.

Now focus on something material, physical, experiential, or tangible that you would like to have. Maybe it is a relationship, a career, a house, a trip, or money. Once you have chosen this, go through the same process of saying whatever it is that describes this third-dimensional property and move back and forth between the word and the Venus Ray. Some examples of this would be: "Radiant health, Venus Ray, radiant health, Venus Ray," "Financial wealth, Venus Ray, financial wealth, Venus Ray."

If it feels as if the connection to your Venus Ray could be stronger, drop the focus on the thing for a few moments and charge the Venus Ray by saying, "Venus Ray, Venus Ray, Venus Ray, Venus Ray, Venus Ray." When it gets solid again, weave the experience that you are choosing to have back in with it until there is a sense of merging between the experience and the Venus Ray.

Begin to tune in to the Venus Ray as a being of light, taking a moment to meet the Venus Ray, to greet the Venus Ray, see, feel, sense, or know the Venus Ray. You may sense the Venus Ray as a color, a sensation, a being, or a vibration. Sense, see, feel, or imagine that the Venus Ray is walking with you into the various areas of your life. Imagine in your mind's eye walking with the Venus Ray through your home and that the Venus Ray, in conjunction with you and your higher self, is offering this fountain of ecstatic bliss to the place where you live. Imagine that your home is invited to resonate with the vibration of joy and those beings that you may live with, whether they are human, pets, or plants, are invited to resonate in the energy of joy. See in your mind's eye this joy and ecstatic bliss awakened within your home and the land that the home rests upon. You may even have a sense of the items in your home sparking with bliss, sparking with joy, coming into that vibration of bliss, that vibration of joy. Feel the heart of your home beginning to fountain this bliss energy in and through and around it.

Walk with the Venus Ray, float with the Venus Ray into other areas of your life and in your relationships, sparking the birthright of joy and the multidimensional pleasure centers within those relationships. Walk with the Venus Ray into the connection to your divine purpose, your divine mission and service. Go into the heart of that divine mission, that divine purpose, and ignite this waterfall, this fountain of ecstatic bliss of the Opulence Ray into your purpose. Move with the Venus Ray into the heart of your finances, activating within the DNA of the heart of your finances the divinity codes of ecstatic bliss. Invite your home, your finances, your relationships, and your divine mission to be in a state of joy.

Now go with the Venus Ray into any other levels of consciousness that draw your attention in your life. Invite your beliefs, intuition, decision-making, health, energy, your emotional body, your sexuality, and your multidimensionality to ignite these divinity codes of joy. Tap into the unlimited supply and infinite fountain of joy. Sense your electric appliances, vehicles, computers, and technology igniting with joy. Sense your water and soil igniting with joy. Sense the food that you eat igniting with joy. Take the next few minutes to continue this process at your own pace and direction.

UNCONDITIONAL JOY

This divine joy, this divine light, this divine love, transcends what you may have previously thought of as the ceiling on your joy. You may have thought that there is only so much joy that you could feel until you became uncomfortable or that surrendering to bliss or ecstasy would leave you feeling a sense of being out of control or feeling as if you may be reckless or irresponsible. But we are not speaking about conditional or circumstantial joy. We are speaking about universal joy, the birthright of joy, the energy of joy, the energy of this ecstatic bliss that your being is naturally attuned to. This ecstatic bliss is your core state and is an anchor point for you that you are emanating from, with, and to. Because of this it transcends anything that may or may not be happening in your external or internal world. There is just a sense of contentment, a sense of peace, or a Zen-like state that is a part of the Venus Ray, this Opulence Ray, which is the happy-for-no-reason vibration and is the understanding of this birthright in the now.

With that being said you may now feel that you are choosing to uptake even more vibration, and that more and more drops of this consciousness are accessible to you. Opulence has a prolific nature to it. Allow this beauty to be prolific, to be exponentiated. It is much easier than you may think to come from joy than it is to experience joy as a result of an external achievement. For as you are in a state of bliss, as you are in a state of joy, you already are where that which you have been seeking is.

You may ask the Venus Ray to help you to develop a practice and an alignment process, now that you have met the Venus Ray—perhaps again, perhaps for the first time, or perhaps more consciously. It can be as simple as stating the following in your mind's eye: "Thought intention, activate the birthright of joy. Thought intention, raise vibration to ecstatic bliss." If you utilize this set point, this answering of the invitation consciously, your manifestation will be rapid, your sense of spiritual connection will be amplified, and your experiences in life in terms of those external manifestations will expand into a beautiful, magical tapestry. So much of what you have seen and have been taught is about striving, struggling, forcing, and an action-oriented way of being. To shift to being where you already are and in a state of joy is the alignment process that will create a life of joy.

SUPPORT EXERCISE
Aligning with Your Desires

The Venus Ray holds your experience and your experience holds the Venus Ray; they are in resonance, in harmony, and they are one. We invite you to do this short Venus Ray meditation practice each day for five minutes.

To begin, call upon the Council of Light that is aligned with you. Move into the awareness of the innermost part of your being, the seed of your being, and elicit or activate the Venus Ray. Spend the majority of the time swimming in the Venus Ray, steeping in the Venus Ray. Once the Venus Ray feels solid, bring in the quality that you want to align with or the experience that you want to have, and move between the quality or experience and the Venus Ray until they merge and you have a sense of having the experience and aligning with the experience. You are within the Venus Ray and the Venus Ray is inherent within your experience. Your experience is inherent within the Venus Ray and you. Bask in this energy until this process feels complete.

THE VENUS RAY AS A BUILDING BLOCK

At its very base this is an alchemical process. If you think about the third dimension, which is energy that appears physical to you and is slow enough to become a chair or a car, it is made up of building blocks. Some people talk about these building blocks of creation being the elements of Earth, Air, Water, Fire, and Akasha. Your body is made up of these elements, yet it also includes as one of its building blocks the Venus Ray. This building block of the Venus Ray is the alchemy, the magic wand, the divine order, and a reason that your natural state is joy and is bliss. The Venus Ray—opulent bliss—is an innate aspect of your origin. If you find yourself on the road of struggle remember that you can choose to get off that road like a train changing tracks and get on the road of the Venus Ray.

SEEING THROUGH THE CHAOS

We would invite you during the next six months to look beyond that which may appear as an unraveling of energy. If you are seeing chaos around you or in the lives of others, train your eyes to look through that chaos into the energy of this birthright of joy. Many are experiencing erratic feelings; you may experience this for yourself where you feel more blissful, more abundant, more on the path, more in that sweet spot than you ever have, and then moving into feeling a sense of separation, loneliness, lack, fear, doubt, or chaos, and you may be seeing this in others too. To be able to see through this erratic movement to the steady, divine state of joy and ecstatic bliss will allow you to be there now.

You may have noticed that when you make a decision to step into a greater level of joy, a greater level of ease, a greater level of grace, or a greater level of clarity, sometimes it feels as if the opposite of that begins to show up in your life. For some this is interpreted as moving "two steps back, one step forward," when really it is just dust that is about to settle. It is like a plane landing in the desert and the dust is flying. The plane still landed. The dust is not an indication that it has not landed. Another example is if you are cleaning your house and in the process of it getting clean it becomes more chaotic or the dust flies. This is not an indication that you were never meant to clean it in the first place or that it is not actually clean when it is done. It is just a surface vibration. When you can train yourself to see beyond the chaos and to just be in that ecstatic bliss in each and every moment, then you will be living unconditionally. It is with great ecstatic joy and ecstatic bliss that we complete this segment in this now moment, knowing that the vibrations and the resonance continue to ripple.

10

THE DIVINE RAY

The Oneness Ray

▲

The web that connects all things, the origin of all there is, the building blocks of the universe. Calling upon the Divine Ray allows you to see things from a heightened perspective and provides the space to go deeper into a state of awareness of the essence of a situation.

TUNING IN
. . . .
The Focal Point

Welcome to this divine transmission with the Council of Light on the Divine Ray. Bring your focus inside and choose a focal point. This focal point could be your breath going in and out or the feel of your heart beating. Allow your awareness of your focal point to deepen through your attention to it. Does your breath exist without you being mindful of it? Does your heart beat without you focusing upon it? Although the answer is yes to both of these questions, there is an enhanced awareness as you focus consciously upon that which is already there. Take a few moments to be mindful of your focal point and when you are ready take a couple of deep breaths and gently return to the present moment.

. . . .

ENTERING INTO
A GREATER STATE OF AWARENESS:
THE FABRIC OF CREATION

The evolution of consciousness is the entering into a greater state of awareness. This is occurring on a planetary and individual level as well as beyond. One of the key elements of the evolution of consciousness is having mastery over your ability to choose what you are being mindful about and what you are focusing upon, not just in your mind or your thoughts but in your whole being and within the fabric of creation.

With that awareness and focus you can receive access to healing energies, healing frequencies, and to meditative states. Your presence can be a therapeutic benefit to others and to yourself, as can the particular modalities that you have learned. You can take the ability to have awareness of subtle energies, of healing frequencies, of a meditative state, into having awareness of the fabric of creation: the underlying rhythm of every moment.

You may call this the oneness web. This is the energetic source or aspect of everything that is energy. It is vibration, frequency, light, and the divinity that exists in every moment. Just like bringing your attention to your breath and to your heart you bring attention to the divinity and the Source energy within each moment.

A DEEPER CONNECTION
TO YOUR INNER KNOWING

One of your desires may be the ability to have a deeper connection to your own guidance system, your internal compass, and your inner clarity. This can be expressed in different ways. You might relate this specifically to what you would call your guides. You might also think of this as having a gut knowing or a feeling.

This can also be expressed as being able to connect to your soul and having the ability to be self-guided, self-directed, and having inner clarity. This is a key marker for living in the evolution of consciousness. This is innate within you. It is not something that has to be learned, necessarily, but rather remembered.

CONNECTING WITH YOUR GUIDES

The thought of connecting to guides is an interesting thing because under the awareness that there is only one, that there is oneness, that all things are connected, some questions arise. "Is the guide outside of you? Is the guide inside of you? Are you the guide? Is the guide separate from you? Are you one with the guide? Is the guide Source? Is the guide an aspect of Source?"

These are all very good questions and intellectual concepts. Depending on how you think you may come to a different realization about the entire concept of having spirit guides and spirit helpers. Your relationship to your spirit guides and your spirit helpers may also evolve over time.

One of the reasons why it can be easier to view a spirit guide, a spirit helper, or a light being as something outside of or separate from you is that it personalizes it and provides a way for you to be able to build a rapport or a relationship. It personifies the energetic essence of the Divine in that spirit helper form just like you would build a relationship with a friend or an animal. You build a relationship with a particular band of consciousness that you identify as a spirit guide.

Do you have access within you to that same band of consciousness because everything that there is and everything there ever will be exists within you? The answer to that is yes. Yet it may be most optimal for you to personify, to have a separate identity with the guide and with the Council of Light.

ENERGETIC EXERCISE
Deepening Your Connection
to the Council of Light

Have a sense of your awareness being drawn to your particular Council of Light group, perhaps setting your intention and putting out the call to connect to them. Allow your awareness of your particular group of Council members to deepen. If you are visual maybe you see your Council group as beings of light, or see them as a particular color. Maybe you feel the quality of energy changing around you and know that their presence is there. If you are auditory perhaps you hear words that are reassuring or you are given some information. If you are kinesthetic the hair on your body may stand up, or you may have an emotional response such as feeling a little teary, or your hands may get hot. There are many different kinds of sensations that are possible for you to experience.

You may not have any sensations even though you have the desire to have them. It does not matter where you are in the remembering of how to connect to realms of consciousness and the infinite intelligence. Just accept where you are and know that wherever you are there exists within you the fully realized capability to tap into the field of infinite intelligence, whether you call it Source, Spirit, spirit guides, or higher realms of consciousness. Set your intention, if you desire, to be even more clear in your life, more confident in your inner trajectory, your inner guidance, and more aligned with your ability as a creator being to enhance this remembering.

You have connected to your particular group of the Council of Light and perhaps you have a very deep, significant awareness of them, or perhaps you have only gone through the motions of the process that has been explained to you. Yet regardless, you have connected to the Council of Light, a field of infinite wisdom, a conglomerate and a complex energy pattern. The wisdom that we are working with together is transmitted and received. This field of energy is expressed as different frequencies, different vibrations, and different textures, and in this moment words are being placed to those different textures, frequencies, and vibrations. The process is happening as a direct transmission, so in addition to words it is also occurring on multidimensional levels.

When you feel ready take a few deep breaths, feel yourself come back into your body and gently bring your awareness back to this time and place.

THE COLLECTIVE FEAR OF CONNECTING DIRECTLY TO DIVINE SOURCE

There is a collective fear that has many different aspects to it. It is the fear of having an awakened intuition, of going crazy, of being ostracized or somehow harmed for having this vision, connection, and ability. There is sometimes the idea that the process of tapping into a particular realm of subtle energies and having a connection directly to the divine source of consciousness is somehow something to be afraid of.

This collective fear is ever present in your history and society, although paradoxically it is becoming more hip to be magical, to be a paranormal and an extraordinary type of person. This is getting into the mainstream entertainment in the form of Harry Potter or movies and TV shows with different forms of paranormal, fantasy beings such as vampires or different archetypes. If there was ever a time in history for it to be cool or hip to express these extraordinary things, it is now moving in that direction.

Yet even within each of those shows and plots there is always the balance being portrayed and the conflict that comes with that. There is the collective paradigm that somehow says that if you are tapped into what is seen as extraordinary abilities—which are actually natural, and a birthright to every single person—it causes undue attention to yourself.

How do you reconcile that one of the major aspects of moving into your own evolution, the next phase of your everyday enlightenment, is to have access to these realms? That is what is happening for everyone whether they want it to or not. Not that it goes against their free will but the capability is being remembered within people who would be the most skeptical about it. How do you reconcile that this is where the planet is moving, and what you have been seeking and desiring to be, with the thought or fear that if you fully align with this it will somehow be dangerous? Here is a meditation exercise to help you do just that.

SUPPORT EXERCISE
An Offering upon the Altar

One suggestion for reconciling this is to let go of the illusion of fear. Continue to focus on your breath, on your heart beating, or whichever focal point you have chosen, knowing that your Council of Light members are here to teach you, support you, and assist you in this process.

Imagine that there is an altar in front of you and that the Council of Light members are surrounding this altar; you are a part of a circle and a team. If you wish, offer this fear onto the collective altar in front of you, this fear that if you really show the intuitive, psychic, wise, visionary, oracular, miraculous, healing part of you it will be dangerous for you. If you choose, place the fear on the altar and know that if you want you can take this fear back at any time. Try this out and see if it is real or is an illusion, and if there is a difference between the real and the illusion.

Imagine that this is an offering that you and the collective have been learning from. This offering has to do with the paradigm of duality and separation. What is being offered as an exchange from the Council of Light on this altar is a combination of different things unique to you.

Imagine that there is a band of light, a book, frequency, belief, thought, feeling, or a symbol that has been placed on the altar. Connect to it and ask yourself if it feels like it is yours. If it is yours then take it and notice if you want to have it next to you for a while or if it feels like something you want to merge with right away by placing it into your heart, your head, or your hands. Maybe it is something that is in the form of a tincture that you are going to take over the next few days, weeks, or months. A gift that comes from this for you has to do with being present; it is a present of the present.

Be with this process for as long as you feel you want to. When you are ready take a few deep breaths, feel your fingers and your toes, and gently come back into your body and to the present moment.

THE DIVINE RAY AND THE ELEMENT OF WATER

Move into the Divine Ray in a more conscious way. The Divine Ray, like your breath or your heartbeat, is always there. It is the web that connects all things, it is the seed vibration that originates all things, it is holographic and it takes many forms.

An example of this is the element of water. You are mostly made up of water; you are like a glass of water, a lake, or the ocean, even though you may not see yourself that way. This water takes on many forms and can be combined with many things. It can make a cup of tea or carry herbs in a tincture. Water can be different temperatures: it can be ice, steam, it can be boiling, and it can be everything in between.

The Divine Ray is like those expressions of water if you think it of it from the perspective of chemistry. The Divine Ray is a block that builds everything. Everything is built from the Divine Ray at its base. You may call this energy or you may have a different name for it, but we call it the Divine Ray.

What is water? It is a combination of frequencies. What is the Divine Ray? It is the chemistry of spirit, of the Divine and the mystery. It is the chemistry that connects us all.

THE DIVINE RAY AS A BLANK CANVAS

How does having an awareness of the Divine Ray assist you in your everyday life? How does it assist you in being an awake being moment to moment? How does it assist you in focusing your thoughts and creating your own connection to your world? It is all a matter of what you are paying attention to.

Although it is not without order, the Divine Ray is a blank canvas. The Divine Ray has a purpose, a function, and a focus. As you bring your awareness onto the blank canvas—the Divine Ray, the web, the hologram, and the Source energy that exists within everything—then you are focusing on a very complex yet simple vibration. It is like the saying "See the Divine in all. Namaste. I see the Divinity within you." It is seeing the concept of healing energy and the unlimited life-force energy in all things. As you bring your awareness to the Divine Ray you feel stillness; there is a clear field of the mind and a place of nonattachment. You are able to see beyond that which is being presented to you.

Let us say somebody gives you a painting of a nature scene. You see trees, the sun, water, and birds. While you are looking at the painting you shift your focus to the blank canvas underneath the paint. Does the blank canvas exist even though it has been painted upon? It does, just like your breath exists whether you are focusing on it or not. As you are tuned in to the Divine Ray—the origin of all things, the energy that creates worlds, the expansive, unified, and clear field—there is calmness, a presence, and an awakeness. You are able to see beyond the illusion of the painting and to be mindful that there is something going on that is in perfect order and that is in alignment with you.

Part of the premise of this is to give you the opportunity to move into an energy of either nonattachment or detachment and for you to decide for yourself. Do you feel like the universe is a friendly universe that is conspiring for your benefit? Are you operating out of the paradigm that all is well and that there is some organized, synchronistic aspect to everything? Is that a preferred way of seeing the world for you? It is not necessary to have that viewpoint but it may assist you in relaxing into seeing the blank canvas of the world, seeing the web of the world, and piercing through the illusion. The Divine Ray assists you in piercing through the illusion.

SUPPORT EXERCISE
Seeing the Painting of Your Life through the Divine Ray

To apply the concept of the blank canvas to your life, imagine a situation that you feel unrest about and have an attachment to. Maybe it is something that you really want to happen that has not happened yet. Maybe it is a person that brings up all of your stuff. Maybe it is a health issue. Whatever it is, just focus on it.

Maybe you do not have any areas of unrest right now, but imagine one that you had previously, or one that someone you knew had. Focus on some area that brings a sense of dis-ease, a sense of unrest, or an incredible sense of longing, urgency, or attachment.

Imagine that this situation is a painting. Maybe it is an angry painting or a wistful painting, a wanting painting or a longing painting. Maybe it is a conflicted painting or one in which there is some residue of war or an inner struggle. That is how it appears to you if you are looking at it from your nonawake eyes, being unaware of the Divine Ray. As you put the Divine Ray glasses on and come from the perspective of seeing from the Divine Ray, it is like the painting becomes misty and you see the clear field of the mind and the infinite intelligence that is pulsing through each moment. You see the expansion, you see the Divine Ray, and you see the web of oneness, the Source, origin, and spirit.

In the beginning of this process things can feel somewhat altered. There can be a sense of grieving that happens when you move into identifying or aligning with a higher realm of consciousness, because it changes the way that you interact with your life and reality. Because of this there can be a sense of the death of an old way of being. Yet there is something within you that very much wants to align with a new way of being: unification, oneness, alignment, expansion, harmony, light, life, peace, and unity.

Imagine that you have, with the assistance of the Divine Ray, stripped away the illusion. It is a part of the prophesy of the New Age that there will be the ability to see everything for what it is: if someone has an ulterior motive in what they are saying to you or what they are doing it becomes transparent. You are able to see that they are being motivated by their own fear, their own insecurity, or they want to get something from you. Everything becomes transparent.

As you look at your painting through the lens of the Divine Ray you also begin to see the right relationship with everyone's connection to it. If your painting involves someone else you are able to see what is motivating them, motivating you, and you are able to recognize that on a soul level the experience has reminded you and the other person to see through the illusion, to grow in some way, and to be a catalyst of remembering. Take a few deep breaths and imagine the Divine Ray completely saturating your picture, bringing a state of resonance and alignment to the situation you have chosen. As you are ready bring your awareness fully back to the present moment, letting go of the picture—the situation—completely.

VIEWING LIFE FROM
A DIFFERENT PERSPECTIVE

Seeing everything from a different perspective can feel like an altered state. If you watch a movie with 3-D glasses, the glasses add a new dimension to the previously flat image. Or like the movie *The Matrix* where Keanu Reaves can see each and every particle of light in everything. That is the kind of awareness that we are talking about. It may not be visual for you, but there is a piercing through and getting to the core of things, to the root of things. You are able to see everything.

As you add the Divine Ray to your toolbox for yourself and others, it provides the space to go deeper. You do not have to have vision for someone else, but if you want to it can provide the space for the person to get to the core of whatever is going on with him or her. You can also call upon it in your own meditation, as it gives you the space to get to the core of something.

ENERGETIC EXERCISE
Connecting More Deeply to the Divine Ray

Focus on your breath and your heart and take a few moments in silence to enhance your connection to the Divine Ray. Notice that more and more of this energy is brought into your awareness. Spend a few minutes exploring the Divine Ray even further. What do you notice about the Divine Ray? How can it support you in your life? In what situations would you call upon it? When you are ready take a couple of deep breaths, move your fingers and toes, feel yourself come back into your body, and gently bring your awareness back to the present moment.

CHOICE

Do you want to live as an awake being? Is this a choice that you are making? Do you want to live in the state of a dream or an illusion? There is a distance to it. It is like living in illusion, duality, and separation without being fully awake. This does not necessarily happen from one moment to the next, although it can, but most people are choosing to evolve in a way that feels comfortable over time. This hesitancy is shifting though.

Draw your focus once again to the Divine Ray and connect in to it, allowing it, relaxing even more. There is nothing you need to do; this is a natural, organic process being guided by your higher self and your free will.

INTEGRATING THE DIVINE RAY

There are various ways that you can choose to integrate the Divine Ray into your life. You may see it like something that you take internally or like a time-release vitamin that spreads its nourishment over time. Or it could be like a muscle that gets developed over time and then you are able to lift something more easily. All of these are perfectly acceptable, wonderful ways of connecting to the Divine Ray. Yet it is important to point out and underscore that the Divine Ray exists naturally within you.

As a human being you are made up of water, and so it is like building a relationship to water by saying, "I am going to drink a glass of water once a day. I am going to put my toes in the water." You already are water so it is not incompatible in any way to your system. Likewise it is not incompatible in any way to your system to fully remember and awaken the Divine Ray in its wholeness.

You may want to set the intention in this remembering and awakening that everything unfolds with ease and grace. You may want to do it in a time-release way, because it is a change in the way that you are connecting to the world. It almost is like a personality change in some ways, but it does not change your essence. Yet it is important for you to state that it can happen in its wholeness from one moment to the next if that is how you would prefer it to happen.

THE BENEFIT OF
LIVING FROM THE DIVINE RAY

What is the benefit of living from the Divine Ray? Why would you choose to awaken it in its wholeness? It is like standing on the inside of a house looking out the window trying to imagine what it feels like to climb a tree or to swim in a pool of water. When you are in the pool, when you are climbing the tree, you have a different awareness than when you are thinking about it from the inside of your house looking out the window. Therefore, you may want to stick your toe in the pool or climb up to the first branch of the tree and see how it feels. A shift in perspective is a shift in perspective.

A HIGHER PERSPECTIVE

Another question you might be wondering about is "Will I still be able to feel? Will I still have emotions? Is living from the Divine Ray like Prozac, like flat-lining everything?" Your emotions are a part of your human experience and as long as you are in your physical incarnation you will have emotions. It is not that your life will become flat-lined from an emotional perspective if you choose to wake up all the way. It is more that you will have a sense of the higher perspective simultaneously with the emotion. In some ways you can feel the emotion even more fully because it is not confused with all the other different paints on the painting. You are able to feel the brown just as the brown without it being glommed on to the entire painting.

Let us say you have a negative emotion. Maybe before living from the Divine Ray you would have that emotion, believe and feel that emotion, tell stories about that emotion, and get into every nook and cranny of that emotion. With the Divine Ray you have the emotion, you feel it, and yet the story you tell about the emotion would be different. Right away you know it is reminding you to pay attention to the stream of well-being that always exists. Or it is reminding you to take some time for you. It has a purpose, but it is not because somebody did something to you, because you have been wronged, or whatever story you might have had from a sleepy place. There is an awakeness to recognizing the intrinsic value of every experience.

With a positive emotion like love, passion, or joy, you can feel those even more strongly because there is a greater resonance to what is underlying those. If you know a little about the idea of joy or you have glimpses of joy, but it does not come as easily to you as you would like, activating the Divine Ray will support you in being able to feel all the aspects of joy.

THE CHOICE TO
INCARNATE AT THIS TIME

On a soul level why do you think you chose to incarnate and to be alive during this time? What about this particular period in history, technology, and the spiritual, physical, and material realms had you saying, "Yes. I am coming in then." What is it that was so compelling that the population on the planet is more than it has ever been, and so many souls have chosen to incarnate during this time? And in particular, why are you drawn to it?

This may be a good question to meditate on because it gives you the invitation to start looking at what is intriguing about this time. What is compelling about it? What is really exciting about it? What is drawing you to it? What is inviting your soul's gifts and talents, your inspirational ideas, your unique essence to shine and to be called forth in a stronger way? It is obvious that this is a rapid and accelerated time. You can look at your technology and other areas and see that there is an acceleration happening.

Maybe like Christopher Columbus you are a pioneer and are discovering continents of consciousness and ways of being that are new and innovative and in alignment with what is to come. Why is it that the average natural lifespan is longer than it has ever been? You can look at this intellectually and see that technology and healthcare make it easier to sustain a longer lifespan. Maybe there is another purpose for it though. Maybe in order to take a quantum leap in consciousness it was important to have lived through many years of the old consciousness, the history, and to be alchemists and transmute that into the new.

It is like the difference between being inside of the house looking out the window at the coming forests of consciousness to being in it. The Divine Ray is a bridge that will assist in this shift in consciousness.

11

THE ENLIGHTENMENT RAY

The Unity Ray

▲

Allows you to clearly see the essence of that which you are seeking, which already exists in the present moment. It supports you in being in union in the now moment and to know that everything you want already exists within you and within this now moment. This Ray is powerful in transcending any thoughts or feelings of separation consciousness and a wonderful Ray to call upon as you are in the process of realizing an expanded state of health, wealth, or happiness.

TUNING IN
Stillness and Inner Union

As we begin this segment with the Council of Light on the Enlightenment Ray, take a few moments to focus on your breath and invite your mind to relax and become peaceful like a still lake. The Egyptian goddess Seshat, who is shown with a seven-petaled flower or star upon her head, is the female form of Thoth. Seshat is related to the clear field of the mind. Have a sense of her presence and her archetypal energy assisting you with this process.

In preparation for tuning in to the Enlightenment Ray, one of the first steps is to come into a greater level of stillness. If this is one of those moments where your mind happens to not be still and has many ripples in the water, then simply be present and accept what is happening in the moment. Rather than trying to fight it,

160

change it, or transcend it, accept that right now your mind may be busy. As much as possible, though, enter into that clear field, that relaxed state.

It is not that you connect to the Enlightenment Ray or to that still place within you from your mind. Your mind may be the part of you that is overshadowing or louder than the stillness. It would be similar to you wanting to do a yoga practice, but having fifty different radios or television shows on in your home or yoga studio. It would be challenging to focus on feeling your body on the mat and doing the exercises. You could still do it, absolutely, and your posture would still look the same from the outside perhaps, but your internal connection to the posture would be different. Beginning with addressing the mind and asking the mind to relax is like turning off the five hundred radio stations or televisions. Yoga stands for union and the Enlightenment Ray is about union, an inner union.

Imagine that in these first few moments, through your intention and through this guidance, you have been able to turn off the louder external signals and begin to tune in to what is already there. Everything already exists within you. Enlightenment, however you define it, is simply living in a light, bubbly, effervescent, humorous, and happy state. Or maybe to you it is that undeniable connection to the Divine within and without in each and every moment, or that expanded perspective to be able to see all there is in every moment. However you define enlightenment, imagine that it already exists in a state of wholeness within you. It is not that enlightenment takes a long period of time to attain or you have to earn it or create it. It already exists in wholeness within you. It is more about quieting down the extraneous environment and tuning in to the wholeness that already exists there.

This first segment of our time together has been about just that, turning down the extraneous environment to bring your attention to something that is there already. Maybe you have had glimpses of it, many moments of connection to it, or maybe you feel like you have no idea that it exists within you. Allow this segment, this time together, to be an invitation to connect to the inner knowing within. Let it be an invitation to connect with the sacred presence, the inner sanctuary, the holy of holies, and to the union within.

Set your intention to connect to the Council of Light. Imagine that you are connecting to your ideal Council of Light frequencies and members and that they are transmitting the Enlightenment Ray to you multidimensionally. Invite your

system to access, receive, and remember the Enlightenment Ray. Allow yourself
the time and space you desire to fully steep in the energy of the Enlightenment Ray.
When you are ready and feel complete with this process, take a few deep breaths
and gently come back to the present moment.

. . . .

EVERYTHING YOU SEEK
ALREADY EXISTS IN THE PRESENT MOMENT

There is the analogy about peeling off the layers of an onion. In a sense
you are peeling away the layers of awareness and tapping into a seed
of consciousness that is the Enlightenment Ray. The core of the onion
exists even when the onion is whole and you can only see the outside
of the onion. What if everything that you have ever been seeking was
already right with you the entire time? What if the confidence, love,
the external manifestation of a relationship, of an experience of having
something, was already in the present moment in which you were seeking it, yet your attention was not able to locate it?

One of the purposes of the Enlightenment Ray is to help you clearly
see the essence of whatever it is that you are seeking as already existing
in the present moment. The Enlightenment Ray is like the blind person
being given a pair of glasses that gives him the ability to be able to see
what is there and has been there all along. You can imagine trying to
find your car keys with your eyes closed. This would be a different process than opening your eyes and trying to find your car keys when they
are in plain sight. The Enlightenment Ray serves the purpose to open
your eyes and your inner awareness to the union that already exists in
all things and at all times in any given moment.

THE ENLIGHTENMENT RAY
AUGMENTS YOUR WORK IN SERVICE TO OTHERS

Tapping into the Enlightenment Ray as you are in service to another, as
you are helping another, turns on the light for the other person to see

what already has been there all along. As you develop your connection and intentionally engage with the Enlightenment Ray while you are in the presence of others, whether it is a formal session, in the grocery store line, or on an airplane, it acts as a field of energy that illuminates what the person has been seeking all along.

Maybe it is about the glasses on the top of their head that they have been looking for, or maybe it is a sense of peace, unlimited abundance, connection to the Divine, health, love, or happiness. Whatever feels as if it is lost begins to be found.

To be clear it is different from handing someone his keys. It is more a turning on the light so he can find the keys himself. These are two different actions. Whether it is Reiki, coaching, massage, teaching, or working in an office, adding the Enlightenment Ray to the modality that you already know upgrades it.

Why is it that you can use a modality, like energy healing for instance, and it works miraculously for one person and it does not seem to work for another person? Nothing seems to have changed. Adding the Enlightenment Ray to energy healing upgrades the modality to be more current. If there is an aspect of a modality where a practitioner is trying to give the client his or her glasses, keys, health, abundance, happiness, soul fulfillment, or spiritual connection, that is a hit-or-miss way for the person to actually receive it. But adding in the Enlightenment Ray lifts the veils of the person whom it is connecting to so she can get the keys and health for herself. She can get the manifestation for herself; as such, she creates a permanent connection to that which has been there all along.

One of the reasons why some helping professions—whether medicine, psychology, psychiatry, or teacher and student relationships—are failing is because those paradigms are steeped in the consciousness that one person has the power to help another person who is powerless. The Enlightenment Ray recognizes that all individuals have within them whatever it is that they are looking for; the role of the practitioner who is working with the Enlightenment Ray is to simply illuminate the space so that each person is able to find it for himself or herself.

It is best to connect to this concept in the beginning from the level of sacred geometry and from the level of the language of light because it is less encumbered than trying to understand it conceptually or intellectually.

THE ENLIGHTENMENT RAY
AS THE "AH-HAH!" RAY

Take a few moments to become aware of that which has already been within you all along. Feel the Enlightenment Ray. Feel it in and around you. Feel it coming into your awareness in a greater way.

In some ways you could call the Enlightenment Ray the "Ah-hah!" Ray; you experience a light bulb turning on and going from the unknown to the known. There is a spark to it and an instantaneous effect as you come into union with that which was previously unknown. Is that not really what a shift in consciousness is? It is shifting from one way of perceiving to another.

BECOMING AWARE OF
YOUR INTERNAL ENVIRONMENT

Many people try to control their external environment and external situations. As you are reading this Enlightenment Ray transmission your body from the outside may be in the same position as it was when you first started reading, yet your inner perception may be in an entirely different place. It may be in such a different place that you are able to see that whatever you have desired exists in the same moment and in the same body posture without anything on the outside of your life having to change.

Will everything on the outside of your life change as you have the awareness of health in the moment of experiencing a disease? Yes. Will your level of financial success change when you have the awareness of financial abundance in the moment that perhaps you don't even have enough money to pay your bills? Yes. Will your experience of your friends, your significant others, your family members, change on the outside when you have the awareness that they are different on the inside? Yes. It is like what Einstein says: trying to solve a problem with the same mind that created it can be a challenge. The Enlightenment Ray is like changing the mind that created it.

ENERGETIC EXERCISE
Tuning In to the Enlightenment Ray

Spend a few moments in a non-mind way tuning in to the Enlightenment Ray. Spend time being with the pure vibration and pure essence of it, allowing all of your sensations. Feel the Enlightenment Ray grow even stronger, and notice how it is even stronger than when we first began.

You are connecting to the Enlightenment Ray now on multiple levels. Invite yourself to feel this clear field of the mind as a result of having attuned to the Enlightenment Ray. It is a sacred choice to live from this place of union, from this place of inner awareness of all there is in each moment. The sacred choice is yours to make.

When you are ready take a couple of deep breaths, feel your fingers and toes, and gently come back into your body and to this present moment.

A SACRED CHOICE

You have had many years of the old forms and ways of being. You have had many experiences that have served you well. It is a sacred choice to choose to live from union, from the place of the "Ah-hah," from the place of the Enlightenment Ray. To be honest it is not for everyone. It is not what everyone is seeking because it is a different way of being.

Perhaps you already have made your sacred choice by being present in this Enlightenment Ray transmission and by hearing these words. Yet you might still be deciding and wondering what this decision is that you are making. What are the benefits, the changes, and what does it all mean to live from the Enlightenment Ray?

In some ways, as was mentioned earlier, it is like turning on the lights or having glasses when you are not able to see. It provides illumination; it provides the ability to find things that you feel are missing. It is like going from tunnel vision to 360-degree peripheral vision and beyond. It is seeing and experiencing the world in increments of wholeness.

FROM DRAMA TO
WHOLE VISION AND UNITY

What is it that you would be giving up if you decided to live from the Enlightenment Ray? There is a certain level of drama that comes from tunnel vision that can be appealing or interesting to the human experience. That would be one thing that you could give up because seeing from the whole vision of things and seeing the whole perspective, the wholeness, and being able to find what has been there all along is quite interesting in and of itself. It has a dramatic benefit to your life but it is not drama, it is not being an adrenaline junkie, it is not stress or experiences of confusion or doubt. It is an experience of whole vision, unification, union, and unity.

You may sit with this decision. It may not be one that you make right now. You may even have a trial period of living from the Enlightenment Ray knowing that you can always go back to the way that you have been living before, even though in some ways once you know it is difficult to unknow.

FINDING WHAT YOU PERCEIVE AS MISSING

From this place of being tuned in to the Enlightenment Ray, begin to look within your own experience and within this now moment for that which you feel is most missing in your life. Maybe it is peace of mind, a sacred relationship with another person, health, money, happiness, or fulfillment.

Pick one thing and then with the Enlightenment Ray engaged allow yourself to find it in your now moment already existing. The love of your life exists in this now moment, financial abundance exists in this now moment, and sacred union with the Divine exists in this now moment. Peace of mind, energy, vitality, euphoria, service, and whatever you desire exists in this moment.

YOU BECOME
THAT WHICH YOU ARE SEEKING

The Enlightenment Ray leverages the laws of the universe. If you apply the Enlightenment Ray to manifestation techniques or the body of knowledge around the law of attraction, there is an aspect of the law of attraction that states that which is like itself attracts more of it. There are exercises that invite you to visualize having what it is that you want. If you want to have a new car you visualize yourself driving that new car. In a way you become, on a vibrational level, that which you are seeking. You become a person who is abundant and you have abundance. You become a person who is healthy and you have health.

This can be a challenging experience for some people when they are feeling like what they want is missing. They cannot find it, and they do not know how to tap into it or how to be what it is that they are not. The Enlightenment Ray leverages the law of attraction, for it enables you to see what you have perceived previously as missing to already exist in your now moment. It allows you to access that which is within and without and above and below in that one moment simultaneously.

If you analyze for a moment the universal principle of "as above, so below; as within so without," it is basically stating that everything is in union with everything else. If there is radiant health outside of you, without, then there is radiant health within. If there is soul fulfillment inside of you there is soul fulfillment outside of you.

WHAT YOU DESIRE ALREADY EXISTS

Let us say you are looking for a relationship or a life partner, and in this example you have not met this person yet. However, they have already been born, they exist on the planet, and they are already formed. It is simply that you have not met them; they are not in your field or orbit of experience. But you do not have to create this person because they are already created.

As you attune to this right relationship with your beloved within, it already exists without and vice versa. It is about coming into alignment, meeting this person, and attracting this person into your life. Sometimes in manifestation—whether it is money, a new home, or a relationship—there is a thought that you have to make the home, make the money, or make the relationship. But in most instances the home, the money, and the person already exist. It is about aligning and bringing into your experience that which is already in existence. The Enlightenment Ray turns on the light so you can see what has been there all along.

KEEPING IT LIGHT

Enlightenment is often associated with an expanded state of awareness, with a spiritual path, and with a relationship with the Divine. This relationship is already in existence in wholeness within you. It is not a serious matter. It is about being light and humorous. If you look at some of the spiritual masters who have attained enlightenment, they are often smiling and almost childlike and laughing. There is lightness and exuberance to their presence. One way of moving into the Enlightenment Ray is being as light as you can be, having fun, laughing, and reconnecting to that childlike innocence that exists within you.

As you are moving about your days, weeks, and months to come, call upon the Enlightenment Ray. Develop a practice of connecting to the Enlightenment Ray in the morning before you begin your day by quieting your mind, calling upon the Enlightenment Ray, and becoming aware of it already having been within you all along.

Notice how your presence illuminates other people. On the physical realm you can help people find things that are lost. It is like you become a seer and are able to find physical things that are lost. On the mental, emotional, and spiritual planes you assist yourself and others to be able to connect to and come into union with that which they felt was missing. Have fun with it, revisit it, and know that the Enlightenment Ray is something to be experienced and not understood from the mind alone.

ENTRAINMENT TO THE ENLIGHTENMENT RAY

To engage the Enlightenment Ray we went through various stages. The first stage was quieting the mind and tapping into the clear field of the mind. The second stage was actively looking for what was thought to be missing in that moment, which is an application of the Enlightenment Ray. In a way, step two is turning on the light, receiving the glasses, and having the "ah-hah." You can engage step two by calling on the Council of Light and the Enlightenment Ray to assist you in tapping into what was there all along that maybe you had not been consciously tapping into. Step three was connecting to it from a nonintellectual, energetic, and holistic place, and then saturating and integrating this light, this Enlightenment Ray.

This divine transmission has served to be an entrainment to

the Enlightenment Ray and a grounding of your connection to the Enlightenment Ray. This subject is so vast it could be presented many times in order to go into the various levels of what is available. The direct connection to it has happened in this segment, and you can learn more about it through your direct experience with it.

PART TWO

Discussions with the Council of Light

Health, Wealth, Happiness, and Other Important Topics

12

MONEY
AND PROSPERITY

Nurturing Your Heart Space

To begin our time together focus on your heart space. Breathe into your heart space and imagine that as you feed and nourish your heart, as you breathe into your heart, it energizes your light body, the light within your subatomic levels, and all the levels of your being. As you breathe into and nourish your heart, feel the light within you expand. Spend some time basking in this light, feeling it nourish and nurture every cell and every part of your body.

As the awareness of your light expands, begin to become aware of the Council of Light beings that are present. Greet your Council and spend a few moments with us receiving any guidance or wisdom as to how to open your heart space even more into the field of prosperity and abundance. When you are ready take a couple of deep breaths, move your fingers and your toes, and stretch in any direction you feel called.

THE COUNCIL MEMBER FROM VENUS

Source energy comes in many forms, including your own form. You are a being of light just as we, the Council of Light, are beings of light. Have a sense of the light within you turning on and expanding as you feed your heart. As we have gathered to speak about the subject of prosperity and money there is a particular council member from Venus that is coming forward at this time that will be the first speaker on the panel. Have a sense of this member from Venus coming more into the forefront.

This is the Council of Light member from Venus coming more into your conscious awareness. The planet Venus, as you know, is related to the energy of love. It is in charge of the house of love and is a place of high frequency. Venus is fifth dimensional and is associated with the energy of the Hathors.

AN UPGRADE IN THE CONSCIOUSNESS OF MONEY AND PROSPERITY

Money like all things is energy; it is currency. There are the various cycles of receiving, having, and releasing money. This is similar to when you have a repairperson come to your home to fix a broken appliance; first, he turns off the electricity. While he is fixing the appliance it is a short-term, temporary time that the electricity is off and you cannot use the electricity. In some ways you can think about the hesitation or the stall that some people experience in the economy or in their finances at this time as an unplugging of the circuitry so that the machinery can be upgraded and replaced.

This is also often associated with your circuit breaker that is targeted to one area of your home. You do not have to turn off the electricity for the entire home. It can be turned off for the kitchen, the bedroom, or other parts of your home. Rest assured that if you are feeling as if things have been turned off or there has been a shortage or a lack of currency in your life, this is just a part of the larger picture. It is temporary and is an important turnaround for the process that is happening.

The collective consciousness—with the help of the news—wants to interpret this as something very dramatic, wrong, negative, and that there is something to be afraid of. As there is a shift in consciousness and a change is happening around wealth and prosperity, there is an alignment with the higher vibration. Things that are unresolved and that move more slowly come to the surface. As the currency is changing vibration and transforms to fit the consciousness of the now rather than the consciousness of then, feelings of upheaval and of unresolved energy may come to the surface if you have any dormant or active fears or worries around money.

SEE THE GOOD IN EVERY MOMENT

The important thing is to allow this currency and energy to keep moving and to know that it is only temporary. It may be that this does not apply to you at all. Things have been flowing and you have not had to have your electricity turned off. For others this dynamic applies quite a bit. Wherever you fall on the scheme of things know that all is well. All is well.

What you choose to focus on is up to you. You can choose to think that the sky is falling. You can choose to see the good in every moment. This outlook in life will determine many future outcomes and experiences. Do your best to align with the person that you want to be. Even if you are not completely behind the idea that not having money is the best thing that ever happened, a part of you can be behind that and see the benefit of it.

The old forms are shutting down. This is a natural part of the cycle. It is on purpose, it has a higher vision, and it has a plan that is in alignment with divine order. Many people on the planet at this time have called for great change, a quantum leap, and have called for what they perceive as injustices to be completed. As you are moving forward in your conscious evolution, for you have chosen to incarnate at this particular time, relax. Lean into the change. Be the person that you want to be until you become that person.

THE COUNCIL MEMBER FROM OCTURIUS

The second member on the panel is coming in from the planet of Octurius. There is a sense of the origin of this transmission coming from beyond the Central Sun in a different galaxy and a different frequency. In a way this is like inviting a guest from a completely different culture. It would be like inviting an Aborigine to speak to you about your life. There is quite a distance of consciousness and perspective from this council member to the everyday consciousness of the human being.

WHAT DOES IT MEAN TO BE PROSPEROUS?

This is the Council member from Octurius coming forward to talk about the concept of prosperity. What is the concept of prosperity? What does it mean to be prosperous? How does one know when one is prosperous? What are the areas of life in which prosperity shows up?

You can see that the energy of prosperity can be directly linked to the fiscal energy of money. That is one form of prosperity. There is also a level of prosperity that comes with the abundance of loving relationships and with the gift of living a life on purpose, a life of fulfillment. Prosperity is the wealth of vitality. Prosperity can be a richness of the soul. The areas of prosperity are infinite.

What has been happening from our perspective on the planet is that some parts of the population have been in charge of certain aspects of prosperity and other parts of the planet have been governing other areas of prosperity. For instance, the Western countries may have had more uniform wealth in the form of shelter, food, and health care, and the types of prosperity that come from the luxury of clean water, clean air, and an abundance of food.

SOUL WEALTH AND MATERIAL WEALTH

You may have an area of the world that is more indigenous, that has less of this material prosperity, but has more soul wealth. It has more soul joy, more brilliance of spirit, and the ability to savor the moment of a smile, a laugh, and a relationship.

One example of this kind of soul prosperity can be seen in Egypt. If you look at many of the Egyptian people who have a fraction of the material wealth of a Western person there is soul prosperity, a freshness, and a playfulness. There is a gleam in the eye, laughter, and a relational community-based prosperity. There is an abundance of the moment. There is an intact account of the soul.

An area like Egypt may not have as much material wealth but does have a great deal of soul wealth, while Western civilizations may have a lot of material wealth but may not have much soul prosperity. There is the sense of something missing for many people who have so much. There is the sense that, "When I have this I will be happy. When this happens I will be happy, secure, or elated." There is a sense of consumption, of looking for that which is missing, that comes from a poverty of the soul and of the relational aspect of the human.

Many cultures that have material wealth are very individually oriented. You as an individual live in your home perhaps by yourself or with a few other people. You earn your own money or you manifest your own money. You do many things for yourself and by yourself. There is an individual type of mentality. In other cultures that are more relational there is a community-based mentality.

NATURE AND PROSPERITY

There are pros and cons to each of these aspects that we are identifying, and there are many forms of prosperity. With an orientation toward the individual there may be a greater sense of independence and a greater sense of the possibility that anything can be accomplished. You may have been, or currently are, very prosperous in one area and yet you may be longing for prosperity in other areas of your life.

People notice that the individual consciousness is impacted, for instance, when something happens in nature that offers an opportunity for the community to come together. An example of this is when nature dumps a great deal of snow in a place like Seattle that is not used to that kind of weather. The result can be that neighbors come out of their homes and spend time together. Normally they may never see one another or ever talk to each other. Or in the instance where there is a natural disaster or a tragedy such as 9/11, there is a call of community that comes together. It becomes less of a focus on the individual and more of a reaching out, connecting, and communicating with one another.

THE GROWTH OF SOUL WEALTH

Part of the shift that is happening is that the prosperity of relationship and community is growing in the Western civilizations. Soul wealth is also growing in the Western civilizations, and if you think about all the different areas of prosperity as if they were a graph and a line and they had different areas like money, health, relationships, purpose, and fulfillment, the graphs may be very high in one area and very low in another.

As this transition is happening there is a greater harmonic resonance with the various graphs occurring in the areas of prosperity. As the balance of right relationship is happening, one area may seem as if it is dropping while the prosperity of another area is soaring. Begin to really take stock of what is soaring in your life and what lines on your graph are rising up. Maybe your creativity is off the charts. Maybe your sense of passion, fulfillment, loving relationships, friendships, or your desire to cook in healthy ways is increasing.

You could look at the area on the graph that seems to have gone down. Maybe it is your portfolio, stocks, your income, or something else. You might think that there is a lack of prosperity that is happening, but that is only one part of the picture. As this member from Octurius suggests, recognize that all is well all of the time. It is a matter of your perception and your choosing to perceive that things are going great, that they are coming into a greater sense of harmony, resolution, and evolution.

THE CONCEPT OF DEBT

The third panel member to speak now is a blend of some of the Council of Light members. There is a particular subcategory of the concept of credit and debt related to credit cards, mortgages, and the debt of owing. Part of why people are feeling that it is a time of financial challenge is that these platforms, these constructs of credit and debt, are seeming to be less available. As the possibility of getting a mortgage or having a credit stream decreases this could create a sense of less money, yet perhaps it is actually generating more money.

There is an infinite amount of financial prosperity that is available. The idea that if one person has a lot then another person will not is a myth; it is an untruth. In reality the universe is exponentially expanding with each person that has a desire. As you have a desire to have more money and someone else has a desire to have more money, and someone else has a desire to have more money, and someone else has a desire to have more money, then this exponential expansion in the realm of money comes to be.

This concept of debt is dying out. It looks as if people have less credit, fewer opportunities to buy a house if they do not have a down payment, fewer opportunities to stay in a house where the payments are more than what they are bringing in, and fewer opportunities to take out more credit. There seem to be fewer opportunities in general, and it seems that things are shrinking. But this is just one way of viewing it. From the perspective of light, there are an infinite amount of opportunities. What is shifting is your ability to access the real, tangible, physical dollars in direct relationship to what it is that you are wanting. There is not as much need to borrow, to have debt, or to have something now that you pay for later. Your access to financial abundance is in alignment with what it is that you are choosing to create in your life: that means you have the cash to buy a car, to pay your bills, and to buy a house.

This means you have access to what it is that you want in a way that is current. It is not a backlog; it is not outdated or compiled with interest, leaving you to feel that you are out of right relationship. As these financial structures that have been so much a part of the Western world are crashing down, it is an opportunity to be able to exponentially increase your direct relationship to funds, currency, and to the energy of money.

What does this mean for you on a daily basis? If you were living off of credit or you were living beyond what it was that you had in the moment, it doesn't mean that you have to not want what you want, or have what you have. It means that the amount of currency that you have access to needs to increase—and in the new consciousness it can easily do so—in order to have the ability to purchase or exchange money for what you want in the now. Once again, where is it that you are looking? Are you looking at what seems to be falling away or are you looking at what is coming forward? It is not a taking away but rather it is a shift from one way of being to another.

SHIFTING THE CONCEPT
OF TIME EQUALING PROSPERITY

What are we moving toward? What is to come? How do we navigate the transition between where we are to where we want to go? One thing that many people are being called to do is to shift from the concept that time equals prosperity.

Here is an example of the idea that time is an exchange for money: you have a job where you work forty hours a week and you make a certain amount per hour, which creates a paycheck. Your time is tied to the amount of money that you are making. These forty hours equal this paycheck. Yet even though this appears to be true, you are not exchanging time for money, or even your gifts and talents for money. Money and prosperity are your birthright, they are givens, and they are not garnered or accessed by exchanging one form of prosperity for another. Time and money are forms of prosperity. They are forms of abundance. You have time, energy, health, and money. These are all forms of resources; they are all forms of nourishment. Allow yourself to become fully resourced.

PROSPERITY AND NATURAL RESOURCES

There are natural resources such as gas. This resource is changing as well. It does not mean that the resources are not there, but the forms and the ways in which they are utilized are changing. This is a good example because as the natural resource of oil seems to be depleted or hard to get, the question of how we can have transportation in a different form becomes more apparent. People begin to look for other ways, other options, and other resources. This is similar to the equation that we are talking about related to currency.

Let us say that time has been the oil that has fueled the automobile of your paycheck. Those two seem to be the only way to get the car to move. The time actually could be the paycheck and could come without the fuel of time. The unstringing of time and space from finances is another thing that is happening. What could that look like? In one minute during the month you could make enough money for the next ten years. That seems impossible, but this is the breakdown of time and space.

TIME AND SPACE

You are infinite and multidimensional. You do not have to be tied to nine to five. Time and space are shifting. Action does not equal outcome. You can, with ease and grace, manifest through intuition, positioning, and being in the right place at the right time. People are getting fired from their nine-to-five jobs and losing their pensions. That might be their experience, but it is also an opportunity to open up to a greater level of freedom, a greater level of living as multidimensional beings, and a greater level of expansion.

BEING ON THE QUANTUM EDGE

Notice your sensations and how you are feeling in this moment. As we are talking about these various subjects they are directly related to certain aspects of your being. Part of your consciousness has been tied to the idea that A plus B equals C. But then you see that A plus B does not equal C; C equals C. As you think about this, things begin to reorient and shift. There is something about wanting to be on the quantum edge, wanting to be on that cutting edge and launch into the quantum fulfillment and exponential unfolding of your joy, bliss, and your conscious evolution.

What has been working in the past no longer applies. You can still do some of the things from the past and get some results. Would you enjoy having radiant health; prosperity in multiple areas of your life; loving relationships; connection to yourself, spirit, and others; and the financial abundance to do what it is that you want? Would it be in alignment with your being to be happy, healthy, wealthy, and prosperous on all levels?

YOU CAN HAVE IT ALL

One of the things that is unique about this time and place is that you can have abundance on all levels of your life. You can have it all.

There may be some areas that excite you more and that you want to develop based on your particular signature energy, your soul's journey, and the themes that you are here to explore. Yet wouldn't it be nice to have energy, to feel healthy, and to have money for you to thrive? How many people on the planet have used the excuse of not having enough money to suffocate or pinch off inspiration or to not follow their soul? How many people have the idea that you cannot do what you love and also have your needs met?

The idea that money is an exchange for life-force is one that is also changing. Life-force is life-force. Money is money. They are not an exchange for one another. You can have life-force, abundance, health, community, connection to spirit, and prosperity on all levels at once.

LOVE

Love is one of the highest frequencies on your planet in its purest form. It could mean many things: the love that you have for one another, the love that you have for yourself, the love that you have for carrots, the love that you have for your car, or the love that you have for the sun. Love can be an emotion, and it is also a high frequency. It is like a vitamin: it fortifies the rest of your body and your being.

PLACING CONDITIONS ON LOVE

There is a sense that in order to have love, to be loved, or to love oneself certain conditions have to be achieved, such as having a certain appearance, lifestyle, body type, or particular qualities. There are conditions around thinking that you have to be this or be that in order to experience love or to have self-love. "I will love myself when I am feeling upbeat. I will not love myself when I am feeling depressed. I will attract a mate when I am at my ideal weight. I will not be attractive to anyone if I am not my ideal weight. This person is beautiful, this person is not."

All of these conditions are tied to the abundance or the prosperity of love, when in reality this is another illusion that is breaking down. There is not one among you that is more lovable than another. You are all special and brilliant and unique in your own ways, but each person is loved. Each person is lovable. Your lovability is not even a question, and the idea that you have to adjust yourself and change who you are and not be who you are in order to have love is another illusion that is breaking down.

You will feel a greater sense of love when you are being authentic to yourself. It does not mean that you do not want to look beautiful, be healthy, strong, exercise, eat good food, take care of yourself, or wear beautiful clothes. You may very well choose to be and express those things. Yet being your authentic self, being true to yourself, can be one of the most exhilarating, intoxicating, juicy experiences. The love is free flowing and you accept who it is that you are: "I accept who I am, I love who I am, I am going to be me even if that may not be what someone thinks they want me to be. I am going to be me even if that looks different than what another person looks like, what another person does, or what another person loves." Love is not contingent on conditions, just like money is not contingent on action or time.

A WEB OF LOVE

As these concepts and beliefs in the universe are changing there is also the idea that you have to exchange one area of abundance for another. Sometimes when people want abundance and they begin to have it they go into an abundance crisis. They go from not being busy at all to being so busy that they end up having less time, less energy, and less health.

Imagine the graph of prosperity overflowing in all areas of life. That is the purpose of this shift in consciousness. That is where the energy of prosperity and money is headed; the money, love, and health are there to support all the other areas. Time, energy, relationships, community, and so on are there. They are interconnected. It is beautiful web of light and divine order.

ENERGETIC EXERCISE
Increasing Joy and Prosperity

Imagine in your mind that you are drawing your own graph. On a scale of one to ten, rate the different areas of prosperity and what is important to you. Notice which areas are high and which ones are low. As you are doing this, have a sense of your particular Council members working with your energy system to increase your joy, and therefore, to increase your prosperity in all areas of your life.

What do joy and prosperity have to do with one another? How are they related? Why is it that when you do things you enjoy it increases your health, wealth, and happiness? It is because on a vibratory level they are resonating at a high frequency. There is Spirit and inspiration in the moment of joy. There is a savoring and a presence.

Have the sense that your joy meter is feeding the graph of your finances and that you are funneling joy into your relationship with money. Allow the joy to overflow. You may ask for help in this process if you need to. Feel all of this delicious joy energy filling the space in and around you. Imagine that you are infusing everything that has to do with your finances with joy, and that you are working with your particular Council members to enhance all of these areas of your life.

When you feel that you have spent all the time that you want infusing your finances with joy, take a couple of deep breaths, move your fingers and toes, and come back into your body and to the here and now.

PROSPERITY AND SECURITY

For some people having abundance helps them to feel safe and secure. For others abundance and prosperity equals a sense of freedom. Whatever feeling might be going on in a person, there is something happening underneath it on a core level.

SUPPORT EXERCISE
Infusing Your Being with the Sense of Security

Begin now by imagining that you are filling the space that you are in with the sense of safety. Fill your being with the sense of security. Feel this sense of security infusing your body, your mind, and your spirit. Be in this immersion of security for as long as you would like. When you are ready, take some deep breaths, move your fingers and toes, and come back to this time and place.

THE UNIVERSE IS CONSPIRING
FOR YOUR BENEFIT

What is security and what does it mean to feel secure? Does having a certain amount of knowledge, money, or particular relationships make you feel secure? Outside conditions do not equal security. Outside conditions can seemingly stand in for the energy of security. Security and insecurity are in a sense like worthiness and unworthiness. From a higher perspective there is not a question of one person being worthy and another person being unworthy. From the higher perspective insecurity and security do not even exist.

You are infinite, eternal, and everlasting. Nothing can be added to you or taken away from you. The universe is conspiring for your benefit. There is this element of trust and distrust; I trust, I distrust, I feel secure, I feel insecure. These are emotional states that then create frenetic energy patterns that may not be in alignment with what it is that you want to be aligned with.

You can, from the inside out, pierce through the illusion of security and insecurity, of trust and distrust. You can decide to feel secure no matter what. You can decide to be trusting no matter what. It does not mean that you are not discerning or that you do not pay attention to things. Your conscious, freewill choice is one of the largest coins that you have. It has increased in value. It is like your conscious will used to be worth ten cents and now it is worth a million dollars. Are you applying your conscious choice?

ENERGETIC EXERCISE
Enhancing the Vibration

Focus on your heart space and feed your heart space with your breath and intention. Say to yourself, "I am a being of light. I am love, I am joy, I am frequency, I am prosperity, I trust, I am in harmony and order. I am laughter, I am peace, I am calm and focused."

Allow yourself to be buoyed and raised up in this energy of light. Feel the light saturate all areas of your being and into your graph of prosperity. When you feel ready, take a couple of deep breaths, stretch your body in any direction, and come back to this time and place.

LIGHT AND A SHIFT IN CONSCIOUSNESS

There is a science and physics to this shift in consciousness. It is like when a strong man goes to a carnival and takes a hammer and slams it down on the platform. The light rises up like a thermometer to various heights depending on how hard he hits it. That momentum, fulcrum, and power lead to the light rising up. The same is true of light. As you focus on the energy of light and pour light into yourself and into your graph, things rise in consciousness, prosperity, and awareness.

As you become more light—which is part of what is happening on the physical plane as the planet increases in hertz, as the Earth moves and accelerates in frequency—you move and accelerate the frequency of your body and the density becomes lighter. You may notice that you are lightening up on many different levels. Focus on this light.

ENERGETIC EXERCISE
The Language of Light

Have a sense of this light language surrounding you and that it is a silent sound. Perhaps you see golden symbols floating in and around your aura or spirals and different images that are specific to enhancing your particular relationship with prosperity and abundance.

This language of light is unique for each person. Just like the octaves of sound have various levels to them, light language has varying levels to it. You might call forth the frequency of the language of light on the higher octave, the medium octave, or more on the tonal octave. Just like the musical scales of sound such as A, B, C, and D, different notes may resonate with your inner being more than other notes. It is similar to the aspects of the language of light. Some aspects will resonate with you more than others.

Just like plucking the strings of a guitar and making a vibration, imagine that you are playing yourself like an instrument. Imagine that with your inner hand you are plucking the strings of your instrument and making the song of you. You are creating, singing, and vibrating your song. In the process you are tuning your instrument just like you would tune a guitar to the particular light language that is pertinent for you. As you attune your individual instrument to the various vibrations and frequencies, you are aligning with your authentic self, to what is important, true, and real for you. You are attuning to what prosperity means to you. Take the time that you would like to fine-tune this process. When you feel complete, take some deep breaths anchoring in your heightened prosperity.

We have provided much information on the verbal level about the shift in consciousness that is happening. We have created a symbiotic synergy with you that addressed your individual needs around this topic. Your particular team of Council members has been and will be, with your conscious choice, continuing to work with you, to encourage you to enhance your joy and, therefore, your health, wealth, and happiness.

THE ALCHEMICAL PROCESS OF SHADOW AND LIGHT

The idea that when you have the things that you desire you will be joyous is outcome-oriented. You can be joyous now. You can make joy out of anything. Just like the Egyptian goddess Kephera, the dung beetle, the scarab, pushes the dung toward the rising sun and gives birth to new forms, you can make joy out of dung.

Your life, the shadow, the dung, is fertile ground and is rich. It is the base metal of alchemy and can be transmuted into gold. Your decision to do so is what transmutes it. Your decision to be a master alchemist, to take what it is that you have, to take where you are and to transform it into what gold means to you, is what it is that you are choosing to do.

Sometimes in the community of light and spirituality there is a resistance to the dark and to what is not working. There is a desire to release it, clear it, and get rid of it. From our perspective, at the base light and dark are the same things. It is a natural part of the process as you move to a higher vibration for the lower vibration to come up to the surface to be included. It is temporary and it does get incorporated back into wholeness.

The saying "If life hands you lemons, make lemonade" is a perfect example of what we mean by alchemy. If you were to throw out the lemons, if you were to throw out the base metal of lead, then you would have nothing to create gold from. You would have nothing to create lemonade from.

TRUSTING THAT EVERYTHING HAS A PURPOSE

Whatever you perceive as not working in your life is the material substance and fertile land to transmute into what is working in your life. It is a perception that it is not working. As we started in this segment, everything is on purpose: it is just that your electricity is off while something is getting fixed.

Trust that if you have lemons, if the electricity is off, there is a higher evolution that is happening and this is part of the plan. You may not have the whole perspective, but it is going in the right direction. Times to come are going to be better than they have ever been, and you have an inherent wisdom that is guiding you. It is time to follow that wisdom with a fierceness, like it is the most important thing in your life. Listen to that inner call, take it seriously, and apply it living from the inside out.

DELIVERING YOURSELF
TO YOURSELF

You have asked to deliver yourself to yourself during this very special time. Now, what does it mean to deliver yourself to yourself? It means that there has been a part of you that has been holding back being you your entire life. As you deliver yourself to yourself you are able to be yourself authentically and in a supercharged way. You can think of how you had been living as a dilution of yourself. When you choose to be you completely, you experience the whole hologram, the whole picture, the longevity, and the brightly shining brightness of all of you.

Now, some of your relationships may beckon you to act in the old way of holding back. You may notice a pattern where, when you want something from somebody, you act in a certain way that you think will get you the result you are after. The way that you act is actually not as empowering as if you would just be yourself with confidence. We are not saying you are a pushover, we are inviting you to take your relationships to the next level, to be yourself and people will appreciate that you're being authentic. If you are authentic then there's more for them to connect to than if you are buttering their bun, so-to-speak. Your level of authenticity is something that will continue to evolve in your relationships.

As you are being more of who you are, as you are living authentically, your signature energy is sending a clear signal and pulse to the universe. This signal or pulse enhances your level of prosperity and money, for as you are being you, as you are showing up as you, the universe and money has a clear signal of who you are and where to bring the prosperity. We have consistently shared that being you is one of the most effective ways to transcend this shift in consciousness, and it is also an often-overlooked yet essential ingredient for prosperity.

INITIATIONS

It is important to acknowledge that your path has been an initiatory path and that the experiences you have had are a part of you. Part of what you will explore in this segment is to identify the initiations in your life. Initiations can be a divorce, sickness, lightning going through you, or a Reiki attunement. There can be all kinds of initiations. Initiation is simply going from one threshold to another.

Take a moment to contemplate the initiations that you have experienced in your life. What are pivotal experiences that you have had in your life that have encouraged you to go from one threshold to another? Can you identify a theme that these initiations have in common? In a sense you are also at a threshold point now, but rather than a crisis being what takes you from this threshold to the next, it is actually your longing, your desire to be, do, and to have more. You have achieved critical mass, you have created momentum, and you have as such created enough momentum that things will begin to change.

MONEY

We would like to take you through an exercise around the energy of money. You are reaching a financial threshold where through your allowing, through spending more time doing the things that you enjoy, more of the abundance that you have been asking for is realized. This exercise with money is unlike any that you have done before.

Attraction and Allowing

Money wants to be a part of your life. Money wants to flow through you. Money is waiting at your door, and you have realized that money is not in direct relationship to action. It is in direct relationship to attraction and to allowing. Money comes from the unlimited source of energy, the infinite energy. Just like Reiki or life-force energy, at its base, it is made of the same material as anything else that you may have in your life.

DRAWING EXERCISE
Infinite Source Spiral

We would invite you to do an exercise with money. Take out a piece of paper and a pen. Leave the center of the paper blank. Now draw a large circle, almost filling up the paper. Choose twelve categories of things that you have done with money and would like to do with money, and write them on the outside of the circle, like a clock. Write one item at noon, the next at one, and the next at two, and go all around the circle of the clock, leaving the center open. The center represents the infinite supply of the universal energy of money.

Starting on the outside of your paper, begin to draw a line between these different outcomes, these different things that you have done or would do with money, and slowly draw a spiral toward the center. You are creating a web into the center, spiraling it into the center, until you connect all of your money choices with the center, the source of unlimited life-force energy in its purest essence. In actuality it is the liquid form of money, or the preform of money. Continue drawing spirals from the outside of your paper into the center of the paper, and then from the center of the paper back out to the things you would do with money. You are spiraling the tangible items into the infinite energy, back and forth, in and out. Know that as you are drawing the finite experiences of money into the infinite energy of money, you are expanding your money and expanding the connection to the infinite supply of money. Take all the time that you would like with this exercise.

The Spiraling Energy of Manifestation

The money spiraling exercise allows you to see that things in physical form exist in a spiral, an evolution of the infinite source, or vice versa: that things spiral back to their source. When you can align or create a connection between the thing that you have drawn and then break it down into and spiral it with the energy of money, then it manifests. Let's say you would like to own your house and that this is the largest financial goal that you have at this time. This would cost (fill in the blank) dollars. This seems like quite a bit of money, however, you are in the house, you are visualizing the house, you draw the house, and then from the house you draw a spiral creating a web from the house into the infinite unlimited source of money. In a sense you only have to touch the vibration of your desire with the infinite source of energy, which is preform money. Just get them to connect.

Let's try this exercise together.

ENERGETIC EXERCISE
Wealth Spiral

Let's say you have your house and you have the unlimited life-force energy, the infinite energy. You take your energetic pen and you draw through your house and you spiral and circle through the infinite energy. Then you bring that energy into your house and then you spiral back into the infinite energy and you bring it into your house.

Again you spiral into the infinite energy and bring it back into your house with the process going like this: infinite, in your house, infinite, in your house, infinite, and so on, until it speeds up and creates this vortex of flowing energy. Visualize it. Money is flowing into your house and your house is flowing out into the infinite, and then it's flowing in and out, in and out, and it keeps flowing this way as long as you are aware of it.

To magnify this process you can state the following aloud, "I command a wealth spiral to spin so that I own (with my family who lives with me) this house with ease and grace. I activate a wealth spiral from the infinite source to this house and it is flowing and spiraling, flowing and spiraling, flowing and spiraling. I activate a wealth spiral."

By activating this wealth spiral you see the individual particles that make up the house and are able to break it down to see that the source is the infinite energy, the same energy as money, and the same energy as divinity. It is a little bit like focusing on a glass vase and as you do so you are able to see that it's actually made up of liquid glass. You do not have to create something new or something outside, it is just a shift in perspective and an inclusion.

You're starting to see the energy of the house, how it breaks down into the infinite source of energy, and how as a part of that there are these connectors that you call money; it is the energy of money that is equated or connected to owning every inch of the house. Bring a spiral of wealth, a spiral of abundance, a spiral of money into your awareness of the energy of the house. You are kissing this wealth spiral into all areas of your life. As you do this you realize that the house or any other area of your life you would like to expand into already holds the energy or the frequency of money and you are expanding this money awareness. It is the law of attraction and it is a vibrational match. It's already there, you're just slowing things down in your awareness so you can see it.

This is a powerful exercise that we would recommend you do on a regular basis. You may choose to do the larger exercise of twelve areas of your life you would like to put the energy of money into, or choose one item a day and focus on that item for the day. You may feel called to use a colored pen that you enjoy or that represents money to you to energize this exercise even further or to simply visualize the wealth spiral.

The money that you are seeking is seeking you. Remember, you being you is like sending your address out to the universe so it can find you and bring money to you.

13

INTERNAL AND EXTERNAL ENVIRONMENTS

You may have noticed since our first conscious contact that at times your emotions and your thoughts have run wild. This is symbolic or indicative of a part of the enlightenment process. As you move into greater and greater states of joy, that which is moving more slowly moves to the surface to be included back into the wholeness.

YOU ARE THE CREATOR OF YOUR OWN REALITY

That you have been drawn to this material is an indication that it is your goal and desire to achieve peace and to be in alignment within yourself regardless of what your external circumstances are. You have recognized that you are the creator of your own reality and, therefore, you are creating all of the circumstances in your life. This is an empowered state to be in. If there are circumstances that you do not enjoy, then you can align with other circumstances through your vibration and staying centered on your own emotional journey.

When you can find satisfaction in every moment, when you can find fulfillment in every moment, then you are free. You are present, you are in the moment, and you are curious about what it is that is in the present moment. You may have noticed that you've also experienced a lot of synchronicities. This will continue to grow.

THE NATURE OF LIGHT

Let's talk for a few moments about the nature of light. Light is radiant particles of molecules that are moving in certain refractory trajectories. When there is light this light absorbs the darkness. It fills the space where there was darkness. This is similar to what you have been feeling with your new orientation toward life; it is not about getting rid of the dark, it is about absorbing the dark into the light because there is much power and vitality in what you may call the dark. As the dark is illuminated it then creates radiance and brightness.

You have been conditioned to think about this in relationship to actual external environments: the light is on or the light is off, you have money or you do not have enough money, you have health, you do not have enough health, you have love, you do not have enough love, you have work, you don't have work. Your internal barometer is yo-yoing with the polarity of your external circumstances. Yet what we are sharing, what is on the cutting edge of the Earth plane, of the new grid, is that your light can always be on internally. Your barometer, your inner journey, can always be one of fullness, happiness, and joy.

YOUR EXTERNAL ENVIRONMENTS

In your own life, you may have projects that you have been working on for periods of time, some of which are coming into fruition and others that may be at a standstill. You may feel frustration arising around the areas that are appearing stagnant, a sense that nothing is happening, and other negativity filling your mind.

Yet know you're in the process of exploring, you have taken some actions, and even choosing to not do something is a decision. There are the external circumstances you're trying to finish, yet there appears to be a holding pattern in the external environment. Perhaps other people who are involved in the project are not calling you back, or you have gone as far with something as you possibly can without additional support or knowledge, or you have reached a plateau in the level of success of this project.

However, your internal environment can move forward without your external environment leading the way. The following exercise demonstrates this process of moving forward internally, and the external environment changes as a result. For the purpose of this exercise, let's imagine that you are an up-and-coming author who is writing your first book and you want to expand your visibility, impact, and success to a global level. Feel free to substitute any project you are working on after you see how the process unfolds.

SUPPORT EXERCISE
Move Your Internal Environment Forward to Expand Your External Environments

Imagine you are in the process of writing and publishing a book and this is your current external environment. Internally you already know that this body of work has been gifted to you for a reason and it has a purpose. It has its own innate intelligence and it is radiating out and people are already learning from it and reaping the benefits of it, and it is a wonderful tool for many, many beings to have.

This has already happened, this already is so, and it is bringing to you financial success, it is bringing to you visibility, and it's bringing to you joy. It is bringing to you all these amazing things. It is sought after by many sources. The publishing of it, the marketing of it, has already happened; it is already done. The copies have already been printed, and they are beautiful, the pictures are beautiful. Now you're autographing copies and you're joyfully watching them fly off the shelves. People are sending you testimonials about how it's changed their life on a daily basis. They are signing up for your other offerings; they are calling and sending you money. They are coming from all different places and it feels so wonderful. It feels so wonderful to be available for the new consciousness that's coming in for you, and to be in this bridging place of having given birth to that which has gone before, and being fertile with that which is coming. It is an amazingly joyful, seamless, and timeless experience.

You have sold ten copies, you have sold twenty copies, you have sold thirty copies, you have sold forty copies, and you have sold fifty copies. Your publisher already wants your next book. You have sold 1,000 copies, you have sold 100,000 copies, you have sold 1 million copies, and you have sold 50 million copies. This book is worldwide and the opportunities that come from it are incredible. You're wealthy and you're happy and you're healthy and you have a vital and vibrant life. This is true. This is all true. It feels good to move forward on your internal journey.

Now take this internal movement even further. You have accompanying products; you have CDs and a workbook that go with the book. They are beautiful. The quality of the sound vibration that comes through the current of these audio recordings is amazing. You have an amazing support team: incredible assistants, a house cleaner, and all the support that you need in all the forms that you need it. It is exciting, it is thrilling, and it is so.

This is the truth of what is going on with your book, and this is the truth of what you're focusing on. The more that you connect to this, the more that you believe this, the more it becomes your external reality. Imagine your purpose vibrating at such phenomenal levels of success that there are more opportunities than you could possibly or would want to do. Then you create a way for people to receive your gifts and talents and offerings on a regular basis and on a global scale.

It is so lovely to have the threshold of thousands of clients in your programs and the people are not only in your programs but they are excited about them and they recognize that it is assisting them in their lives. This can be your focus; you can spend time creating a detailed process.

Throughout this entire process you have learned something incredibly valuable. You have heard it from others, but the practice of it is something entirely different: you can experience bliss and joy internally in every single moment. You can stay on your center. You can have a rich life, a wealthy life, and a fulfilled life.

This process can be enhanced through writing. Use the following exercise to put into words what you want to expand in your life.

WRITTEN EXERCISE
Move Your Internal Environment Forward
in an Area of Your Choosing

Have a pen and paper nearby. Call upon your personal Council of Light and take a few moments to connect with us. As you connect with us, feel yourself moving into a greater state of joy and peace. As this peace expands, bring your awareness to an area of your life that you wish to expand in your external environment. This topic could be a project, a relationship, your health, your finances, whatever you would like. Once you have decided on this topic, go into an even greater state of joy and peace as you are loosely holding this topic in mind.

Now take out your pen and paper and write the topic on the top in its fully-realized state: "I am a best-selling author," "I am in a state of radiant health," "I am in a passionate, nurturing, and loving relationship." Then start moving this topic forward by writing about it in detail. Knowing that it already exists and is fully realized, walk yourself through the stages.

Write the next natural step, and then the next one, and then the next one, until you come to a place of feeling great. Take all the time that you would like with this exercise. When you feel complete, take a few deep breaths and state out loud, "So it is!" Then just sit back and watch your external environments show up to match the internal movement you have created.

You many need help visualizing what your fully-realized external environment would be. We offer the following list of suggestions and questions to ask yourself, which will lend you an idea of how to give your external environment more detail and substance. Simply stated, you choose a subject and then you play it forward, imagining what your end result is.

Step 1. To begin, choose a subject that already exists in your life that you would like to enhance and amplify. You have started writing a book, yet you would like to see it published and become a bestseller. You have money in your account, yet you would enjoy having it double, triple, and quadruple.

Step 2. Acknowledge all of the wonderful things about your subject, and all of the things that it has inherent to it. Acknowledge and appreciate that which has been wonderful, beneficial, and already working about the subject.

Step 3. The magnitude of your subject is without limit, therefore, the next step is to double the success you already have. If it is a dollar amount you double the amount of dollars, then double it again, then double it again. If it is books sold, you double the amount of books sold and the way people find the books. You expand and grow the subject, doubling and doubling until we have expanded the scope of the project beyond your imagination. It has gone way beyond the bounds of what you had previously thought possible.

We created new neural pathways with this exercise by taking it further than you had taken it before. This allows the space for the brilliance of that which you are choosing to manifest. It's a simple exercise, and it's one that you can do on a regular basis to assist you in focusing on the growth of your external environment in a way that is fun, glorious, and expansive.

MASTERING YOUR
INTERNAL ENVIRONMENT

We feel as if you have an understanding of how to continue to actively and internally move forward with things. There is really only a slight difference between this internal moving forward and the external moving forward. You know how it feels to have things in your life going well, so you can call up this feeling as you are moving forward in your internal environments and new areas of your life. Your number one focus right now is your mastery of your internal environment.

Remember you are incredibly gifted. You have abilities that nobody else on Earth has. Continue to practice moving your internal environments forward. We will continue to support you on the energetic planes. The main thing is to enjoy your life. That is all for now. We look forward to our continued relationship and we invite you to meet with us at least one other time this week, if that is possible, and practice this exercise again.

14

BELIEF PROCESSES

We spoke in the previous section about taking an internal emotional journey, focusing your internal environment on what it is that you are choosing to create, and moving this dynamic into the completed experience. In this chapter we will discuss the belief processes that aid in this manifestation, and how you can enhance them.

THOUGHTFORMS AND BELIEFS

Thoughtforms and beliefs are the container around that which comes into physical form. For instance, if there is a desire, a projected emotional experience that is outside of the landscape of the belief, then it takes that much longer to come into form, or it has to shrink in order to come into form. In this segment we invite you to access your ability to work with thoughtforms and beliefs in a very general and nonspecific way that will address all of your individual beliefs.

In the past you may have used words, beliefs, and thoughtforms very specifically to move your limiting belief into a more expanded state. For example, if you believed "I can't have what I want," you would create an affirmation that counterbalances that belief: "I know that I can have what I want now, and with ease and grace." If you have a belief like "I believe that money doesn't grow on trees," you create a new belief: "I now choose to know that money comes to me easily and frequently." These are more specific, individualized beliefs; we are offering you a process that can widen the belief systems in a general way that also covers or includes the individual belief system. Entrain for a few more moments to this consciousness.

SPOKEN EXERCISE
Affirmations to Widen the Vessel

We would invite you to write down the following affirmations and to read them every day for the next thirty days, once or twice a day, and notice how it opens up the width of that which you are choosing to create. It widens the vessel. When the word God is used, please replace it if you would prefer with your word of choice: Divine, Source, Goddess, Good, Infinite, Nature, or whatever term is true for you.

"I believe I am God, I trust myself as a creator being. I am one with my creations. I am aligned with the infinite; therefore everything is available to me. Instant manifestation is safe. Instant manifestation is safe and governed by the laws of divine and cosmic balance. Anything is possible. I can be, do, and have all that I imagine. I am a spark of the Divine, a cohesive energy pattern drawing to me the perfect opportunities, circumstances, places, conditions, and people. My soul is joy."

THE POWER OF GENERAL AFFIRMATIONS

You can see that we did not speak about money, health, or houses on the ocean; we used general affirmations or beliefs rather than individualized affirmations. The reason we went this route is because general affirmations go inside your consciousness in a way that creates that which you are choosing much more easily. In this way, a general affirmation doesn't have to bypass your attachment or resistance, which can often be present when you want something specifically.

REPLACING A HABIT

When you stop a habit, when you quit smoking for instance, it is more successful if you replace this habit with something else. Perhaps going for a walk, chewing on a toothpick, running, or having something else that replaces the habit. The Council of Light, as you can tell, has provided very practical applications of how you can begin to replace the internal dynamic struggle, the habit of negative emotional patterns, and belief systems with active processes.

The ancients have used mantra, pranayama breath, and sound current to provide the space for alignment to occur, and these are viable techniques. We are offering additional ones that we feel will address the discomfort of the modern day and the average person who is overstimulated and overwhelmed and who has an internal dialogue that is running out of control.

BECOMING CURRENT

As we said earlier, as the consciousness on the Earth continues to shift, things are going to continue to dissolve in ways around you—this is a good and necessary thing. The more that you can feel at peace and at ease the better. We would encourage you to complete the projects that you are able to complete to free up your energy, as well as create a demarcation point from that in which you were engaged at a previous vibrational vantage point.

WRITTEN EXERCISE
Finish Projects and Dissolve
That Which Is No Longer Current

Take a few minutes to contemplate your life. Notice what projects you are ready to complete. Also identify areas that you are feeling called to just let go of. Take some time to write down what you are choosing to dissolve and what you are choosing to complete so you can become energetically current. Then create some guidelines as to how and when you would like to complete these areas and projects. Remember to include patterns that are no longer serving you, as well as physical items like cleaning out your closet. If you find an area that you have been stuck in for a long time, create a plan that includes getting added support. Take all the time that you would like with this exercise.

JOY AND FUN

You can have fun and joy in every single moment regardless of how it may look to you or whether it is in a subject that is fun or joyous. This is what your bliss team (a combination of light beings solely dedicated to your bliss) is helping you with. This is what you are moving toward; you can have fun in each and every moment. We are repeating this several times as you are getting more attuned to our energy and more energized through the process, and also because it is something that's worth repeating. It is worth repeating to say that you can have fun in each and every moment.

It is up to you to have fun, to find the fun in it, to find the joy in it, and if you have the curiosity to look for what is fun you will find it. If you are looking for the stress or feeling of being overwhelmed in the situation then you will find that as well. It is all about what you are looking for in each moment. It is for the fun of it these days that you are working; it is for the fun of it these days that you are in relationship; it is for the fun of it that you spend time with your friends and your family; it is for the fun of it that you travel; it is for the fun of it that you have kittens, or plants; it is for the fun of it that you take a shower; it is for the fun of it that you eat; it is for the fun of it that you exercise; it is for the fun of it that you drive; and it is for the fun of it that you do or don't do anything.

Saying that you are doing something for the fun of it carries an entirely different energy than if you say it is for work, for finances, or for the saving of the planet. Those all have a different frequency of tonality than simply saying that it is for the fun of it. When you say it is simply for the fun of it—and that it is so much fun—then you're able to allow things to be what they are. Saying that it is for the fun of it, that you are creative, elicits the fun in your internal and external processes. This is a mantra and a way of being, a belief that we encourage you to take on. Notice as a side benefit when you do things for the fun of it how fun your life is and also how successful it is.

Let's say that you have a goal and your goal is to have 1,000 clients purchase a product you have for sale. You realize this goal supports you to be financially free, have soul fulfillment, and have an impact on the planet. Those are all lovely, lovely things and wonderful intentions. But what if you said that you had 1,000 clients purchase your product for the fun of it? That does not minimize the significance and the respect that you have for the benefit of the product; however, it creates a different vibration and a different attractor field to it. If you add that it is for the fun of it that you are choosing to do anything, it will not only be a more joyous experience, and one in which you will feel more alignment and more safety, but it will also prove to be more successful.

In order for you to connect more directly and easily with us, bring your awareness into your cellular memory. Just like using a thumbprint to open a door is a form of recognition, access through your conscious choice the memory of the Council of Light's signature energy that exists within your cells, and as the Council comes in there is a cellular recognition. As this cellular recognition happens, as it is a match, it is with great ease and grace and joy that we are able to communicate. Now that this has been established it will become less necessary for you to go into deeper states of meditation for us to connect. We know you enjoy moving into a relaxing state so you may choose to continue to do so. We are simply saying that it is not necessary.

YOU MAKE IT ALL UP ANYHOW

Let's work with the premise that you make it all up anyhow, so why not make up something really great? This is a concept of exercising your imagination or your ability to make things up, but in a way that feels grounded and real, not out of the ballpark of your current situation. It's like making up a really nice and juicy story.

Let's use the example of 1,000 people purchasing a product that you have. You have a vision, and this vision is to support the people of your planet through the tool that you have, which is this product. These 1,000 people flock to you, they find you with ease and grace, and they get your product joyously. You love every moment of it. You enjoy the miracle of them finding you, of them buying it, of them having it, the amazing experiences that they share with you, and the miracles that they experience as a result of the product. In the meantime you have become free yourself and you manifest the experiences that you enjoy, and most of all you have fun throughout the whole process.

Another story is that a company contacts you, in direct relationship to your intention, and that company has 1,000 employees, and they would like to support their employees. As a gift to their employees they purchase 1,000 of your products. You are given a gift and the company is transformed.

Or let's say there's a neighborhood and all of the neighbors want to do something for the environment. They realize that the best thing that they can do for the environment is to uplift themselves and to allow their own vibration to come back into love and homeostasis, which is the purpose of your product. They find you and they ask you to create products for a 100-block radius for all the families in this area. What if you, through the multidimensional layers, had 1,000 people purchase your product right now? What if it were the truth right now that you have 1,000 people with your product in their hands? How does that feel right now? You are, on a day like today, enjoying time with us and through your own enjoyment you are supporting 1,000 people to have their own enjoyment and to be their happiest selves. It feels so great.

Now take the story into the "I" form and in the present: "I have 1,000 people who have bought my product and it is such a blessing and such a joy. It is so much fun and I love every minute of it. Thank you, thank you, thank you, thank you."

It was for the fun of it that we did this exercise, and in the process you were able to experience different scenarios that would achieve this goal. This allows you to explore infinite possibilities and expand your capacity to imagine even more than you previously thought was possible.

WRITTEN EXERCISE
Write a Story About Having Your Goal

We would encourage you to make up a story about a goal that you have or an area of your life that you would like to expand. Make sure to include at least three ways that the goal can come into fruition. Then focus on this story for a six-week period, bring it into your awareness, read it, and visualize yourself in the story. Bring it into your awareness as often as you can.

YOUR GOALS ARE DIVINE

Remember that the Divine inspired your goal; it was not something that you created on your own. There is power in knowing that your desires are God-given. Yes, you are God, but knowing that your goals are spiritually based enhances in your particular situation, although not in everybody's, a deeper level of trust in the happening of it.

There is some part of you that feels that if you are forcing something, if you are manipulating it or doing it solely for the money, then it is less than if it were a gift from God, if it were meant to be, or if it were for the joy of everyone involved. All of these things feel better than feeling as if you were taking advantage of people through this goal. This is true—it was given to you by God and you are the steward of it on a conscious level. But we would remind you that it happens on the multidimensional level and there is only a very small fragment that you are conscious of.

OBSTACLES AND OPENING THE WAY

The only obstacles are the ones that you have created. Because you have created them, you have the power to uncreate them. You know what they are made of, you know what their purpose is, and you know this from the level of your multidimensional being. We, the Council of Light, are openers of the way and you have this energy of opening within you. You are also an opener of your own way. The next exercise may appear simple, but that is because you are reclaiming what is yours to begin with.

SUPPORT EXERCISE
Opening the Doorways

We will spend the next five minutes together opening the doorways of these obstacles so that they are no longer obstacles. They are clear channels of light, of love, of health, and abundance, because these divine qualities are your natural state. Pause for five minutes to let this truth settle into your being.

YOUR ESSENCE AMPLIFIES
YOUR EXTERNAL ENVIRONMENT

One of the things that closes the gap between your misalignments with what it is that you are choosing to manifest is the recognition of your essence. As you focus and concentrate on your essence, as you know that your essence, your soul, and your signature energy are eternal, there is a qualitative vibration to you that is whole and transcends time and space. You can connect to your essence when you're in the experience of wanting something that you do not have. Connect to your essence in the now, and connect to your essence in the past. You will find that it is your essence that is the common denominator between the having and the not having.

Sometimes people think that if they had something that they do not have then they would be an entirely different person. Let's say you suddenly go from having the financial wealth that you have now to having extreme financial wealth as a billionaire. There is a part of you that thinks that your values will change, that what you value will be different, and you will become a different person. You will do totally different activities, there will be this incredible internal and external transformation, and you won't recognize yourself.

In actuality you—as an essence—will stay the same whether your finances are modest or whether you are a multimillionaire or billionaire. You will still value your relationship with the Divine, creativity, intimacy with your beloved, and the exploration of assisting on a planetary level. You will still value a beautiful home, spending time with your friends or cats, and going to the movies. Your essence and your activities will not be as drastically different as you might think, and this will allow you to align with the external circumstance much more quickly.

BELIEFS AND WAYS OF BEING

One of the most important things that you can do right now during this extraordinary time in consciousness is to allow yourself to be radically different than you were the day before. We are not talking about your essence but about the beliefs and the ways of being.

Suppose your old self was stressed, worried, and believed that you had to work hard in order to make money, or you had to clearly appeal to the mainstream in order to make money. You spent a lot of time and energy worrying about things, forcing things, praying for things, wishing for things, and basically your overall energy field was chaotic and noncohesive.

Then the next day you allow yourself to be cohesive and to know that things are easy. You allow yourself to be in alignment with your Source and to be in alignment with abundance. You as an essence have not radically changed during the shift of those two different sides of you. It is more that your essence is allowed to shine through; it is brighter and it is more prominent. Your values and your signature energy remains the same in its purest state.

We will spend a moment energizing this concept so it becomes more grounded and understandable. Allow yourself to be different one day to the next in your beliefs, feelings, experiences, and in your manifestations, yet at your core know that your essence remains the same.

We have spoken about many things: the idea of doing everything for the fun of it, the idea of making up your own reality, the idea of aligning your essence with your greater yet-to-be to eliminate the gap. Now we would like to introduce wisdom about your physical environment.

YOUR PHYSICAL ENVIRONMENT

Your physical environment is undergoing a radical adjustment. When we speak of your physical environment we are referring to your body, your temple, your home, and your planet. As your physical environment is undergoing this radical change there are some activities that we would offer or recommend for you to do to assist in the stabilization of your physical environment. You might anticipate that we are going to speak to you about detoxing and eating healthy and getting plenty of exercise and water. All of those may be beneficial, but we are actually going to speak to you about the pollutants of your thoughts on your physical environment.

How many years have you have slept on the same bed? You are not the same person as you were in the year you got it. Your thoughts have gone into the fabric of the mattress. They have become embodied in the mattress, for example. As you are lying in bed and you are different in this year than you were last year, your mattress sees you as the same. Your mattress relates to you in the same way.

It would not be practical for you to get rid of everything in your physical environment that you have had for an extended period of time. Although it may be time for a new mattress, it makes more sense to have a tool with which you can update everything to your current being, your current vibration, and your current now. As such you can also overlay onto physical objects your vision of who you are. It's like the concept that the universe doesn't know the difference between you being a millionaire and you visualizing yourself as a millionaire. The same is true for your physical environment, your body, your home, and your planet. These objects do not know the difference between you being healthy, happy, holy, and wealthy, and you visualizing yourself as happy, healthy, wealthy, and holy.

SPOKEN EXERCISE
Three Steps to Enhance
Your Physical Environment

State the following declarations out loud. You may find this exercise even more potent if you stand up and move into a powerful posture with your body.

> **Step 1.** I call upon the energy of pure divine love. I ask that this energy of pure divine love move and awaken in my body, my home, and the planet. I activate pure divine love in all physicality in and around me.
>
> **Step 2.** I neutralize anything before it comes into physicality that is not in alignment with pure divine love.
>
> **Step 3.** I program all physicality with the infinite spring of health, wealth, joy, and fertility.

Repeat the process again, declaring these statements out loud, clearly, and confidently:

Step 1. I call upon pure divine love to infuse all physicality within and around me including my body, my home, and my planet.

Step 2. I neutralize any vibrations before they take physical form in my body, my environment, and my planet that are not in alignment with pure divine love.

Step 3. I program all physicality with health, wealth, and joy.

We will deepen our connection to you and ask you to repeat these simple statements:

Step 1. Pure divine love inhabits all physicality. My body, home, and planet are programmed with pure divine love.

Step 2. Pure divine love inhabits all physicality. All physicality is neutral.

Step 3. My body, home, and planet express pure divine love through health, wealth, and happiness.

Take three deep breaths to complete this process.

THE IMPORTANCE OF YOUR PHYSICAL ENVIRONMENT

Why is it that we are spending time on your physical environment? This is your point of focus, this is where you connect to one aspect of your consciousness, this is where you are. It is something that is overlooked quite a bit; however, it is also something that has been known about for thousands of years. The feng shui consultant knows that your environment is impacting your wealth, health, and your joy. The energy-space-clearing person knows that your environment can take on energy that can impact your vitality, health, joy, and life. The interior designer knows the power of having a beautiful environment.

This information is not new. People feel the weight of their physical environment holding them down or in a pattern that is not freeing, and there is a desire to declutter, to live a simple life, or to have more things to assist in shifting this feeling of being weighed down by the physical environment. This is also one of the reasons why people are overweight. This is another subject, but we will introduce it here: the weight may represent the old self that has been dragged forward longer than it needs to be.

As you declare these statements, as you practice them, as you bring them into your awareness, you become current and your physical environment is nourishing you, your health, your joy, and your wealth. You will also feel inspired to make changes in your physical appearance and in your physical environment. The energy of pure divine love will address everything now without having to change anything. Now is where you are. Now is where you can help yourself. Now is where we can access you. When you are perfect then you will be in a different now. We want to assist you where you are, meet you where you are, and provide tools to allow you to become or reveal to yourself your biggest, brightest self. We are excited for you and you are right where you need to be. Enjoy, and have fun with it.

15

POSITIONING

You may have noticed in your life—perhaps more so recently—that there are times when you feel like you are making progress and times where no progress is visible. In this chapter we will explore what these different periods mean to you and how you can best position yourself to be ready when the time comes for change.

TRUSTING THE CYCLES OF YOUR LIFE

We invite you to relax into and trust the process of the cycles of your life. There may be days where you are very busy and other days where you are less busy and less is happening. However, there is the same amount of potential and growth that is occurring in days that are busy and days that are spacious.

In this moment we invite you to become more aware of the cycle that is happening in the unseen realms, particularly during the times that are more quiet. In some ways it is like the arcade coin pusher game that you may have played as a child, where you have a coin that you would put in a slot, and you would try to place it so it lays flat next to coins that are already in the game. Then as the bar that slides left to right comes into contact with the newly positioned coin it creates a momentum that pushes the money off to the side (and ultimately into your pocket). Things in your life are inching in the direction of coming down the chute; they are getting closer at times when you take an action and others when you don't need to take an action. Both aspects of the cycle of life create more momentum and traction through which things can manifest in physical form.

We are describing a bit more in detail the qualities of the energy of manifestation to assist you in understanding the importance of all the cycles. Ruminating, what you would call waiting, and things not happening as quickly as you would like are all important, because that is when things are lining up, organizing, and coming into the next vibration of density so they can come into physical form. The process of moving something from inspiration into form is one in which a vibrational shift occurs. The idea or energy of money is moving more quickly than the manifestation of money. By honoring the cycles in your life and adding the energy of joy you can move energy from the ethers into physical form.

EVERYTHING HAS IMPORTANCE, SIGNIFICANCE, AND PURPOSE

Imagine that every time you have wanted more money you have accrued more money in an energetic bank. In fact you have millions of dollars in your energetic bank. Yet how do you cash the check of your financial etheric bank? It is similar to the critical mass that we have discussed in the coin game; everything lines up and then it comes into form. It is based on the principles of quantum physics as well as all that you know about vibration, sequence, and divine order.

Right now, imagine that today there is not so much that you have to do. You could go to the movies, talk to friends, lie on the couch, read a book, meet with us, work on an appreciation journal, work on projects, or do many, many things. On a day like today it is not so much about doing what is visible or pressing but more about using your inner guidance to choose what activities to do. Are you choosing to do things that bring joy, that feel peaceful, and feel enlightening, or are you choosing to push forward and take action just for the sake of taking action? Are you feeling impatient or are you feeling patient? Are you feeling happy or are you feeling sad? These are all parts and parcels of things and on some days like today, going to the movies, relaxing, having fun would be that perfect placement of the coin that would kick everything off. On a day like today meeting with us could also be that perfect coin that kicks everything off. On a day like today taking a nap could be the perfect coin that kicks everything off.

CHOOSING THE NOW TO
LEAD AND GUIDE YOU

We are verbalizing something that you have known for quite a while, which is that everything has importance, significance, and purpose. The many facets of expression and experiences are equally important and equally significant. Yes, there are some events and some moments that create a quantum leap or quantum momentum, yet it is based on the day-to-day movement and the momentum, back and forth. It is the action of putting the energy in, putting the coin in, and seeing where it falls and how it impacts everything else.

You can also do things that are on your mind, do things that feel like piddling around, that you know would enhance your quality of life, especially when you have the time to do them. For instance, doing laundry on a spacious day is different than doing laundry when what you need to wear tomorrow is in the dirty laundry. Working on a long-term project on an open day is different than working on it when you have a deadline to get it out tomorrow. There is a relaxation to the doing that has a different quality. There is also a lot of power and potency in doing things under a deadline, which we like to call a joy-line.

However, in the scheme of things, to operate from a place of ease and grace and do things when you have free time, from that place of slowly getting to it and relaxing into it, is a nice way of doing things. It is different than all or nothing. The other thing that is nice about this is that you are doing things as they are coming up into your awareness. It's not artificially planning what it is that you are going to do. Imagine that this morning you felt like lying in bed a little longer and you did, you felt like calling a friend and you did, you felt like meeting with us and you did. This unfolding experience of inner guidance is different than preplanning that tomorrow from nine to ten o'clock you are going to do this and from ten to eleven o'clock you are going to do that. There is an allowing for the now to be the leader in what you are choosing to do, and as you are choosing the now to lead you and to guide you there is an alignment that occurs—an alignment with your energy being focused in the now.

One of the benefits of doing things when you have the space to do them rather than in an accelerated or condensed, deadline-oriented format is that it allows you to simply be in the now. It allows you to focus on the thing in the now without any challenges. For example, you need to get your house ready to sell for a move sometime in the future. You know that you need to paint the house and get rid of some of your belongings at some point, and you don't know when that is. It could be a year from now or it could be a week from now. It's something that needs to be done and doing it in advance— because it is something that you would like to do—allows it to be completed for when it's needed. You become ready even if it is not time to move forward, which brings you further along your path. It's like taking action as you feel called to positions you right on the edge of being pushed into this chute in the game, rather than being five or six steps away.

As you are living your life from your intuitive plane, following your guidance, and letting your activities be dictated by what you are feeling moment to moment—and what seems to be important moment to moment—then more of those things are right on the edge of manifesting from nonphysical to physical. It's like you are moving all of the coins halfway over the ledge, so maybe all it takes is a lovely time with your friend or spouse at dinner to push things over.

POSITIONING TO BE READY
FOR THE NEXT PHASE OF YOUR LIFE

How does this work with money? It is similar to what you have been doing with the above exercise as you become a person whose house is ready to go on the market. As you become the person that is abundant, then you are right on the edge for when the money comes in. You've already become that person, and you've already taken the steps that it would take to move from where you are to being the person that would have that level of abundance.

When it's time for it to drop in, you are right there, ready. You don't have to go through "Do I deserve this, am I ready for this, what do I have to do to make it happen?" You are already primed. You are being positioned on many different fronts to be ready for the next phase of your life. This is a good day to rest, to be in, to play, to be in the present moment, and to have all of those options that you are looking for— allow yourself to be where you want to be. In choosing your activities you set the tone from the inside out.

TRUSTING THE PROCESS

There is also a trust in this level of being where you know that you will be able to have enough of whatever you need at the time. If you need time you will have it, if you need energy you will have it, if you need resources you will have them. Sometimes as you look at what you could do on a particular day and if you want to hang out and relax, one thought that can come up is "If I am not doing something 'useful,' am I maximizing the time that I have been gifted? Do I trust that there will be enough time when I need it, that I can use this time for something that will bring me pleasure? Do I trust that there will be enough money even if I am not making money today, even though I know that there is that infinite supply of money?" The cause and effect of taking time to enjoy, once you get the hang of the concept, is that it is through joy that greater health, wealth, and happiness happen. It is through your alignment with the higher vibrational energy of play and bliss and relaxation that you're in alignment with your dreams. Add joy and pleasure to your to do list and watch how your success skyrockets.

The concept of positioning is highly beneficial to embrace, for knowing that you do not always need to be going, going, going, doing, doing, doing is key to the changing times. There will be times that are more accelerated. There will be times that are more compressed. There will be times that are more fluid and expansive. Today could be one of those days that is more fluid and expansive. One of the benefits that you receive from your work with us is the greater understanding of the role of joy in your health, wealth, and happiness.

16

HEART AND SOUL

Your ancestry and your family tree extend beyond your biological family; every human has a spiritual, multidimensional soul lineage as well. In this chapter, we will discuss the different origins of the soul, the divinity in every soul, and ultimately what this means for your own heart and soul—your Source and your joy.

THE SOUL'S LINEAGE

Part of our purpose in working with you is to assist you in being able to connect directly to your origin, to your Source, and to the aspect of you that encompasses all that there is.

We will begin this divine transmission with looking at the soul's lineage and the lineage of where you come from. You may have a strong connection to the Egyptian lineage. You may go as far as to say that you are a child of the gods and goddesses of Egypt and that you are also a god or goddess of Egypt. You have a connection to us—the Council of Light—and in that sense you are the child of galaxies, stars, and galactic energy.

You may have a connection to India, the Celtic or Peruvian lineage, or another kind of lineage. If you think about lineage and genealogy, it is often about your family of origin. Begin to think of yourself as a divine being and that your family of origin includes the Divine, gods and goddesses, stellar consciousness, the heavenly realms, the fairy realms, and all of the magical creatures.

REVERENCE

You have been conditioned to think of yourself as a human and that the human is devoid of the Divine. To say that your ancestry is of the gods and goddesses, the stars, that you are a star, and that you are the Divine breaks through many layers of old conditioning and old patterning. To really know that you are the Divine is the ultimate in resonance and alignment with self-love.

There is a certain reverence in your relationship to the Divine. There is a certain reverence that has been conditioned and dogmatized in religion, that there has to be a certain humbleness as you are connecting to the Divine, there has to be an intercessor such as a priest, and that there has to be this separation between you and the Divine. There is an unhealthy aspect of reverence that has been dogmatized in religion: the ritual has the power, not the individual.

However, there is also the positive and healthy aspect of reverence that we are asking you to connect to in your relationship with yourself and the Divine. This is to have the same level of resonance with your divine self that you would have for someone that you think of as holy, a spiritual teacher, or someone who you think of as ascended. In interacting with that person there is an honoring, a sense that the sacred inhabits this person, and a sense that something magical or divine is in and around them.

The part that does not work so well in reverence is the pedestal consciousness: that this person is more than you are, has something that you do not, that you need to bow down, and that you are not in equal relationship with them. This is in some ways how people approach their relationship with their guides, allies, gods, goddesses, or the Divine— that it is not an equal partnership. Reverence is an equal partnership and comes from a place of equality and a place of honoring, peer-to-peer, and Divine-to-Divine.

YOUR BIRTHRIGHT AS A DIVINE BEING

We invite you to begin to think of yourself as a spiritual master. We know that you have contemplated this concept consciously or unconsciously and feel that you are in varying degrees aligned with this concept. Perhaps you feel far away from this concept or perhaps you feel close. Begin in earnest to develop a relationship of reverence with yourself that is based on seeing yourself as a spiritual master and a divine being.

One of the reasons that we have started this segment by speaking about your ancestral lineage and that you are the children of the Divine beings and gods is to begin to create a concept and new neural pathways for you to see yourself not as a child of God, in the sense that you are not the Divine, but that your heritage, your birthright, is as a Divine being.

We could speak about this for a long time and it would still not balance out the amount of conditioning you have around thinking about yourself as a human being. This conditioning leaves you feeling finite, and there is often a sense of being all alone. There is often a sense of feeling separate and disconnected.

As you begin to recognize that you are not separate from your Source or your origin, you will see that you are human and human is implied in the definition of Divine. The language here is funny because it is speaking as if spirit and matter were different, or human and divine were different, when in actuality they are the same.

ENERGETIC EXERCISE
Unlocking Your Spiritual Heritage

Spend a few moments breathing into your body, breathing into each of the parts of your body, scanning from the top of your head to the tips of your toes, and directing the breath into each body part as you do. Now connect to your skin: notice the template, consciousness, or energy equivalent of union that is present now that you can connect to at the level of your skin. You may notice your skin vibrating, pulsating, and communicating with this consciousness and energy. This energy is coming through the Sphinx and is being transmitted through the Sphinx to you.* It provides a lock and key so that you are able to unlock the unity consciousness within you and the knowledge that you are a Divine being with a heritage. Take all the time that you would like awakening your spiritual lineage, and when you feel complete stretch in any direction your body feels called.

SACRED TRAVEL

One reason that you are called to travel to sacred places is to reconnect to ley lines that directly connect you to your Source. For instance, some people travel to Ireland, Wales, or Germany because their ancestors are from those places, even though they were born in America and they've never been to those places. There is a sense that going there reconnects them to the line. There is a sense of reawakening a cellular memory. As you travel to the places that you so desire, you are like a lock and key that unlocks that spiritual heritage. You don't have to go to the physical location; you can connect energetically to the land. However, going there is also a wonderful experience. There is something about being there that resonates and awakens.

There is the energy of the region that you live in that is being made available as a part of your heritage. Where you plug into consciousness is in direct alignment to who you are and what would be helpful for you. Just as there have been many people who have lived in the same land where you are currently living, there are bands or

---

*To connect more deeply to the power of the Sphinx or to take a spiritual journey through the temples of Egypt, see Danielle Rama Hoffman, *The Temples of Light: An Initiatory Journey into the Heart Teachings of the Egyptian Mystery Schools* (Rochester, Vt.: Bear & Company, 2009).

layers of consciousness. Where you tap into these bands or layers of consciousness is part intention and part resonance; you will naturally draw to you that which resonates with you. Five different people could go to Egypt and tap into five different aspects of the consciousness that's available in Egypt. Or five different people could go to Spain and tap into different consciousness depending on their heritage.

There is an aspect that we are bringing in about connecting to the heritage of where you live now that will assist you. One purpose of doing this is that it will assist you at feeling at home where you currently live regardless of your spiritual lineage or your origin. It will enhance a sense of feeling at home on the Earth, even if your origin is that of a star and you may have previously felt a sense of restlessness. For in this moment you can energetically connect to your origin, to the lines of your spiritual heritage, and as such feel at home wherever you are, without the restlessness. Then as you travel it can be with the pure desire to explore for the sake of connecting and exploration.

HEART AND SOUL

We have spoken about your Divine heritage, of the powerful reasons why you are drawn to certain locations or power places, and we will pick up the thread of reverence and your relationship with yourself. The topic that we want to speak about is the heart and soul and why the heart and soul are so important to living a joyful life. Just like you can go to a power place and feel fortified, strengthened, or nourished, you can also connect to your heart and your soul and feel fortified and nourished. They are access points to your origin and are doorways, gateways, portals, and avenues for you to connect to your Source.

The description that we are going to use is not literal, it is more symbolic. Let's say within your heart center or your high heart center (located at the thymus) there are trillions of drops of consciousness of your origin, and located in your mind there are three drops of consciousness of your origin. This is an exaggeration but if you are connecting to your heart, following your heart's desires, and following your soul's longings, you are swimming in the ocean of your origin in a way that is much stronger than if you are wrapped in your thoughts, emotions, or your physical needs moment to moment. You are a multifaceted being and in some ways, if you choose, this segment is about orienting yourself to reside within your heart and, therefore, within your soul. As you move through your life you are seeing and experiencing your life connected to your origin and your Source.

ENERGETIC EXERCISE
Developmental Stages and Alchemy

Focus on the back of your heart center in between your shoulder blades, and in particular around your spinal column. Allow the back of your heart center and your spinal column to open up wider to receive your connection to joy. The back of the heart center is one of the largest places where you are able to receive energy and consciousness. It is also one area that oftentimes people close down because there is a fear that they will be stabbed in the back, or that something else bad will happen if they are not protecting the back of their heart center.

Allow the protection to drop away. It is counterintuitive in some ways, but the more wide open your heart is the safer you are. There is a vulnerability associated with living from the heart or being wide open in the heart that can make you feel as if you are open, unprotected, or exposed to danger. However, if your heart is completely open it is a safe vibration and frequency from which you can move through your life, for the heart is inclusive and is the vibration of unity consciousness. In unity consciousness the question of safe or unsafe is no longer relevant, for you are in a state of deep connection and union with self as Source.

Now focus on your spinal column, in particular in the cervical spine in the neck. Imagine a soothing-colored energy cascading through the spinal column in the neck. Allow this energy to open and relax your neck and your spinal column even more. In the past, you may have had an old pattern surface in the neck where it gets tight, or goes out of alignment when you try to connect to Source. Allow yourself to call in that perfect template and temple for your neck to be able to connect with Source and stay in alignment and balance.

Now bring your awareness to your digestion and your spleen on the left side of your body, under your ribs. There is some cleanup that is happening on the digestive level with the spleen and the energy of sadness, sorrow, or worry. It has to do with little routines that you have and little ways that you move in the world. Begin to drop some of those and know that you are safe and that you do not need to have your routines in order to thrive. Your routines are helpful but you do not need them. It is less about the routines and more about the reason why you have the routines.

If you have worry and you're worried about getting somewhere on time, or you're worried about having something happen in the perfect way, or you're thinking about different kinds of things, then it is taking you from the now. Focus on the energy of trust.

Take a few deep breaths and anchor into your cellular memory the knowledge that the results, movement, and shifts that you are experiencing in your life are permanent. The yo-yo movement of moving forward and moving back is unnecessary. You have upleveled, and you are now on this new level ground.

Does the caterpillar think that it's going to become a butterfly? Who knows? But its evolution is to be a butterfly. The tomato seed has everything within it to become the tomato. Also innate within you is all that you need to become who you are. Take a few breaths and allow your awareness of yourself to become current with who it is that you have become. When this process feels complete, stretch your body, and when you feel ready, return to this time and place.

THE STAR SEED

What does it mean to be a star seed in the human divine form? This high heart area that was spoken about earlier is also the location of the star seed or the soul seed. As you connect to this area you are able to connect to your soul and to the seed and origin of you. Your origin is in the stars; one way to look at it is that you are connecting to that heavenly consciousness and stellar chi.

ENERGETIC EXERCISE
Connect to Your High Heart Chakra

We are working now with you on your heart center and the soul seed at the high heart. Breathe in a very soft, light pink-violet into the high heart and into the soul seed located at the thymus. Now breathe a golden energy into that area. The color is a like a golden metallic pink beyond what you see in your physical realm. It is an energy color. This process is symbolic. As you connect to your high heart chakra and to the energy of self-love, you are connecting to more droplets of consciousness of your essence, soul, signature energy, and origin.

Spend some time in this process, and when you feel ready take a few deep breaths, stretch and move your body, and gently return to this time and place.

FREEWILL CHOICE

In this moment there is a decision point to be made; the free will is being activated and asked a significant question for the evolution of the soul and your life. There is the opportunity to blow the ceiling off your capacity to experience joy. There may be some residue or some fear that you are completing that is impacting you unconsciously in making the decision to say yes to more joy. You will not split. You will remain in the wholeness if you have more joy.

Are you choosing to uplevel your capacity to experience joy? State your choice aloud. "Yes, I am choosing to expand my capacity to experience joy," or "No, I am not choosing to expand my capacity to experience joy." Know that your answer is being recorded in your Akashic Records and is being taken into consideration on the level of your soul's evolution.

THE ARCHETYPE OF JOY

Joy is a funny archetype. If we look at clowns, jesters, stand-up comedians, and those that are embodying fun or joy there is a certain level of kookiness or quirkiness that is associated with them. These archetypes are often made fun of. They allow others to project onto them for the spirit of fun.

When you have been truly silly there may have been consequences or judgment in the past. For example, as a child if you were having a giggling fit or being silly, adults may have told you to be quiet. As you are expanding your capacity to experience joy one thing that might come to mind is the underbelly of the archetype that asks the question, "Does it mean that if I choose to have more joy that I will be the butt of all the jokes, and that I will be thought of as crazy, silly, or not taken seriously?" As you are expanding into greater joy and you have sensations surface like a fear of losing love, community, or connection, tap into your Rays of Light toolbox. You could call upon the Emerald Ray to amplify your essence and in that field of consciousness you will be tuned in to living your life for *you*. Or you could call upon the Peace Ray to create an illusion-free bubble in which you are free from what others could think. Call upon the Love Ray to drop the barriers between you and your sense of wholeness. As you are in a higher vibration these sensations will simply melt away and you can realize the joy you are designed for.

CONSCIOUSLY EMBODYING
THE ENERGY OF SOURCE
TO EXPERIENCE JOY

There is the willingness to experience joy on a more frequent basis that is directly tied to your consciously connecting to the aspect of yourself as Source energy. If you are playing in the realm of duality, struggle, separation, self-doubt, and of self-deprecation, then there is a separation from your union. Think of your negative emotions as indications that you have come into resistance or separation from your Source. That's all those feelings are. They're indicators or guidance for you to recognize that you have become separate from Source.

There has been an overidentification with striving that has been creating a distortion in experiencing joy. For instance, it seems more interesting if a person works hard for something than if they just happen upon it. There is something valued in your society around hard work, struggle, and sacrificing that is actually an indication of separation.

As you are choosing to increase your capacity to experience joy and connect to your heart and soul, you are choosing to consciously embody the knowledge that you are Source. If you think about the ascended masters that you know or have heard about, some of them—like Buddha, or even those that are or have been in body, the Dalai Lama or Sai Baba— usually are smiling, laughing, silly, and there is a levity and a lightness to them that is synonymous with their union with the Divine. The more connected to your origin and your Source, the happier you are. The more you feel separate from that, the lonelier you feel and the more struggle or separateness you experience.

ENERGETIC EXERCISE
The Kaleidoscope of Your Heart

Return your focus to your heart. The Council of Light has already worked with your high heart with a pink metallic energy. Think about your heart like a kaleidoscope: a myriad of different combinations of energy, beautiful colors, and beautiful textures that is multidimensional and multifaceted. Imagine that you are looking through a kaleidoscope and that you are changing the lens on your heart to be able to see different facets and create different patterns. Through your intention, align in this moment with a pattern that feels the most openhearted and relaxed.

Focus on balancing the front of your heart with the back of your heart energy. There's more energy in the front of your heart than the back of your heart. Allow some of the beautiful energy in the front of your heart to go to the back of your heart.

We are taking a few moments of silence as you are stabilizing your strongest connection to the portal of your heart. When you feel ready, take a couple of deep breaths, move your body, and gently come back to this time and place.

THE ALCHEMY OF THE HEART

Connecting more to your heart and your soul leads to an increased capacity to experience joy. In some ways it is like going to the beauty shop. Let's say you are having your hair colored. The color is applied, then you have to sit under the dryer. The timer goes off and your hair is rinsed. An alchemical process happens as your hair is changing color. It is not that you walk into the beauty shop and you go from being a brunette to being a blond in one second; there is a process.

The process that you are in is similar. You are changing color, so to speak, to the color of the heart and the soul. You are in various stages of this entrainment process, and it will continue even longer after this time together. But you will come to a strong enough, stabilized place and be in the right color. This is what we are waiting for and assisting you with, and you are engaging your free will to orient yourself to come from the heart and the soul.

When you are in a state of love, when you are in a state of open-heartedness, you are in alignment and there is unification, inclusion, and expansion. We recognize that we are throwing around the words heart and soul, which are associated with many different things. Our definition in this case is the portal or the access point to the consciousness of unity, wholeness, and divinity.

ENERGETIC EXERCISE
Connecting Heart with High Heart

Imagine the kaleidoscope of your heart and the metallic pink of your high heart. Connect the two with an infinity symbol (a figure eight). The top of the figure eight resides within the high heart and the bottom of the figure eight resides within the heart center. In between these two is the center of the infinity symbol.

Begin to allow the high heart energy and the energy of the soul to flow in this infinity symbol into the heart and allow the heart energy to flow into the infinity symbol and into the soul. Allow this infinity symbol to mix, merge, mingle, and unify the heart and the soul. You may feel different sensations in your physical body as this is happening. Then allow a color to come to you that represents the energy of self-love, and begin pouring that color into the infinity loop.

Your new operating system has been awakened, installed, and remembered so that you are now running the consciousness of your heart and your soul. Spend a few moments having a conversation with this aspect of you receiving guidance, perhaps about how to have more joy in your life, or just simply allow the wisdom of your heart and soul and your heart and soul's desires to become more conscious to you. Spend a few moments receiving this download and having this interaction. In a sense your compass has been reset to align and direct you to following the path of your soul and your heart. This will make things easier in your life.

Take an internal picture of your energy system and your being the way that it is right now so that you can call upon it in the future. One main aspect that we would point out about the way that your field is right now is that it is in a state of coherence. You are a receiver and a transmitter and you are receiving and transmitting at all times. Now you are receiving and transmitting in a coherent fashion, calling to you those perfect people, places, and opportunities.

When you feel ready take a few deep breaths, wiggle your fingers and your toes, and gently return to the here and now.

We feel as if we have reached the highest energetic at this time, and so we will complete our verbal transmission and invite you to take some time, for the energy is still coming, to shift your focus back to the present moment.

17

HEALTH

Receiving the Energy of Love

Focus on the space in between your shoulder blades on the back of your body behind your heart chakra. Imagine that there is an emerald-green spiral of energy that is about three feet away from the back of your heart center. This energy portal is spiraling and absorbing any tension in between your shoulders related to feelings of having to watch your own back, any constriction or contraction around receiving, and in particular any discord or dissonant energy that is not in alignment with the emotion of love as well as the pure vibration and essence of love.

From our perspective there is no such thing as worthiness and unworthiness. It is not a matter of you needing to change at all in order to be able to receive love and energy. It is simply a decision on your part whether to receive love. Within your mind's eye decide to receive the energy of love, knowing that you are safe and that your physiology has natural capabilities of discerning and filtering what is in your highest and best good and what isn't.

The human body is multifaceted and multidimensional; it has many different layers to it. There is what you would think of as the physical body: blood, bones, muscles, and organs. There's also what you would think of as the energy system: chakras, subtle bodies, emotions, and so on. In actuality there are trillions and trillions of aspects to your individual health, your individual brilliant system, and your physiology.

When there is disease, when there is an absence of health or perceived absence of health, there can be a pinching off or a constriction from the energy of love, high vibration, and joy. We have begun this session with the back of the heart chakra because it is one of the largest areas in which you open to receive support and nourishment.

At your base and the subatomic level of your being you are light. Therefore, you are the same as we, the Council of Light. The matrix and the fabric of creation are divinity and unity. The natural state of this light frequency is in a bandwidth of consciousness. This light frequency is in harmonic resonance, accord, and a vibrational frequency that is in constant harmony with the symphony of all of the light within your body. When we speak of the body we mean your entire being.

In order to activate your optimal functioning and health program we invite you to connect to your etheric body, your energy body, and your body of light. Some traditions call this the merkaba, the ka, the aura, the soul, the Tree of Life, chakras, subtle bodies, astral bodies, the Akashic realm, spirit, and divinity. Regardless of its name, have a sense of connecting to your light body. As you relate and connect through your intention to your light body, notice an exchange of energy pulsing through you. This is an activation and enhancement of sorts.

Spend some time in this process, and when you feel ready take a couple of deep breaths, stretch, move your body, and gently come back to this time and place.

······················

MOVING FROM DUALITY TO UNITY

As we further discuss the topic of health, it is important to come to a vibrational frequency, a vibrational awareness, or understanding of what is meant by health. One definition of health that may be very common for you is the idea that everything is feeling good: that your body is energized, vital, and healthy. Yet even the definition of health in and of itself is connected to when you don't have health. If you have disease or an illness, that definition of health is somehow tied up with the definition of the lack of health. That is not the frequency we are vibrating with when we use the word "health," because to us health is movement, health is light, health is wholeness, and health includes everything. Health is unity. As you evolve your definition from health as it has been based in separation and duality to a frequency or vibration of wholeness, then your awareness of your health can be present in any situation.

From our perspective, this is really the true freedom that we are offering to you through this material. You can live beyond your experience. You can be aware of your health, your vitality, your vibrancy, and your wholeness when you have disease. You can be aware of and connect to your wealth when you have the flow of money going out. You can recognize that there is happiness within each and every moment. There is joy within each and every moment, even when you may be feeling sad. That may seem like a simplistic concept that is perhaps more challenging to embody, and yet what if you could recognize that your health never goes away even when you have a disease, even when you die, even when you're sick? Your health is still something that is constant and continuous. That's the only way that really makes sense when you evolve from the compartmentalization of duality, separation, and lack into unity, wholeness, and oneness. In oneness your health still exists and in oneness you are eternal. Health at its base is another form of light.

THE EFFECTS OF THE SHIFT IN CONSCIOUSNESS ON THE CONCEPT OF THE BODY

As we are connecting to you and working with your light body and physiology, we want to talk about a shift in consciousness that is happening on the planet that impacts the physiology and the functioning of the system. Some people speak about this shift of consciousness as a step in the journey of ascension, enlightenment, and of entering into the Golden Age.

Once again, regardless of what you call it, there is a changing of the guard on the level of your body. Your being or body has in the past, from the perspective of your thoughts and your beliefs, been thought of in compartments or as individual parts, such as your arm, your toe, and your head. It's been a process of seeing different parts of your body rather than seeing it as a whole. This concept of the body having different parts has been placed within the context of an incarnation in which you are born in a young body and then as you move throughout time and space, which doesn't actually exist, you become an old body. There has been a sense of disease or wellness. There has been a sense of youth, vitality, aging, and decay.

THERE IS ONLY UNITY

All of these concepts are tied to the belief system that is anchored in polarity or duality. Even if you experience a lack of health in your perception you can look for the well-being that exists in that moment. This is a skill you develop. Let's say you have pain in your body. What would happen in the old paradigm is that as a part of your body hurts, you forget that the other 99.9 percent of your body doesn't hurt. It becomes the loudest thing in your perception. But if you know that you're safe and you train your body and your being to look for the 99.9 percent that is expressing wellness in that moment, you're able to see that what exists is actually wellness.

In actuality the body is synonymous with spirit and with light. There is no separation between body and matter, spirit and matter, and human and the Divine. There is only unity and there is only oneness.

The entire concept in which you have been conditioned, the collective consciousness around things being separate from other things, is part of the illusion that is falling away. When we approach this from a vibrational level it has been thought that the body is moving at a slower density than the spirit. In actuality these are merged together as one. They are not different vibrations or different parts. They are creating a unique pattern and hologram.

HEALTH IS THE OPULENCE OF LIGHT

Health wholeness in a state of opulence is what is being vibrated at this time. It is an evolution of your previous conception about health that expands it to be beyond the duality or the lack of having or not having. Health is the opulence of light, the abundance of light, the abundance of consciousness, the abundance of energy, and it is moving at a vibration in which there is a flow of vibration.

Health is a vibrational flow. What is known about the vibrational flow of the universe is that it is a wellspring that is infinite. It is always there, it is a given, it is a constant. This is what we would invite you to recognize and to move beyond through this entire text. We invite you to remember this capacity, to have the awareness of your health, wealth, and happiness as being the building blocks of the universe and that they are the givens in your life. When you evolve all your definitions on a vibrational level, you are able to recognize that these resources—which in the past were tied into separation or lack, you either have them or you don't—are always there. Then you move beyond the conditionality of your existence. Then you move beyond the illusion of any kind of lack or separation.

We have spoken a lot about unity consciousness and about oneness. What that really provides access to is your capacity to be at one and to unify with all there is. When you are feeling like you have a situation where there is a lack of health, you could access the wholeness of health to consciously be able to unify with the health that resides in that moment. Your infinite being is always in a state of health, wealth, and joy. As you are evolving your consciousness and your energy to be in the infinite nature that you are, then that in a sense embodies the wholeness of your being. It includes the disease and the ease; it includes the illness and the vibrancy. It is all in a state of oneness.

USING UNITY CONSCIOUSNESS
AS A TOOL

You can use oneness and unity consciousness as a tool when you've left your awareness of the wholeness of the health that exists within you. When you are feeling as if something is out of balance, as you return your awareness to the whole mechanism you can recognize that the whole mechanism is in a state of balance and vibrational flow. The physiology, including the energy physiology of the human brilliant system, is magnificent. Sometimes what you would call a lack of health, like a fever, is actually the mechanism that the system utilizes to maintain the equilibrium or homeostasis of the whole that exists in all moments and in all times.

ENERGETIC EXERCISE
Unity, Wholeness, and Light

As we take a few moments of silence, allow yourself to engage with the concept of unity, wholeness, and light. Allow this light body to come into your awareness, as your entire body and being is light. The concept of density and the idea of your flesh is an illusion. At its base you're only light. Begin to see and connect to the wholeness, matrix, greatness, and light pattern of your being.

Spend some time connecting to the light of your being. When you feel ready take a couple of deep breaths, stretch, move your body, and gently come back to this time and place.

PHYSICAL OVERLAYS, DNA,
AND LIGHT CODES

Everything at its base is made of the same thing: it's all made of light. You may think about everything in the universe being made of the elements of Earth, Air, Water, Fire, and Ether or Akasha. You can think of your body in terms of the liquid in it being Water, the matter or the bones being Earth, the circulatory system being the electric impulses or Fire, your breath being Air, and your blueprint, your Akashic field, being in this energy of Ether. Everything in the universe is made up of these elements, and if you break it down even more and you go deeper into it, at its base it's only light.

One way to look at this is in the DNA. You have four letters in the DNA—A, T, C, G—and these four letters make every single part of your body. It is the order in which they're configured and the order in which this library of consciousness is read that determines what becomes what. They will be a protein or a bone or some other element. At its base and on a physiological level within your body and the DNA, it is made up of these four elements, four letters, and four energies.

When there is any imbalance in the system, it is as if these letters are being read from a place that is out of order, out of alignment, or not optimally functioning. You may have a sense of an inner librarian rereading all the codes and activating the light codes within you so that all of your physiology is being read from its optimal place.

NEUTRALIZING AN ALLERGY BY
SEEING FOOD AS LIGHT

Let's take something like food allergies as an example of a type of imbalance that people may experience. Food has been changing on the planet as you have been evolving. Your ability to get nourishment from food is what's important. It's not so much about the food itself. As you think about food being made up of certain units of energy of light, it is light ingesting light. As you are eating you are eating light and you're feeding the light within your body. If you relate to food on this level it surpasses or circumvents any allergy of food because you're not connecting to the overlay of the food; you're simply connecting to it at its base, which is light.

Food allergies exist in the first dimension. On this level you have foods that aren't nourishing or supporting your body in an optimal way. Many people who take food allergy tests come up with everything that they are "allergic to." Eliminating all these foods, when there is a slight sensitivity or chronic allergy to them, is not as practical as connecting to these foods as light from a place of strength and light within your own being. It is always helpful to meditate on and energetically connect to the light that makes up all foods, even ones that you are allergic to. However, if you have a severe food allergy (such as those causing anaphylaxis) it is not recommended to physically confront the allergen unless you have the guidance of a medical professional.

Imagine that you have all of the food groups in front of you and that they are being x-rayed: you can see wheat, animal protein, sugar, fruit, vegetable, grains, legumes, and all of the different foods on the planet as light. As you begin to see everything in front of you as light, then this neutralizes the "allergy." All we have done is go into the matrix of food and bring our awareness to the aspect of food that is light and focus on it long enough so that it is nourishing and feeding the light within you. As you take in food, imagine that it is actually turning up, feeding, and enhancing the light within you.

SLEEP

Sleep is an experience of regeneration and where the body receives nourishment. This nourishment goes through and bathes the different organs and is a way you get to unplug, or plug into a different dimensional dreamtime.

You could look at the process of sleep like being in a solarium of light for the number of hours you are asleep. You might sleep eight hours or maybe for two or ten. Maybe the number of hours of sleep you get is erratic. Sleep disturbances have become more and more common as the energy on the planet increases, evolves, and shifts.

As you look at the process of sleep like sun for a plant, the plant absorbs nutrients from the sun in its growing process. This is the same as the way your light body connects to the energy of sleep. Sleep is your time to absorb nutrients of light and to enhance the light within you. It is a little tricky on a conceptual level to imagine because sleep is not something outside of your body like food. Sleep happens within your own body.

Sleep is a shifting from day to night and from active to inactive, which is not exactly accurate because it is an active state as well. Have a sense of any sleep disturbances that you may have, any overlays that you have on sleep, any ideas that if you don't get enough sleep you won't have enough energy, and allow these concepts that you have about sleep to dissolve. Allow sleep to be what it is, which is light: light that feeds your light. That's it. At its base it's light that feeds your light.

MOVEMENT

Like sleep, movement or exercise is another form of light feeding your light. Just as we have gone through the subject of food and sleep, set your intention to focus on the energy of movement without having to call it exercise, and see that movement is a way that your system accesses and connects to light. As you begin to go through this process it becomes clear that the different states of your being all have one underlying purpose, which is for you to enhance your light and to connect to different forms of light.

You can think of yourself like a bee that is going after pollen: all aspects of your being are opportunities to plug into, connect, enhance, and to turn on light. By light we mean divinity, energy, and Source.

RELATIONSHIPS

We have worked with food, sleep, movement, and we have worked with the energy that you receive in connection to others when we began this segment with focusing on the back of the heart and the energy of love.

Let's focus now on your relationships and your connection to others.

This is a very interesting category as it relates to the shift in consciousness that is occurring on planet Earth at this time. During the Piscean Age relationships were steeped in the energy of polarity. You were giving or you were receiving. You had the power or you didn't have the power. You loved or you were out of love. There was also a great empathic aspect of the Piscean Age because one of the many benefits of the Piscean Age was the development of the individual concept and the structure of you as an individual. Because of the structure that you have created for yourself as an individual you are able to unify and to connect to oneness.

It is like an electric plug that has a very distinct shape that can plug into the unlimited source. If it didn't have a shape there'd be no way to connect. Or it's like you are a key and you can plug into a lock and unlock what's there for you. The Piscean Age was about becoming the key, forming the key, and forming the structure. The Aquarian Age is about unification, the awareness of wholeness, and the recognition that all is one.

You may be empathic, feel other people feelings, and not be able to discern what's yours and what's not. You might caretake in a way that's out of balance, be inclined to be overly responsible, have an underappreciation of self, and a lack of self-love. As the energy continues to shift on the planet the pattern of empathy is dissolving. Therefore, the idea that other people energize or exhaust you is simply that: it's an idea. It's no longer an active aspect of the new paradigm of consciousness. The idea that someone can harm you or is dangerous is also one that is based in the old paradigm. You are eternal: nothing can be added to you or taken away from you. The idea of death, that your body ages and dies, which is an aspect of your relationship to yourself, is also one that is only a facet of the whole.

Imagine that your relationships are a way for you to connect light to light even with people who you may have found in the past toxic or "energy vampires." As you connect to these people from an aspect of light you are able to see their essence and are able to connect to their light. It becomes contagious; you see their light, they see your light, and it all becomes light. Your relationships, regardless of what state they are in, are another way that you connect to light and another way that you will be able to get even more nourishment and nutrition in the future.

ENERGY

We want to speak about the concept of the energy and the idea of being energized and vital or being tired and exhausted. Your concept of energy is an important way that your body receives a nourishing access point of light. In the following exercise engage your conscious will to shift your concept of energy to be infinite.

ENERGETIC EXERCISE
Light Energy

Breathe into your body. Move your awareness into one cell in your heart. Dive down into the DNA of the cell. Set your intention to access your beliefs around your personal energy.

Sense, see, feel, or imagine that a pile of beliefs around your personal energy and the idea that you are tired, not tired, or somewhere in between have been identified in your DNA. Imagine light pouring over these beliefs and dissolving any overlays they hold. Notice that in actuality only a small percentage of the energy that you have available to you is being utilized. You have access to unlimited energy in every moment. You have felt this at times when you have been especially excited or passionate about something and you seem to have endless amounts of energy.

Imagine this light dissolving any overlays that you may have around a lack of energy, and know that we are working with your system around this concept, because it is an important concept that relates to your sense of feeling good. When you feel good you are able to align and express more of your purpose, more of what brings you joy, and more of what brings you light. Enlightenment is a process of becoming lighter and moving into the light.

As the light continues to pour onto these outdated beliefs they dissolve. As you dissolve any perceived limitations around your boundless access to energy, have a sense of the greater light body of Source and that what you associate your being with is only one light body. Have a sense of connecting to the infinite light body of Source, Spirit, the Divine, God. As you connect to this infinite light body you are able to see that this infinite light body includes everything in your experience every moment: everything that you can touch, see, feel, everyone that you can talk to, every job that you could have, every illness that you could experience, and every life experience. The light body of the Divine is in all there is; it is omnipresent and is in every aspect.

With the absence of these overlays you can see your entire being as receptacles, filaments, and docks to which light can be connected. Feel the receptacles in your DNA opening to receive more light. Receive the light that you haven't previously absorbed from your loving relationships. Receive the light that you haven't absorbed from your sleep, from your food, from your movement. Receive the light of the Divine within and without. Spend the next few moments receiving more and more light into your cells, feeling energized, recalibrated, and expanded.

INFINITE AND BOUNDLESS HEALTH

Part of what we're restoring as we are exploring the concept of health is the recognition that it is boundless, it is infinite, it is omnipresent, it is always there. As you tune in to it as a wholeness and you tune in to it as a multidimensional awareness, you see that it exists on all levels of your recognition. You move your definition of health into it being based in unity consciousness, it being based in opulence, it being based in overflowing.

WEALTH IN ALL PARTS OF YOUR LIFE

That is why we have also been looking at the energy of light, the energy of love, the energy of relationships, the energy of sleep, the energy of movement, the energy of food in the subject of health to provide the multidimensionality, the capacity to be able to plump out your definition of what health is, your awareness of what health is, and to recognize that it is multifaceted. Just like wealth is inclusive of much more than just the amount of the money you have or just finances, you're wealthy in many areas at the same time.

It's the same with your health and it's the same with your happiness. Your happiness is not something that is just in your emotional body, and it's not based on an event that's happening. To be able to consciously choose to be connected to an internal state of health, wealth, and happiness is something that is available to you at all times. Tune in to opulent health, opulent wealth, and opulent happiness. Tune in to the opulence of this oneness.

This gets into so many deeper layers. What we really want to tell you is that even if you die you're in a state of health. We understand that might sound crazy or abstract. Yet from our perspective—and this is what we feel you're really wanting in your new awareness on the subject of health—there isn't anything that's ever wrong.

That is what you're recovering and remembering during this shift in consciousness increment by increment. You're remembering your connection to what is always there and what is always there is your infinite nature, your health, your abundance, your happiness, and your joy. It's always there. Yet how much more fun could it be if, rather than carrying the baggage around health and especially aging—because that's another subject that we feel we could also express an interesting perspective about—rather than continuing on the conditionality that as you age then you get disease and illness, you could just slowly choose to let go of your physical form and remain in the health that's always been there?

HEALTH AND WHOLENESS ARE ALWAYS HERE

One way to convey this subject in a way that doesn't challenge your core beliefs, even though that in a sense is what we're asking you to do, is to think about it as simply an energy location. Let's say you go into your house and the house represents health. In this case, you're outside your house in the yard. The health still exists in the house.

You go up the stairs and you're closer to the health in the house, and then you go into the house and you're in the same location as the house and the health. Then you go up to another floor and the attic and you're still in the health and the house. Then you go to sit on the roof and you're still in the vicinity of the health and the house. Then you leave your house and you drive fifteen miles away. The health still exists except that you're no longer in the location of it. That's from our perspective what is happening; you simply are in a different location from the wholeness that is always there. It doesn't mean that whether you are in your body or out of your body you are any more or less healthy; the health always exists.

YOU'RE HAPPY, HEALTHY, WEALTHY, AND WHOLE AT ALL TIMES

Rather than trying to understand this from your mind, vibrate into this and know this for yourself. Does this feel true to you, does this feel light for you, does this feel like a relief, and does this feel that it can liberate you from having to live a conditional life? You can move from the idea that you can only be happy when this is happening, you're only healthy when this is happening, you're only wealthy when this is happening, to reclaiming that you're happy, healthy, whole, and wealthy at all times in every single moment. Which is more empowering and which transcends the illusion? It isn't an either/or and it's not a competition. You are who you are and you are where you are and there's no judgment as to what that is.

Yet because you've asked for greater support and greater assistance during a time when you are experiencing a lot with the body, because the body is no longer moving at the vibration of density that it used to be moving at, and because it is and always has been one with light, with the faster vibration and the faster frequency you may be experiencing some niggles with your body. Your body may be calling your attention in certain ways to circle back and include it into the wholeness, into the oneness. Yet it's not because it doesn't have health within it at all times, it's simply because it's been at a different location or dimensional frequency.

Our biggest tip for you in terms of enhancing your health is to really be in the multidimensionality of the frequency, vibration, and speed that is you and that is beyond and inclusive of only the body. The more that you're occupying your full territory as the infinite being that you are, then the more that you're in that state of health.

ENERGETIC EXERCISE
Opulent Vibration of Health

Bringing the Rays of Light into the Central Column

To begin, find yourself in a seated position. Bring your awareness to your spinal column and to the central channel of energy that goes from the top of your head down to the base of your spine, and up from the base of your spine to the top of your head. You can think of this as a pathway, a road map, or a channel of energy. To generate optimal health we recommend bringing in the Rays of Light into the central column or spinal column so the Rays of Light may restore the optimal frequency of the energy system in the body. As the energy system is restored to its optimal functioning then that enhances overall health of the entire body and the entire being.

Relax for a few moments and make a decision or choice to be in alignment, to be in connection, to be in communion with your natural state of well-being. Well-being is a definition of health that is more encompassing because it allows you to have the awareness that the well-being exists in each and every moment no matter what the external circumstances. That is the awareness that we're energetically vibrating at this moment. As much as you can, see whatever is happening in your external environment as simply something in your external environment, not the whole picture, not the indication that there is or isn't health, because health always exists. Abundance always exists, happiness always exists, and the flow of well-being always exists. By utilizing the Rays of Light you're returning your awareness to the capacity to tap into the flow of this well-being, this health, wealth, and happiness, no matter what is occurring in your life.

In the seated position call upon the Council of Light that is pertinent to your wholeness, your multidimensionality, and your optimal brilliant system. You may notice that there are some Council members that are coming into your awareness that you haven't noticed before and there may be some that were very familiar to you that are more in the background. Allow this well-being team, this oneness team, this unity consciousness team, to come forward. As this oneness, unity consciousness, well-being team is coming forward, state your choice for this mini-session with us. What is it that you would like support around, what is it that you would like help with specifically for this exercise around your sense of health? Your sense of health can be the body, it can be wealth, it can be anything. We want to invite you to have a very open view of health.

Once you've shared with us what it is that you would like support around, you can just let go of that. Know that on a higher self level you may have also added something to this intention that you may not consciously have verbalized or have an awareness of.

Now call upon the Love Ray and vibrate the Love Ray at the space above your head. You may imagine that the Love Ray is a ball of light or a beam of light and that you're either calling the ball light of the Love Ray down into your body from the head or you are having the Love Ray create a beam of light that then is shining down through your body. You'll know which way to go. It may also be a spiral. Move the Love Ray from above your head down into the third eye of the forehead, feeling the Love Ray creating connections, creating communion, creating access, and breaking down and including back into the wholeness any partitions or separations that you have between you and your health. Feel the Love Ray breaking down and including back into the wholeness your capacity to perceive in the third eye the health that already exists in your life right now, the thoughts that enhance your well-being, and that you're able to access them through the Love Ray.

Then gently bring the Love Ray down into the throat, into the words that you speak, into your self-expression, and into your communication. Feel the Love Ray absorb back into the wholeness, back into the oneness any overlays, anything that you've wanted to say that you haven't said, any partial expressions, and any infrastructures that you have had a groove or a rut of negative thinking about. This groove or rut of negative thinking is absorbed into the Love Ray.

The pathways that you may have had in the past of telling old stories or a lack of health—feel all of that being absorbed. Bring the Love Ray into the thymus in between the throat and the heart; the thymus is where the high heart chakra is located and the high heart chakra is a place of self-love. Beam and call in the Love Ray into the high heart chakra. This high heart chakra is bringing the concept of self-love into oneness, into unity consciousness.

Now drop the Love Ray into the heart center, the front, the back and the sides of the heart center. Feel the Love Ray entering into the heart center and circulate through the circulatory system out into the body like the blood gets pumped through the heart. Feel the Love Ray getting circulated through the heart center into the blood, into the lymph, into all of the cells, and then drop the Love Ray into the solar plexus, which is the space in between the ribs. Stay here for a few moments, letting the Love Ray absorb in this area of the body any place that you've created a separation between you and your health, and between you and your well-being.

Drop the Love Ray into the navel center, awakening and opening the navel center. Drop the Love Ray into the second chakra below the navel center and then drop the Love Ray down into the root chakra. Let it rest at the root as well as above the head and the crown and imagine that there is communication between the Love Ray at the crown and the Love Ray at the root, and then back up from the root to the crown. It's like a tennis ball being passed, but it's passed through all of the energy centers of the spinal column. With the Love Ray vibrating in each of the energy centers, also have the awareness of the nervous system, the bones, and muscles being filled with the Love Ray.

Then imagine that below your feet is the vibration of the Joy Ray. The Joy Ray is pooled in a pool that's wider than your physical body. It's at least nine feet in all directions, and you're standing in this pool of joy. This pool of joy has a mirror image that is at least an arm's length above your body. This mirror image of the pool of light of the Joy Ray below you and the pool of light of the Joy Ray above you creates a beam of the Joy Ray that you're standing in the center of. It is spherical and it is circular. You're standing within nine feet in all directions, at least, of the light of the Joy Ray, and this Joy Ray shines all through and around you. As it shines you may have the awareness that you're in a hologram of the Joy Ray. You have the Love Ray within the spinal column in a vertical manner and the Joy Ray is a hologram around you in a spherical manner.

Call upon the Divine Ray and imagine that you're adding one drop of the Divine Ray to your crown center. As you add one drop of the Divine Ray to your crown center, you're connected to divine knowing, and as you're connected to your divine knowing, you can ascend or descend into this spiral of consciousness of awareness. As you descend or ascend into this spiral of consciousness of awareness, allow the Divine Ray to inform you of that which you already know about your current situation.

If you are experiencing what you would consider an unpleasant sensation such as a lack of health or some symptom that the Divine Ray has brought to your awareness, notice what it is that you have chosen to separate yourself from that's showing up as this lack of health. What it is that you have chosen to shut down? Now that you've turned on your awareness again, does the lack of health still exist?

Bring a drop or several drops of the Rainbow Ray—Wholeness Ray—into the navel center, letting the Rainbow Ray reconnect you to the joy of living.

Bring a drop of the Emerald Ray—the You Ray—into the root chakra, connecting to a master cell in the root chakra. A master cell is a cell that holds all of the information of you in a state of wholeness. By bringing the Emerald Ray into the root chakra you are recalibrating your system to say yes to life as you. This Emerald Ray in the master cell is tapping into the divine blueprint of radiant health, wholeness, and well-being and broadcasting that into the root center, as well as the infinite awareness that you are you eternally, connecting you to the flow of your soul and inviting in more of the energy of your soul, of your infinite nature, of your divine self, and allowing you to tap more into that.

It is understood that this incarnation is something that has a span or some decades or years attached to it and that at one point you will choose to leave your body and go back into the oneness without your physical form as it currently exists. Sometimes what appears to be a lack of health is one way for you to be able to go back into the oneness when it's time to walk out of your body. Yet you can also choose to walk out of your body without having a disintegration of the physical form.

What is occurring now by bringing the Emerald Ray into the root center is a reconnection to your broader self, your nonphysical self, your energy self, your multidimensional self, your infinite self, your divine self, and your eternal nature that is always flowing so that you can be connected to that flow of well-being always and in all ways. There may be times that it is in your highest choice to have a disconnection to the health that's always flowing. Yet by tapping into the well-being of your eternal nature, the vastness of your soul, in those moments you are cultivating your internal environment and your awareness in such a way that you can feel at peace and you can realize the health that exists within that moment.

Become aware of the Love Ray within the spinal column, the Joy Ray being a hologram around the entire body, the Divine Ray at the crown chakra, the Rainbow Ray at the navel center, and the Emerald Ray at the root. This exercise is enough to reconnect you to your wholeness, to reconnect you to the flow of well-being, to reconnect you to that oneness, that wholeness that is your radiant vitality, your radiant wholeness, your radiant oneness, the flow of health that exists in each and every moment, the flow of wealth that exists in each and every moment.

Now that you are in this place, ask yourself if any of the other rays would be of benefit for you in this moment. Maybe you would like to call upon the Forgiveness Ray or the Solar Ray or the Venus Ray of Opulent Bliss or any of the other rays. Allow yourself to be in these energies and follow the guidance that you get. Take as much time as you would like, asking for any guidance and be with us until you're ready to come back to your waking consciousness.

WIDENING YOUR INTENTION
BEYOND HEALTH

We have provided this exercise in the subject of health because we have the awareness that it is something that you desire more support with.

Yet for us to just focus on one aspect like health is not accessing all that is possible. Even when you use this exercise for something that you have around health, a lack of health or a perception of a lack of health, we would always invite you to widen your intention in the beginning to include even more. You can utilize this exercise as an example of what you could do in any subject—such as manifesting greater wealth, manifesting greater joy, and manifesting greater love.

You can invite the Rays of Light into your life, into different areas of your body, into your finances, your home, or your relationships, and ask that the Rays of Light go into those areas in a way that will create a recalibration to your oneness, to your wholeness. What we know is that all is well and that you are all and that there isn't ever anything that's wrong, that there isn't ever anything that's missing, that you're not separate from anything, and that in the larger perspective that is the flowing universal light. Yet we also have the awareness that that's not how it feels to you at times. You can use any of these tools, any of the Rays of Light, and call upon us to help remind you again and again that you are exquisite, that you are an infinite being, and that you have creative capacities that you are evolving into a greater awareness of in each and every moment.

INFINITE LIGHT

Through this session you have retrained your being to connect to the light in all there is. As you do this, the infinite supply becomes available to you. You are able to see that it exists within every moment, and you begin to look for it and seek it out. You as a light being have been training yourself during this segment, and even before this, to find the nourishment, light, health, and well-being in every moment.

We close this segment with the divine truth that you are the epicenter of universal consciousness; the Rays of Light and the tools that we share with you as well as our dynamic ongoing connection are those that will cultivate the remembering of this divine truth.

18

HAPPINESS
AND MAKING JOY

TUNING IN
. . . .
Light Language and the Central Column

To begin our time together, focus on your spinal column and the space around it, which is also known as the central column or the pranic tube. The central column is wider than the physical spinal column.

Imagine that there is a golden light in the form of sacred symbols moving in and around your field, aura, and the space around your body, and that these symbols that are aligning with your system will be integrated and absorbed. It is like a puzzle piece that fits together or putting a square peg in a square hole. There's something about your particular system that is a perfect fit for these golden sacred symbols and this language of light.

As you are connecting to your central column, notice the sensations as light language is absorbed into your system, making way for more and more happiness in your life. Your central column is one of the widest areas through which heavenly and earthly chi flows; the energies from above and below flow through your central column. On a physiological level this is where much of your life-force is channeled and where important nerve endings and other vital parts of your body are located. See in your mind's eye more of these golden symbols come into the space around you, informing you of your internal makeup, which is light.

Have a sense of your unique Council of Light forming. For this particular segment the representative from the planet Venus is present among your Council members. Venus is often associated with the Hathors, or Hathor, the goddess of dance, sensuality, bliss, music, and ecstasy.

Imagine that more and more of this light is coming in and around you. This light represents the energy of happiness, freedom, and bliss, regardless of outside circumstances. Your system is going through a process of uptaking, bringing in, and absorbing light and happiness. We are describing this process as being outside of you so you have a concept to connect to, but it is actually an internal process. As you absorb it from outside, it also awakens from within. As you are connecting to this light and energy, imagine that you are giving yourself permission to absorb more of this light and energy.

Spend as long as you would like in this process, and when you feel ready, take a couple of deep breaths, stretch, move your body, and gently return to the here and now.

. . . .

TRANSCENDING THE ILLUSION

This process is similar to what you may have heard about vitamins. If you take vitamins that you are not able to absorb then you don't get the full benefit of what is within the supplement. The same is true of food and the same is true of your life. You could imagine that your life is like this supercharged, incredibly nutritious vitamin of happiness and yet your system doesn't quite know how to take up or absorb or access all of the happiness.

One of the purposes of this segment is to help you to be able to absorb the nourishment and the happiness that is already there. This process is also about transcending the illusion. We are not saying that when you have all of the circumstances exactly to your preference that isn't creating or enhancing happiness or your ability to take in happiness. We're simply saying that happiness does not have to be conditional. It does not have to be based on your conditions being perfect.

Your conditions are always perfect from our perspective, even when you feel tired, hungry, cold, lonely, or some other condition that you may not prefer.

ENERGETIC EXERCISE
Spirals of Light

Breathe into your body and imagine that the light language that has been coming into your field and connecting to your pranic tube, the space around your sacrum and your spinal column, has been preparing the way for your innate ability to awaken and connect to happiness. Set your intention to absorb more of the light and freedom that is in your life in this moment.

Some of the sacred geometry and language of light looks like small corkscrews or spirals. A drill sounds more invasive than this process, but just like a drill can go into something that's hard and spiral in and make space, these corkscrews of light are softening and opening and creating space in your system so that you can absorb more of the happiness that's there.

Spend some time in this process, and when you feel ready, take a couple of deep breaths, stretch, move your body, and gently return to the here and now.

ANYTHING IS POSSIBLE

There is the thoughtform that if you are not achieving happiness all the time and if you are not an enlightened being in this moment then you are doing something wrong and are failing in some way. It would be our suggestion to not use the statement that "you can be happy regardless of outside circumstances" to frustrate you or to create a sense of "less than" or failure if that's not your current experience. It's not our intention to say such a thing as an invitation for you to use it against yourself at a later time. It's just to say that anything is possible. Anything is possible. It may not be your choice, it may not be your soul's expression, yet it is possible. Stringing together more and more moments of happiness may be the progression of how it unfolds for you.

THE DEFINITION OF HAPPINESS

There are many different definitions of happiness. Happiness can be associated with an emotion, or happiness can equal a particular experience, feeling, or condition. Yet our view and definition of happiness is wider than a particular emotion, such as smiling, laughing, feeling upbeat, or feeling positive, although those could all fit under the umbrella of happiness.

Happiness is really a sense of freedom that you feel inside of yourself. It is not equated with happy, sad, up, down, inconsistency, or consistency. It's always strumming through you, it's always in your environment, and it's always there. Happiness is beyond polarity and duality. It is like a river flowing.

HAPPINESS IS
BEYOND A STATE OF BEING

You have experiences where you feel like you've felt held, connected, free, expansive, in the moment, light, and carefree. Those are the times when you're connected to the vibratory and energetic template of happiness. We're expanding the definition of happiness to be beyond a state of being and an emotional state to be more inclusive of a wellspring, a template, and a paradigm in which you feel free and open.

There's often a striving for the perfect recipe for happiness, success, love, or for whatever it is that you desire. There's this thought that if you find a certain magical combination of thoughts, feelings, affirmations, goals, intentions, living in a high vibration, or whatever your individual recipe would include—eating well, sleeping, exercising, whatever it is that you value—that once that recipe is perfected then you will be able to feast upon the gourmet meal of happiness, success, love, peace, soul fulfillment, or health.

We want to invite you to unhook from the immense amount of pressure that you may place upon yourself to achieve this perfect recipe, because everything already exists in a state of wholeness. You don't have to bring together the individualized components in the recipe to get to the wholeness.

SUPPORT EXERCISE
Working with Your Higher Self

We want to spend a few moments working with you to assist in lifting any sense of inner desire to be perfect and any sense that certain actions equal particular results. We are not saying that this doesn't happen and that if you do things that you know make you feel good then you'll have a life of feeling good. But this way of approaching it is not as related as you might think.

We will be working with you for the next few moments and you may notice different sensations. The key component in this is that we will be working with you rather than for you. We will be working with your higher self, soul, and the part of you that knows you are already in a state of wholeness.

Spend some time in this process, and when you feel ready, take a couple of deep breaths, stretch, move your body, and gently return to the here and now.

RELEASING THE IDEA
OF THE PERFECT RECIPE

We would encourage you to move away from the idea that to experience x, y, and z and the things you prefer is contingent on what you do, say, think, or where you are. This is a part of the paradigm that is crumbling.

You may have had experiences in your life where you've tried everything that you know and have explored a certain area of your life but are still left with the feeling that you have not achieved the results you would like. There's no nook or cranny that you haven't explored or that you haven't grown from and no issue left that you haven't processed or cleared. Yet a particular area is still the same.

Suppose you have always wanted to have a loving relationship with a life partner. You have gone to counselors, done your inner work, and had relationships with people, yet the caliber of union with the beloved that you are seeking has not shown up.

Perhaps you have wanted to find a career that is incredibly fulfilling on a soul level and that brings joy and also supports you financially. You've explored all of your feelings about career and money and you've really gone into great depth of introspection and outer change. Yet you still don't have a fulfilling career on a soul level that supports you on all levels, including financial.

Or what if you have a bodily condition, a health issue, a perception of your weight, or some part of your body you may not like and you've done everything you know to do on the inside and the outside to really shift into a place of health, self-love, into your ideal, optimal, and happy weight. Yet it still seems to elude you and feels like it is always one step beyond.

We're describing these scenarios to say that if action or finding the perfect recipe equaled the ideal creation, manifestation, situation, and circumstance, then you would have already achieved everything that you had wanted, which hasn't always been the case.

UNPLUGGING FROM
THE OLD PARADIGM

We're mentioning these examples to prove that the old paradigm hasn't worked and to demonstrate that you can unplug from those beliefs. If you take yourself off the hook of having to be perfect and having to find a particular formula, as we said earlier, there is a sense of space that comes with that.

Yet in order to unplug there has to be a reason to unplug. You might ask yourself, "Well, if I'm not going to believe this, then what am I going to believe? What actually is my universal belief? What is my truth? What is the law of the universe and the universal truth that I would rather focus on or align with?" The new paradigm is that happiness is available at all times. It is not sometimes there and sometimes not. It's always there.

The shift in consciousness occurs as we move away from the Piscean Age and into the Aquarian Age; there are different beliefs and ways of being within those different zodiac signs. We are inviting you to shift from one paradigm to another. The new way of Aquarian energy does not have to be anything like the Piscean energy, although you can honor what you have done in your life so far under the old energy, which has gotten you to this moment and has been an invaluable asset to the shift in consciousness.

The process need not be difficult or challenging. It can be quite simple to align with the new consciousness because it's always been there. Aligning with the template of happiness will provide you with a sense of freedom, lightness, connection, and the experience of being held.

THE ACCESS POINTS TO
THE TEMPLATE OF HAPPINESS

As we bring in even more access points to the template of happiness, we invite you to awaken, ignite, recalibrate, remember, research, and resource this template of happiness within your own system. Nothing is outside of you. Everything that you desire is within. Throughout this divine transmission your ability to absorb and connect to happiness has increased.

Have a sense for yourself if this is something that you are choosing to align with. Is it something that you are willing to give a try? It's one thing to express concepts and to share wisdom, yet we are very interested in how the concepts and the wisdom play out in your everyday life. You have a PhD in trying to control your conditions to create happiness, and so perhaps you would like to experience or remember another way of connecting to happiness.

We want to also stress, because we're speaking in absolutes, that we know that you are a master, that you do this naturally, and that when you're not paying attention happiness just sneaks up on you and there it is. That's the nature of it: when you forget to think about what would make you happy, you just all of a sudden fall into it. Again, it's not difficult, challenging, or a skill that you have to learn; it's natural and innate. Now is the time to move forward.

SUPPORT EXERCISE
Choosing Happiness

We will spend a few moments now in silence with this template of happiness. In your own way you are making negotiations with this concept and template of happiness. Just like any decision you make, connecting to a sense of expansion and freedom will create different experiences in your life.

On a soul level it's a choice. It is a choice to move into the template of happiness and a choice that you are making from all levels of your being. This is your negotiation time to see how much you want to go into it, how far, and if you want to dive into the well directly, absorbing and awakening this template.

Focus on the space about two inches below your belly button, and imagine a cross section of your body. If you were to place a horizontal line through your midsection about two inches below your navel, this would create a grid inside of your body. Imagine that this template of happiness, this golden light language, is merging, absorbing, aligning, and coming to life in this particular area of your body. This may look like a grid of light and you may have a feeling of yumminess, bliss, joy, ecstasy, and a feeling of a kinesthetic quality almost like the texture of honey that is decadent and fluid, yet substantial.

Or you might hear the sound of this template. Bring your attention and consciousness into that area of your body and to the connection of this grid. Notice the template in this particular part of your body and how it's communicating and resonating with the rest of your being and consciousness.

Notice as this process is continuing to deepen and stabilize within you. As we're completing this segment we want to provide you with some strategies, recipes, and formulas to connect to this template, even though we just told you that formulas, recipes, and strategies are unnecessary. It is sometimes the habit of changing the way of doing something that is important.

We would encourage you to use this process as a practical, everyday, tangible experience and expression in your life. If you would like to do a meditation as a process of connecting to the energy of happiness as we've described it, you would begin by focusing on your spinal column and the pranic tube of your central column. Visualize calling upon the language of light, this golden sacred geometry. Bring it in from the outside of your field, and see it swirling in and around your pranic tube, your central column, and then from that place allow it to absorb. The next step is to focus on the grid in the midsection two inches below the navel center and spend time concentrating and meditating on this part of your body.

This is a quick meditation that you can do if you find yourself in the habit of trying to change or shift things, or if you want to have a short meditation to connect to the energy of happiness.

Spend some time absorbing the energies of this template of happiness, noticing the sensations of space and freedom. When you feel ready, take a couple of deep breaths, stretch, move your body, and gently come back to this time and place.

THE DESIRE TO STOP A HABIT

Continuing a pattern that's become a part of you can be an unconscious process. Stopping a pattern such as smoking, eating sugar, complaining, or whatever you've wanted to stop can feel like fumbling around in the dark.

It's a process that can be mutable or mercurial or hard to locate. To tell you to stop planning, organizing, doing your formulas, recipes, thinking that you have to be perfect, or controlling your conditions in order to be happy is a little ethereal and intangible because it can be, to varying degrees at various times in your life, so automatic.

KEEPING A JOURNAL

You may want to keep a journal or a small notebook as an action step with you over the next days, weeks, or however long you feel called to do. In this journal write down every time you have a thought or an action where you're trying to change your condition in order for it to be the recipe or the formula for happiness.

Let's say you're in one of those situations that we mentioned earlier about health, career, wealth, love, or whatever it is, and you find yourself thinking or doing or trying to create that perfect combination of things in order to achieve it. Instead, just write it down. We're not saying if you want to be healthy and vital physically that you stop eating well, exercising, and doing those things that bring you a sense of peace of happiness. What we are saying is that if you find yourself doing a lot of the monkey-mind thinking, ruminating, the "if this person would change then I would be happy" kinds of things, you write those thoughts down.

If you find that you're trying to push, force, or control something or holding yourself to an incredibly high standard of perfection, just take note of it. As much as possible give yourself permission to stop it and allow what is already within you to emerge.

OUTSIDE CONDITIONS ARE
NOT NECESSARY FOR HAPPINESS

Suppose you find yourself in one of those situations related to something outside of you: "If only my boss didn't do this," for example. Rather than thinking about how to change them or how to change the situation, go into your pranic tube, take some deep breaths, call upon the light language, and breathe into the template of happiness. Look for the happiness that is already there rather than focusing on the condition to change.

Having the ideal conditions, happiness, health, wealth, love, and soul fulfillment, and all the things that you want, will enhance your sense of happiness. We're not negating that, yet we want you to know that those outside circumstances or conditions are not necessary in order for you to feel happy or to connect to this broader concept of happiness, which is the sense of freedom on all levels of your system.

ABSORBING THE HAPPINESS
THAT IS ALREADY THERE

We invite you to trust that this will be an intuitive process that unfolds naturally. Rather than focusing so much on getting the conditions exactly right, we're inviting you to focus on your ability to absorb the happiness that's already there.

Many people talk about the emotion of gratitude. Focusing on what you appreciate shifts your perspective of looking for what's working in your life. That's similar to the concept we are describing, yet what we're talking about is more about enhancing your ability to absorb than your ability to see it. The process we're describing is instinctual and natural.

You don't have to see your digestive system absorbing the nutrients of food. You wouldn't want to be in there watching the whole process as it's happening. We're talking about focusing on your ability to absorb, not your ability to see it or to take action to create it. It's about your ability to absorb the stream and flow of happiness that's in each moment.

THE ILLUSION OF DUALITY

This is a time where the concept of duality—light and dark, good or bad, a preferred condition and unpreferred condition—is accelerating and the realization that everything exists in wholeness is awakening. Within each part exists the mirror image of that part, so rather than focusing so much on whether something is either this or that, there's a move to focus on including it all: to include what isn't working in your life, what is working in your life, and to see the wholeness in that. The ability to see something as manifested, knowing that the nonmanifest exists, means you can connect to it in its wholeness.

As a vibration accelerates and increases the time delay between the unpreferred condition and the preferred condition begin to blur and merge. That's when you're able to see that it's all one. The wholeness and the happiness are always there. It's not either/or, half full or half empty. It's about inclusion, embracing, allowing, receiving, absorbing, and it aligns you with the oneness that exists in each moment.

ENERGETIC EXERCISE
Focusing on the Language of Light

We invite you to once again focus on the language of light and these corkscrews of golden energy and various sacred geometry shapes and sounds in and around you. Notice that you are now able to absorb even more of this golden energy than you were when you first started.

Set your intention to allow the absorption of the happiness that's already there to increase in a way that's comfortable for all levels of your system. Happiness is already there and it's a matter of focusing on your absorption and inclusion of it.

As you are ready, take some gentle breaths and begin to connect to your body even more fully, perhaps wiggling your toes or your fingers, or stretching your body in any direction, and gently come back to this time and place.

A NEW ERA IN YOUR LIFE

Living from joy is the beginning time of a new era in your life. You are moving into a time in which you are truly a creator being; you are creating each moment, and each moment after that. The fabric of what you are creating is joy and this joy will begin to be without bounds. It will transcend activities, it will transcend health, it will transcend finances, it will transcend sleep, it will transcend food, it will transcend everything you know.

You are making joy, just like when you make love you make joy. How do you make love? You make love by stimulating, expressing, and exploring, as well as being in a very relaxed state. During this transition of moving into a relaxed state you may feel a desire to let go, to unplug from activities and people, to have a period of time where you are going through your life at a slower pace so you can get into a truly relaxed state.

In the process of this letting go you may feel a shedding of your old identities and ways of being, and there may even be some grief or sadness associated with this process. If you notice that you still respond with a layer of stress when you have something that you need to do, know that this is unnecessary and will shift as you enter into the new state of being in joy. This is a time where you can feel joy regardless of what you are or aren't doing. Simply live in the now and be the best you that you can be in each moment and resonate with that which is pointing you in the direction of joy. Feel the joy in every now moment.

We would like to take your awareness of making joy even one step further, for you are the creator of your own experience. You can create joy out of anything, truly out of anything, by shedding everything, which is what you are doing. By shedding your identity as a friend, as a daughter/son, as a wife/husband/single person, as your work, you are allowing yourself to be you without form, without identity, or even without purpose in some ways. You may feel guided at times to move into a state of reclusiveness so that you can unplug more and more and more from the ideas and the consciousness of those around you. Through this shedding you can create joy.

SPOKEN EXERCISE
Releasing Contracts of Obligation

As the creator being that you are, state the following choices out loud in alignment with your free will:

"I release myself from contracts that I have made around being the one who takes care of others at the expense of myself. I release myself from contracts that are no longer serving me with my family, loved ones, and all those who may seek my guidance. I am not bound to anyone. I am not creating for anyone. I am free."

MAKING JOY OUT OF THE FRICTION

For you to feel purpose without purpose is an ideal state. There is a deeper level of trust in what is happening, a deeper level of understanding, and knowing that what is happening is an ingredient in the joy. Sometimes in making love there is the friction that creates the pleasure; this friction is what really gets your juices flowing.

You do not need to be off balance when there is friction or if you feel annoyed that things are the way that they are. You do not have to change anything or strive for anything, just allow what is to be. This way of being has brought you great peace at times in the past when you could simply allow yourself to be regardless of outside circumstances. If you have been grumpy rather than happy this is also part of the process of letting go and surrendering. Allow yourself to use the unhappiness as a part of the creative fabric of joy.

THE GIFT OF A RUBY RED DIAMOND

We would like to end this segment of the conversation with the gift of a ruby red diamond. If you would like you can place it in your heart. This ruby red diamond is the generator of the sense of joy, making joy, and creating joy. Would you like this gift? If so, internally say, "Yes," and take a few long, slow deep breaths to receive it.

From this enhanced perspective of making joy you can see that there is nowhere to go and nowhere to be and nothing to do and nothing to achieve. It is simply all for the pleasure of it, for the joy of it, and for the lightness of it. Enjoy.

19

HEALTH, WEALTH, AND JOY

One of the things that is so beneficial about working with the Council of Light is our accessibility, practicality, and the simplicity of what we bring forward. The Council is coming into this divine transmission based on your individual matrix. Be open as always to receive direct guidance and notice sensations throughout this segment, for it is a time of self-guidance and self-direction. It is for the joy and the pleasure of it that we come together and share in this way.

THE SPIRIT REALM

We would like to start by talking about the spirit realm, also known as the realm of guides, angels, helpers, and aspects of the Divine. There are different symbiotic relationships between the human and the spirit realms. Not to say that the human isn't spirit, because the human is spirit, but you have different guides that are more in alignment with your particular signature energy. The belief system that there is one Source, one divinity, or monotheism, says that guides and allies are aspects of that one Spirit and divinity. As you get to know these aspects of the Divine in an individualized way, like working with a certain guide or ally, then you get to know that aspect of the Divine within yourself.

Similarly, you have a divine quality and characteristic that you are most connected to or that is an expression of you. As you get to know yourself and other people, you get to know aspects of the Divine as well. The Divine is everything so there is nothing off-limits and nothing that isn't divine.

This is like the Egyptian pantheon and the different gods and goddesses that have unique archetypal energies but are all aspects of the one Divine. It is leveling the playing field and saying that the human race is also made up of angels, spirit guides, gods, and goddesses. The more that you begin to see the people in your life, especially in those moments that really ring true as being Spirit speaking to you, the more you're able to access the divinity in every moment; your relationships with one another are becoming more and more endearing, rich, and vital in various ways.

We have started this conversation by acknowledging that you are a god or goddess, that you are a spirit guide, an angel, archetypal energy, a totem, or other words that you have to express this concept. We are beginning the conversation this way to say that there are different allies and guides that are more pertinent to a developmental stage than other allies and guides. Just like in your life some people come and go, your allies and guides also come and go.

Some allies and guides are signing off, their time is complete, and others are coming on. When there is a major transition in your life there is a changing of the guard in the realm of spirit, angels, and allies in your guidance system. Simultaneously this also happens in the lives of the people that you know. Specifically what we are saying is that some of your relationships end and new ones come on board, while some of your relationships change (in other words, you have the same person in your life but the relationship gets upgraded).

This also happens as a mirror image in the spirit world. Set your intention that those 100 percent pure love-light helpers and guides that are pertinent to your now and your forward movement are present with you. Thank and bless any of those guides and allies that have been with you previously that are no longer pertinent to your now and your forward moving now, and send them back to the Source from which they came.

DECLUTTERING AND LETTING GO
WHILE SENDING LOVE AND GRATITUDE

An area where decluttering is often spoken about is in your physical space. Decluttering your physical space is a really wonderful thing to do. It provides a lot of fresh energy and vitality. We would invite you to also think about decluttering your relationships; there is a time of letting go of some, rearranging others, and bringing new ones in.

Call upon the higher selves of all those people in your life and spend a moment sending love and appreciation to all the people that have been in your life in the past year, all those people that you've passed time with, shared experiences with, the ones that you've loved, the ones that drove you crazy, and all the people that have been a part of your life.

Expand this appreciation to the people behind the scenes. For instance when you go to the grocery store you may see the person at the check-out line but there are so many people behind the scenes of getting the food into the grocery store. Expand your love and appreciation to every single human being that has been a part of your year directly and indirectly, sending love and appreciation, acknowledging all that's gone into every single moment of your life during the year.

So many people, so many details of the simplest things: the people that work the electricity and the phone lines, your car, home, the place where you work and the people that you work with, the people that you've shared classes with, the people that you've shared your gifts and talents with, and on and on. Acknowledge the web of all those gods and goddesses in human form that have been a part of your life in the past year. Call upon the higher selves of those people and also send them love and appreciation. State that you're calling upon the higher selves of those people that are pertinent to your now and your forward movement to come.

GUIDES AND ALLIES
PRESENT AND FUTURE

You are choosing to take a quantum leap in your life and you're putting out the call for those that want to come with you. As such you're also untying yourself from the potential of not going because you want to stay with a certain energy, frequency, or person. There is a grieving process as relationships come to a place of completion, yet you have chosen to move forward.

As you're sending back to Source those guides that aren't pertinent to now and calling those that are to move forward with you, if you desire, do the same with the people in your life. Send the ones that are no longer pertinent to your now back to Source and call upon those ones that are going with you where you're headed and to those that you haven't met yet.

There is the saying in real estate, "Location, location, location." It's similar when you are on a path of evolution, change, and of expanding your consciousness. Your environment, the people you're around, and the places that you go have a certain vibratory field. It doesn't mean that you can't go forward without them but it can be easier if you're surrounded in the location that supports your forward movement growth.

We're allowing some space and time for this process to happen organically and naturally and know that as you're setting this intention now there is a time delay in some of these experiences. Some of your relationships still have a shelf life and an expiration date that's beyond this moment but may not be in the future.

When you have a relationship with a certain ally or guide that's close and deep and one that you've developed, oftentimes it's because your signature energy is compatible with the signature energy of that guide or ally. Your divine qualities and the divine qualities of that ally are either a match or an opposite; there's something about that guide that you're missing that they bring in, or there's something about that guide that you already have that's being matched up.

Let's say you've been connected to the energy of horse as an ally. Horse has to do with strength, courage, and freedom, and that's been something that you've really needed. There's a certain aspect of the horse that has to do with the third-dimensional material plane while your forward movement has to do more with the galactic level of consciousness. You've already integrated the qualities of horse but staying close to the horse will, in a sense, hold back your forward movement of where you're headed on the galactic plane.

Simply said, we, the Council of Light, are becoming more prominent at this time and are inviting you to work with us more because there is a simpatico, a synergy between our frequencies, the consciousness of where you're headed and the consciousness that we have to offer. Believe it or not, not everyone wants to have joy in his or her life. Those who do will benefit from having a relationship with us.

VENUS

The Council member associated with the planet Venus is coming more into the energy of this divine transmission. You may feel a qualitative difference in the energy that's stepping forward. We are working with you, your astrological chart, and the setting of the planet Venus in your astrological chart, this love energy and opening the accessibility of this galactic love to you.

You may, if you have your chart, want to look and see where Venus is in your chart. If you have had your astrocartography chart done, which has to do with what physical locations are good for you to visit and live in, see where your Venus is. An example would be if your Venus were located in the Nile. The Nile would be a place that would feel like home and you would be able to access love easily. Even if you don't have that conscious information right now, connect to the energy of love.

ENERGETIC EXERCISE
Falling in Love with Yourself, Buoyancy, and Space

Move into the elation that's associated with falling in love: that giddiness and joy of falling in love, that feeling, memory, idea, and experience of how good it feels to be loved. Perhaps remember the beginning of a romantic relationship where everything is imbued with a fairy-tale feeling of love—with excitement, anticipation, and elation.

As much as you can, set your intention in a very concentrated way to fall in love with yourself. Energetically now in the moment, imagine that you are the person of your dreams and fantasies and that you're enraptured, exhilarated, and ecstatically in love with yourself. There is a sense of falling, floating, surfing, and a sense of being held. This is falling in love, falling in love, falling in love with yourself. Spend some time in the warm embrace of this love energy, letting it move in and around you.

With the Venus Council members still predominantly present in the energy makeup of this divine transmission, connect to the energy of Pluto that is associated with the body and radiant health. The Council member of Pluto is becoming more prominent at this time to assist with your physical makeup and matrix.

Part of the physical imbalances that you're experiencing have to do with the upgrade and the transition of the physical form from one way of receiving fuel to another way of receiving fuel. It is similar to cars that have shifted from gas to the hybrid or electric way of fueling.

You are becoming more and more buoyant in your physical form. More and more space on the subatomic level is the foundation of the particles of your body. If you were to dive deep within yourself and go all the way down through the nucleus and into the subatomic levels of the cell you would find that place where there is only space and only light. That space and light is beginning to expand its territory to not only be in the subatomic planes but to be in the atomic plane. What happens when the cell changes from being battery packed or sourced from this space to becoming the space, battery, and light is that things have to shift around and change.

Having the need to pay attention to your body as things come out of physical balance allows more light and more space to come in. If you've been having any pain like headaches, back pain, hormonal imbalances, any disease processes in your body, or you've been experiencing a low level of frustration in your body, all of these are related to the shift on the energetic plane to becoming atomically and subatomically made up of light or space. Buoyancy more accurately describes this process than the term "light."

Imagine that your connection to Pluto and your body is expanding more and more in your physical form, and within the structure of this divine transmission you're able to accelerate the process with ease and grace for all the levels of your body.

If there's an area that feels tight, is out of balance, or tends to be weak, imagine that you're able to call up the space into that form. It'll feel like, "Oh, there's more space in there!" You may have done a yoga class, a walk, or some experience that makes you feel like you have more space in your body and that things aren't as dense or condensed. This is the sensation that you're experiencing at this time. You're breathing in more space into that part of your body; you're inundating and saturating it with space. Space, space, space, space, space. There's an opening and a lengthening and a lightness that comes from this space.

As we're working with you and with the members of the Council of Light, imagine that each planet is associated with each aspect of your life. We've worked and are working with Venus, the energy of love and your relationship to yourself and to others. We are working with the Pluto consciousness and the energy related to the physical form and health.

As that's continuing to happen, have a sense of connecting to the Central Sun and the council member of the Central Sun coming more and more into the forefront of this divine transmission. The Central

Sun has to do with prosperity and abundance on all levels. Feel in your third eye, pituitary gland, hypothalamus, and your pineal gland a connection to the Central Sun as a beam of pure, undiluted prosperity, a thinking download of consciousness. It is not a question of whether or not you or the universe is abundant or whether or not you are prosperous. It is a given. If you look at the grains of sand on a beach, there are an infinite number of them. If you look at the prolific nature of a cherry tree, there are more and more cherries on the tree.

Spend some time soaking in this pure download of prosperity consciousness, feeling it saturate every cell of your being. As you are soaking in this download of prosperity, contemplate the abundance that is already in your life. Imagine writing a list of every single physical thing that you have in your life, every apple in your cupboard, every sock, shoe, pan, every piece of furniture, and every dollar; you notice that you would have an abundance of hundreds if not thousands of physical things. If you were also to write down all of the experiences that you've had, you would have thousands and thousands of experiences in abundance.

Now that you have acclimated to the prosperity energy of the Central Sun we want to work more deeply by moving into the undiluted consciousness of the Central Sun. If you find that you're experiencing resistance to any of these consciousness bands that are coming in, just breathe, allow, and know that it's happening on the multidimensional plane and that you can integrate it with time and space.

To allow the full spectrum of consciousness that is available from the Central Sun to saturate your body right now, we will allow the energy to flow without talking about prosperity at this moment. Let the pure consciousness in, letting it flow in and around you.

Now have a sense of the energy of the zodiac sign of Gemini coming in. This zodiac sign and the Council member associated with it for this moment has to do with the soul's expression. Have a sense of this Council member and this zodiac sign amping up your soul's expression of your gifts, talents, and your soul's purpose.

It's like the strings on a guitar. You're playing different notes that you've gathered together in this divine transmission to harmonize these notes, different bands and streams of consciousness. They are like the major chords of your life. Spend some time feeling your being harmonize, and expand on these different notes and streams of consciousness.

Imagine that all the Council members associated with the energy of joy, which are all of us, but present and pertinent to your now, are coming forward and that this joy energy is abundantly in surplus. The Joy Ray is the Ray of Light and the ray of consciousness that enhances joy. It is not an intellectual concept. It is an experience of joy. There is a desire to try to construct joy, to try to figure it out or process it in the mind, yet it is something to be experienced.

You can make joy just like you make love. You can make joy out of any situation and any experience. For now imagine that you are in this energy spa of joy and you're absorbing this joy. Even if you don't feel it now, know that you're receiving it on different levels. Feel within your system more space, more love, more joy, more prosperity, and more of your soul. And when you feel ready, take a few deep breaths, wiggle your fingers and your toes, and gently come back to this time and place.

JOY AS THE EXPRESSWAY TO ENLIGHTENMENT

From our perspective, joy is the fastest and most direct route into the greater yet-to-be. It is our purpose, as we have stated, to enhance joy. We could have chosen any divine quality to enhance—freedom, love, trust, or beauty—yet we, this intergalactic council of thousands and thousands of light beings, have chosen collectively to enhance joy because it is the essence of the evolution of consciousness. To understand it on a frequency and vibrational level, it is beyond even the emotion that you associate with joy.

Joy is larger than that; it has a certain alchemical reaction when it is alive within a person, just like certain colors of glass when they're melted together go through an alchemical process that creates a color that's outside of them. When you melt ivory and blue glass together, there is a brown that goes around the blue—it's not a part of the ivory or the blue originally, but when they come together with heat it sparks and creates a third thing.

As the human system in this now comes into contact with the Joy Ray, it sparks an alchemical reaction that vibrates and elevates. It aligns the system and it creates, in a sense, a third thing. It is this third thing that is the key to the process of enlightenment, expansion, unfolding, and becoming. It is on purpose that we have chosen joy as our purpose. We are here with you to enhance your joy in a nonintellectual way because it does create this third thing, and a part of this third thing leads to the health, prosperity, fulfillment, and happiness that you want.

ENERGETIC FINE-TUNING

As this energy is stabilizing and as you begin to feel more centered, more yourself, and more alive, when you have an experience or have a moment that isn't one that you prefer it feels even worse or more drastic than it did before you felt as good as you felt. In a way you become an energetic fine-tuner. You're in that high frequency and high vibration and you drop in your vibration. It feels so much worse than if you hadn't been in that high vibration to begin with. Yet it doesn't take as much to move back into the high vibration as it did before.

We know that you experience moments that feel funky, stressful, or out-of-sorts, and you can get frustrated with yourself or wonder why you feel so bad when you've done all this work and you've changed so much. It's that the degree of your awareness has heightened. It's like a professional musician who can hear the tones of different notes, so when a note is off-key it sounds more dramatic to them than it does to someone who has an untrained ear. Or like a photographer notices the high quality of a picture where the layperson may not notice the subtle differences in the quality. Or like a chef that is used to eating amazing food and can taste the difference if something is a little bit off.

We feel that you have become the chef of energy, the photographer of energy, the musician of tonality and of energy. When things are a little bit off, it's more dramatic or drastic than it was ten, twelve, or twenty years ago. This can become even more motivating because you don't want to stay there for any length of time.

The energy is continuing to build and strengthen. Keep your focus on the different members of the Council and these different qualities and your connection to Venus, Pluto, Gemini, and the Joy Ray. Focus on keeping the quality, tonality, and harmony of energy where it is now.

ENERGETIC EXERCISE
The Central Column, the Central Sun, Venus, Pluto, Gemini, and Wisdom Energy

Focus on your spinal column. Feel the Joy Ray moving through your spinal column and flushing out anything that isn't beneficial to your being. Feel the energy vibrating and illuminating the Joy Ray in between each of the vertebrae in your spine, the central column, and in your pranic tube, the space around your spine. Focus on the Joy Ray in the spinal column.

Now focus on the Central Sun and the energy of prosperity and abundance. Imagine that it is a color, whatever color comes to you. Direct the Central Sun's color to fill up your entire being and overflow out of your system into your bank account, wallet, credit cards, bills, expenses, assets, and everything that you own. You're saturating the Central Sun's prosperity energy into all of your relations that have to do with finances and prosperity. Allow it to saturate all of your finances. Take all the time that you would like in this process.

NEUTRALIZING THE CHARGE FROM DEBT

Part of what's happening when you direct the energy and intention in this way is that your connection to the electronic forms of prosperity such as credit cards becomes neutralized. Notice that any large emotional charge you have around your credit card charges is an opportunity for you to really allow yourself to expand in this level of finances. For many people finances can be a reason they give themselves for why they don't do certain things that their soul is calling them to do. On a soul level, and in this time on Earth, it really is a time of having it all—not just on the spirit plane but also on the material plane. Your desire to have it all: to have financial security, to follow your soul's callings, whether that's a class, a trip, a pair of shoes, a car, or whatever it is. That desire to expand is natural, the soul's calling is natural, and to have that manifest on the material plane is natural.

The feelings that come up when you think about the credit card debt are just an opportunity to clean up some old ideas or beliefs so that you can return to that limitless feeling. Oftentimes for people there is something underneath what it is that they want. They want money but underneath that they want freedom or security. Like the law of attraction states, what you are you attract. As you connect to the consciousness of security, and you don't need to have the money to connect to the consciousness of security, you begin to attract more of that security. It is a balance.

We're not suggesting that you do everything that your soul desires on a financial level and that you use your credit card because you have a desire to do something. That has a potential to create more stress than it does benefit. Move at your own pace and it can be more loving to wait to do something without having to have the sense of going into debt for it. There is no such thing as debt and it doesn't really matter, only if it bothers you. You can decide to not have it bother you. We know we're saying it's simpler than it feels, but it really is simple.

One more thing we want to add about money, because it is a topic that is pertinent to a lot of people, is that oftentimes you don't even need the money in order to have the thing. For instance, you could say you need a certain amount of money in order to have a home, but you can live in the home without owning the home. Or you could want a pair of shoes and someone could give you the pair of shoes. You don't have to have the money to have the shoes. Begin to focus more on the things that you want than how much they cost. If you want to take a trip to Egypt, focus on being in Egypt and having the experience of Egypt. If you want to have a new car, focus on having the new car more than the dollars that it would take to have the car. Your focus is on the thing that you want, not the money that you need in order to have it.

ENERGETIC EXERCISE
Oracular Wisdom

Feel yourself connecting now to the Council member that's associated to wisdom. Have a sense of a really yummy, delightful wisdom energy coming in. There is a connection to Delphi, to the Oracular tradition, and inner wisdom that you are also connecting to from past lives. Focus on this wisdom energy coming in. There's a zone that you get into that you want to be able to call up on demand. This zone is a sweet spot of knowingness that's where you want to be. When you're there it feels joyous.

Think about living in joy, being that sweet spot, and that zone that you get into when you're in a state of knowing. When you're in a state of knowing, implicit in that is being connected to your Source and yourself. You're having more and more of those moments. Keep focused and stabilized in the energies of Venus and love, Pluto and health, the Central Sun and wealth, Gemini and the soul, and the wisdom plane that you are bringing in. Spend the next five minutes grounding and saturating these energies.

YOUR BECOMING IS A PROCESS

As you're learning how to call up that sweet spot on demand, you're able to be more consistent in it regardless of other people. But as you've been learning, it feels a little challenging at times when another person's energy gets in the way of your awareness of your sweet spot. You might wonder if they're going to support the changes you are making in your life. Are they going to support, respect, and not discount your knowingness? As you're developing your own connection and respect to your knowingness, that will begin to stabilize more and more.

We could go into a story about the patriarchy and giving away your power but it doesn't really matter anymore; basically when you feel disempowered in a relationship it's happened within yourself. There isn't any assertion that anyone can take your power from you. The relationship of empowerment that you have is with yourself and to be able to maintain that regardless of who's around you.

You may have times when you have the sense of being uprooted. It's like when you transplant a plant and there is a level of shock that the plant goes through as it's moving into and growing in its new pot. You may have had major milestones in your life with children going to college and moving from the house, or you had a change in a job that you've been in for a long time. There may be a part of you that doesn't want to be in motion and wants to be in the pot or in the earth and grow.

Yet there's something important about movement on a soul level. The part of you that wants to root and doesn't want to be in motion is resisting being in motion. However, on a soul level there's a part of you that's been asking for the transmutation, growth, and evolution that comes with movement. Openheartedness needs to be on the move for this to happen. It's like the nomadic lifestyle, like a turtle's ability to have its home on its back, to be able to move and stay grounded and stay centered regardless of what's happening.

There is a lot of expansion that comes from being uprooted. We would invite you to stay mobile during those periods when movement is happening even though it doesn't feel very good; you're heading somewhere, and when you get there and put your roots down you'll be in a different place than if you were to put your roots down now.

Be gentle and as loving as possible with yourself. You're in the right place. You have grown exponentially. Take yourself off the hook and lower your expectations of yourself so you don't have so much pressure. Allow yourself to be where you are.

To return to the coasting analogy from the Rainbow Ray chapter, think of your life as a bike ride. There are parts of a bike ride that are uphill and you have to pedal. There are parts where you go downhill and you can coast. Do some things to make life easier for you. Maybe you get some food that's already been cooked rather than going through the process of cooking it. Maybe you don't do the laundry one day to give yourself some time to take a nap. If things have movable deadlines or there are ways that you can do them more easily, let yourself do that for now. Let yourself build in some coasting time and coast where you're able to, and then you can go back to doing the laundry as it needs to be done or cooking more elaborately. But for now give yourself some space and stay on the move, stay in the change, and be as gentle as possible because when you land it'll be in a really yummy and exquisite place.

SPOKEN EXERCISE
Honor Your Self-Expression

Now focus on the energy of Venus and the energy of love that relates to relationships. Breathe this love into your throat area. Fall in love with yourself, with what you have to say, with your contribution to the world, and with what it is that you are here to do. There is a thought that some things that you may have to say are important and other things aren't important. Or other people may have things to say that are more important. Write a story about yourself as if you are a wise woman or a wise man, as if you are a sage and a wisdomkeeper, and that you're on the leading edge of expression; every word that comes out of your mouth is to be savored, applauded, and loved by those around you, and you are valued by you.

There are some patterns that you may be completing around self-monitoring of your expression. A part of you in the past may have been afraid to talk in front of large groups or move into a leadership or a teacher role, and you may be hesitant because you're afraid you won't say the right thing. But there is no wrong thing.

Imagine as you're creating your reality that you are telling yourself stories and saying really amazing things. It's kind of like thinking about someone whom you consider really self-flattering and self-centered and who is always going on about how great and amazing they are and how they say the best things in the world. There are probably people that you have met that when you listen to them you think, "Wow, they have the best life and the best experiences." Or they'll talk about their house and you think, "Oh, my goodness. They must have the best house in the world." Then you go to their house and it's just a house.

We want you to get in the habit of flattering yourself and talking yourself up—of walking around and saying, "Wow. I have a lot to contribute. That was a great thing to say." Even if you don't believe it, for now go through the motions of self-flattery. The belief will catch up in time.

We have accomplished much together in this divine transmission. We have provided a direct connection to the members of the Council that are related to the areas in your life that are most important to you. We would encourage you to call upon us, to create a connection and a relationship with us, and to call upon those members that are most pertinent to what it is that you want to create in your life.

BEGINNING
THE NEXT JOURNEY

It is a very exciting and potent time on Earth. There is so much that has happened in the previous now moment and more that will happen in the next now moments to come.

We have enjoyed being your guides on this journey. It was our honor and the fulfillment of our purpose to watch you grow, meditate, and remember the divine parts of yourself that always were there. We were there as you experienced the Rays of Light; expanded your joy; invited new meaning into your concept of health, wealth, and happiness; and now you are taking all this awareness into your future. It will seem exponential and as if so much more than you could possibly imagine happened and was transcended. Part of that comes from living more in the now and in the moment. Enjoy the ride, the journey, and the fun you will have at your destinations.

DIVINE TRANSMISSIONS PROGRAMS AND PRODUCTS

To support and enhance your personal growth and spiritual evolution please refer to the additional Divine Transmissions programs and products below and visit our website, www.divinetransmissions.com.

JOY PODS

Ready to deepen your connection to the vibration of joy? Join these monthly live transmissions with the Council of Light, Thoth, and other light beings to renew and enhance your natural state of joy. Receive your first month for only $1 when you register with the coupon code, Joy.

THE ENERGY SUPPORT PROGRAM

This innovative and transformative program is a wonderful addition to your journey through *The Council of Light*. It supports your system to move into and maintain a high vibration, allowing you to reach your goals in a fraction of the time.

DIVINE BIRTHRIGHT ACTIVATION PROGRAM

Step into your Divine Lineage Birthrights:
Manifestation, Bliss, Abundance, Purpose, and Union

This premier five-day life-changing immersion is designed to systematically support your being to permanently activate your system to unity consciousness and access your birthrights.

THOTH'S MAGIC ACADEMY

Five Areas of Ascended Mastery
(Akashic Records, The Scribe, Architect,
Merchant Priests/Priestesses, and Alignment)

This year-and-a-day-long magic, mastery, and ancient wisdom academy is for those souls who feel an inner call to take a quantum leap in consciousness and to uncover, illuminate, and share their unique contribution during this extraordinary time.

DIVINE AWAKENING

1:1 Consciousness Evolution with Danielle, Thoth,
and the Council of Light

Each year Divine Transmissions opens up five spots to work privately with Danielle, Thoth, and the Council of Light. These in-depth mentorship programs are designed to heighten your personal connection to the Divine and elevate your consciousness so you can amplify your capacities to play, intuit, manifest, and thrive.

MONEY MUSE

Panel of Light Beings

This three-part home study course guides you step-by-step into a new relationship with money.

THE TEMPLES OF LIGHT
MULTI-SENSORY MYSTERY SCHOOL SET

Book, Six-CD Set, and Sixteen Essences

This home-based mystery school guides you on an initiatory journey through thirteen of Egypt's sacred sites. Each sacred site is a portal to ancient wisdom that can assist the modern-day pilgrim with everyday life issues and struggles—love, purpose, money, and health—and the deeper questions of enlightenment and our divine origin. You set the pace that is right for you, perhaps connecting to one temple a month or a week. Engage all your senses—including visual, kinesthetic, and audio—and embody the heart teachings shared by each temple. Read the chapter about the temple in the book that comes with the set and follow the suggested exercises, listen to the correlating guided meditations on CD, and take the corresponding Temple essence internally.

FRANCE AND EGYPT TOURS

Journey to Egypt or France and experience direct initiations, meditations, and accelerated transformation in the heart of these sacred sites and land.

To order any of the programs and products listed above and to find out about new offerings please contact me, Danielle Rama Hoffman, and my team, at my website:

www.divinetransmissions.com

Or e-mail us at:

Danielle@divinetransmissions.com

ABOUT THE AUTHOR

Danielle Rama Hoffman is a divine transmitter and scribe of ancient and innovative wisdoms for the purpose of elevating consciousness and inspiring personal growth. She is a leader in the shift into unity consciousness, living from joy, purpose, and prosperity as divine creator beings. Danielle supports spirit-centered lightworkers, visionaries, coaches, and personal growth enthusiasts to access their inner divinity so they can confidently share their purpose and unique contribution prosperously (unencumbered by fear, shame, or doubt) and manifest the life they desire. She is the author of *The Temples of Light,* creator of bestselling, life-changing, and divinely-guided programs such as Divine Birthright Activation, the Money Meridians, and Thoth's Magic Academy. She leads tours to Egypt and hosts Heaven on Earth retreats in Southern France with her husband, Dr. Friedemann Schaub.

INDEX